Writing
and Revising
A Portable Guide

Other *Portable* Volumes from Bedford/St. Martin's

WRITING
and REVISING
A Portable Guide

SECOND EDITION

X. J. KENNEDY

DOROTHY M. KENNEDY

MARCIA F. MUTH

Bedford/St. Martin's   BOSTON ◆ NEW YORK

For Bedford/St. Martin's

Vice President, Editorial, Macmillan Higher Education Humanities: Edwin Hill
Editorial Director for English and Music: Karen S. Henry
Publisher for Composition and Developmental English: Leasa Burton
Developmental Editor: Brenna Cleeland
Publishing Services Manager: Andrea Cava
Senior Production Supervisor: Lisa McDowell
Marketing Manager: Emily Rowin
Project Management: DeMasi Design and Publishing Services
Senior Art Director: Anna Palchik
Text Design: Sandra Rigney
Cover Design: Donna Lee Dennison
Composition: Jouve
Printing and Binding: King Printing Co., Inc.

For information, write: Bedford/St. Martin's, 75 Arlington Street, Boston, MA 02116   (617-399-4000)

ISBN 978-1-4576-8233-9

Acknowledgments

Text acknowledgments and copyrights appear at the back of the book on page 259, which constitutes an extension of the copyright page. Art acknowledgments and copyrights appear on the same page as the art selections they cover. It is a violation of the law to reproduce these selections by any means whatsoever without the written permission of the copyright holder.

Preface for Instructors

The second edition of this compact and flexible book continues to offer clear guidance on every stage of the writing process, from generating ideas and planning to revising and editing. With its affordable price and process-oriented coverage, *Writing and Revising* can be used as a classroom text or as a quick reference, accommodating many different teaching needs. Whether students are developing brief papers or more complicated essays drawing on multiple sources, *Writing and Revising* encourages students, bolstering their confidence as they strengthen the skills necessary for writing projects in college and beyond.

In accord with the practical advice of an insightful group of reviewers, this revised edition has added many new professional and student examples while retaining its concise advice for students. Now divided into three sections—Processes, Strategies, and Resources—the first three chapters help students begin on sound footing by explaining key processes. The opening chapter on writing includes a spotlight feature on audience and purpose as well as a new online threaded discussion on writing processes. Chapter 2 on reading includes a spotlight on literal and analytical levels plus new coverage of critical reading responses and of reading online and multimodal texts. Chapter 3 on critical thinking includes a spotlight on evidence with new activities for using varied sources.

In the second section on Strategies, Chapters 4 through 7 guide students through generating ideas, planning and organizing, drafting, and developing their points. Each chapter presents practical strategies to help students develop a strong foundation, improve their papers, and build their skills as college writers. For example, the rich and varied strategies for developing ideas guide students in everything from giving examples and providing details to adding visual evidence. The revision strategies in Chapter 8—now illustrated in two student drafts—encompass macrorevising for purpose, thesis, audience, structure, and support and microrevising for emphasis, conciseness, and clarity. Chapter 9 on editing and proofreading adds new sections on developing a college voice and style to its focus on fixing likely problems. Its handy Quick Editing Guide reviews grammar errors, effective sentences, punctuation, mechanics, and format.

The last section—Resources—turns to common yet challenging expectations of college writers: arguing persuasively, integrating evidence, and crediting sources. Chapter 10 on arguing emphasizes choosing an arguable issue and forming a thesis. Next, it presents strategies for making claims, selecting evidence and using it to support appeals, reasoning logically, avoiding fallacies, and developing three common types of arguments—taking a stand, proposing a solution, and evaluating. Chapter 11 on integrating sources covers evaluating and critically reading sources, avoiding plagiarism, capturing evidence from sources (quoting, paraphrasing, and summarizing), and building an annotated bibliography. Chapter 12, now a separate section for crediting sources, provides dozens of new examples showing how to cite and list sources in both the MLA and APA documentation styles.

Throughout, this text offers practical help to students such as

- tables, charts, figures, and other visuals that clarify concepts and serve as quick references for review
- abundant and varied illustrations of strategies, especially for discovering ideas, drafting paragraphs, and developing supporting material
- frequent individual and group activities to guide students as they practice and apply the processes, strategies, and resources presented
- checklists to help students accomplish critical tasks that can improve their processes and drafts
- extensive coverage—a chapter apiece—of revising and editing, including concise explanations, examples, and checklists for fifteen common editing issues
- practical advice about making argumentative claims, selecting evidence, supporting appeals, and reasoning logically
- consistent connections between strategies for selecting and presenting information and its eventual role as supporting evidence
- discussion of plagiarism in the context of academic ethics and best practices for avoiding problems

- comprehensive illustration of conventions for citing and listing sources, innovatively organized around two key questions: Who wrote it? What type of source is it?

NEW TO THE SECOND EDITION

New final chapter on crediting sources provides dozens of new examples showing how to cite and list sources in both the MLA and APA documentation styles and expands the coverage previously offered in Chapter 11 with more documentation models for multimodal sources.

Revised writing samples and visuals offer students fresh examples on composition techniques and strategies. New excerpts include writing from wide-ranging sources and writers, contemporary and classic.

Stronger reading-writing connections including a full-length professional writing sample—journalist Clive Thompson's essay on "The New Literacy"—a new section on Reading Online and Multimodal Texts, and a new student revision in response to a peer review.

Seventeen new examples of student writing processes, including an online threaded discussion with an instructor and five students, a formal outline for organizing a research paper on wetlands, a selection from a student interview essay, and a student's accompanying critical response to Clive Thompson's piece.

More advice on writing in the digital age, ranging from a new section on Reading Online and Multimodal Texts to generating ideas through e-journals and blogs to citing e-books.

New editing advice in sections on Refining Your College Voice and Polishing Your College Style.

Quick reference numbering of the activities makes this feature easier to find and easier to assign during class or for outside writing.

ACKNOWLEDGMENTS

Thanks to those who thoughtfully reviewed and helped shape the plans for this book: Laurie Buchanan, Clark State Community College; Polly Buckingham, Eastern Washington University; Emily Chamison, Georgia

College & State University;. Arline Davis, Bellevue College; Emmeline Gros, Georgia State University; David Magill, Longwood University; Amy Norton, Pierce College; Bob Nowlan, University of Wisconsin-Eau Claire; Matt Schwisow, Highline Community College; and Paul Zajac, The Pennsylvania State University. Special thanks to Kathleen Beauchene, Community College of Rhode Island, for sharing her class's threaded discussion on writing processes. Thanks also to the students, seventeen new here, whose work has enriched this book by illustrating many points of value to other college writers: Cristina Berrios, Linn Bourgeau, Betsy Buffo, Sarah E. Goers, Kelly Grecian, Stephanie Hawkins, Alley Julseth, Cindy Keeler, Heidi Kessler, Dawn Kortz, Emily Lavery, Schyler Martin, Daniel Matthews, Angela Mendy, Susanna Olsen, Shari O'Malley, Lindsey Schendel, Erin Schmitt, Joshua Tefft, Leah Threats, Joel Torres, Lillian Tsu, Donna Waite, Arthur Wasilewski, and Carrie Williamson.

At Bedford/St. Martin's, many people have contributed to the evolution of this small book. Joan Feinberg, Denise Wydra, and Karen Henry initially conceived of the project and supported the first edition development. Brenna Cleeland acted as developmental editor for the second edition and senior editor Martha Bustin helped supervise the second edition in its early planning stages. Karin Paque was instrumental in tracking down new reading selections, and Jennifer Prince assisted with locating a replacement reading. Credit for a smooth production process goes to Andrea Cava and Linda DeMasi and to copyeditor Leslie Connor. Thanks also go to Sandra Rigney and Donna Lee Dennison for the book's attractive design and to Pablo D'Stair for clearing permissions.

As always, Marcia Muth is grateful to the inspirational student writers and revisers in her writing workshops, sponsored by the School of Education and Human Development at the University of Colorado Denver. Special appreciation goes to Mary Finley, University Library at California State University Northridge, for conference-paper selections and for ongoing expert advice. Thanks, once more, to Rod Muth, University of Colorado Denver, for encouraging her own writing and revising.

GET THE MOST OUT OF YOUR COURSE WITH *WRITING AND REVISING*

Bedford/St. Martin's offers resources and format choices that help you and your students get even more out of your book and course. To learn more about or to order any of the following products, contact your Bedford/St. Martin's sales representative, e-mail sales support (sales_support@bfwpub .com), or visit the website at **macmillanhighered.com/writingrevising**.

CHOOSE FROM ALTERNATIVE FORMATS OF *WRITING AND REVISING*

Bedford/St. Martin's offers a range of affordable formats, allowing students to choose the one that works best for them. For details, visit **macmillanhighered.com/writingrevising/formats**.

Paperback	To order the second edition, use ISBN 978-1-4576-8233-9.
Bedford e-Book to Go	A portable, downloadable e-book is available at about half the price of the print book. To order the Bedford e-Book to Go, use ISBN 978-1-4576-8928-4.
Other popular e-book formats	For details, visit **macmillanhighered.com/ebooks**.

SELECT VALUE PACKAGES

Add value to your text by packaging one of the following resources with *Writing and Revising*. To learn more about package options for any of the following products, contact your Bedford/St. Martin's sales representative or visit **macmillanhighered.com/writingrevising/catalog**.

LearningCurve for Readers and Writers, Bedford/St. Martin's adaptive quizzing program, quickly learns what students already know and helps them practice what they don't yet understand. Gamelike quizzing motivates students to engage with their course, and reporting tools help teachers discern their students' needs. *LearningCurve for Readers and Writers* can be packaged with *Writing and Revising* at a significant discount. An activation code is required. To order *LearningCurve* packaged with the print book, use ISBN 978-1-319-01172-7. For details, visit **macmillanhighered.com/englishlearningcurve**.

i·series This popular series presents multimedia tutorials in a flexible format—because there are things you just can't do in a book.

- *ix visualizing composition 2.0* helps students put into practice key rhetorical and visual concepts. To order *ix visualizing composition* packaged with the print book, use ISBN 978-1-319-01171-0.
- *i·claim: visualizing argument* offers a new way to see argument—with six multimedia tutorials, an illustrated glossary, and a wide

array of multimedia arguments. To order *i·claim: visualizing argument* packaged with the print book, use ISBN 978-1-319-01170-3.

Portfolio Keeping, Third Edition, by Nedra Reynolds and Elizabeth Davis provides all the information students need to successfully use the portfolio method in a writing course. *Portfolio Teaching*, a companion guide for instructors, provides the practical information instructors and writing program administrators need to use the portfolio method successfully in a writing course. To order *Portfolio Keeping* packaged with the print book, use ISBN 978-1-319-01173-4.

MAKE LEARNING FUN WITH *Re:Writing 3*

bedfordstmartins.com/rewriting

New open online resources with videos and interactive elements engage students in new ways of writing. You'll find tutorials about using common digital writing tools, an interactive peer review game, Extreme Paragraph Makeover, and more—all for free and for fun. Visit **bedfordstmartins .com/rewriting**.

INSTRUCTOR RESOURCES

macmillanhighered.com/writingrevising

You have a lot to do in your course. Bedford/St. Martin's wants to make it easy for you to find the support you need—and to get it quickly.

TeachingCentral offers the entire list of Bedford/St. Martin's print and online professional resources in one place. You'll find landmark reference works, sourcebooks on pedagogical issues, award-winning collections, and practical advice for the classroom—all free for instructors.

Bits collects creative ideas for teaching a range of composition topics in an easily searchable blog format. A community of teachers—leading scholars, authors, and editors—discuss revision, research, grammar and style, technology, peer review, and much more. Take, use, adapt, and pass the ideas around. Then, come back to the site to comment or share your own suggestion.

Contents

PART ONE

Processes

1

Writing Processes

You are already a writer with long experience. In school you have taken notes, written book reports and term papers, answered exam questions, maybe kept a journal. In the community and on the job, you've composed tweets, text messages, e-mails, letters, and perhaps reports. You may have designed your social network pages, blogged about your interests, or even tried your hand at writing songs or poetry. All this experience is about to pay off.

Unlike parachute jumping, writing in college is something you can go ahead and try without first learning all there is to know. In truth, nothing anyone can tell you will help as much as learning by doing. In this book our purpose is to help you write better, deeper, clearer, and more satisfying papers than you have ever written before. We encourage you to do so by diving into writing—experimenting, practicing, and building confidence as you expand your writing strategies.

WRITING, READING, AND CRITICAL THINKING

In college you will perform challenging tasks that enlarge what you already know about writing. In fact, you can view each writing task as a problem to solve, often through careful reading (see Ch. 2) and objective thinking (see Ch. 3). You will need to read—and write—actively, engaging with the ideas of others. At the same time, you will need to think critically, analyzing and judging those ideas. To help you assess your own

---

WRITER'S CHECKLIST

- ☐ Have you addressed your audience?
- ☐ Have you achieved your purpose?
- ☐ Have you made your point clear by stating it as a thesis or by unmistakably implying it?
- ☐ Have you supported your point with enough reliable evidence to persuade your readers?
- ☐ Have you arranged your ideas logically so that each follows from, supports, or adds to the one before it?
- ☐ Have you made the connections among ideas clear to your readers?
- ☐ Have you established an appropriate tone?

---

achievement, you will use criteria—models, conventions, principles, standards. In large measure, learning to write well is learning what questions to ask as you write. Throughout this book, we include questions and suggestions to help you accomplish your writing tasks and reflect on the processes you use to write, read, and think critically.

A PROCESS OF WRITING

Writing can seem at times an overwhelming drudgery, worse than scrubbing floors; at other moments, it's a sport full of thrills—like whizzing downhill on skis, not knowing what you'll meet around a bend. Surprising and unpredictable as the process may seem, nearly all writers do similar things:

- They generate ideas.
- They plan, draft, and develop their papers.
- They revise and edit.

Although these activities form the basis of most effective writing processes, they aren't lockstep stages: you don't always proceed in a straight line. You can skip around in whatever order you like, work on several parts at a time, or circle back over what's already done. For example, while gathering material, you may feel an urge to play with a sentence until it clicks. Or while writing a draft, you may decide to look for more material. You can leap ahead, cross out, backtrack, adjust, question, test a fresh approach, tinker, polish, and, at the end, spell-check the tricky words.

Generating Ideas

The first activity in writing—finding a topic and something to say about it—is often the most challenging and least predictable. (For strategies for generating ideas, see Ch. 4.)

Discovering Something to Write About.   You may get an idea while talking with friends, riding your bike, or even staring out the window. Sometimes a topic lies near home, in an everyday event you recall. Often your reading raises questions that call for investigation. When a particular writing assignment doesn't appeal to you, your challenge is to find a slant that does interest you. Find it, and words will flow—words that can engage readers as you accomplish your purpose. (See the graphic below.)

Discovering Material.   You'll need information to shape and support your ideas—facts and figures, reports and opinions, examples and illustrations. Luckily you have numerous sources of supporting material to make your slant on a topic clear and convincing to your readers. You can recall your own experience and knowledge, you can observe things around you, you can converse with others who are knowledgeable, you can read materials that draw you to new views, and you can think critically about all the sources around you.

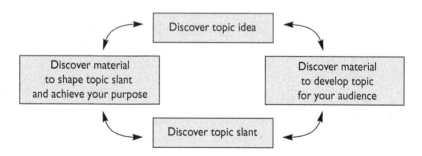

Planning, Drafting, and Developing

Next you will plan your paper, write a draft, and then develop your ideas further. (See the graphic on p. 6.)

Planning. Having discovered a burning idea (or at least a smoldering one) to write about, and some supporting material (but maybe not enough yet), you can sort out what matters most. (For planning strategies, see Ch. 5.) If right away you see one main point, or thesis, for your paper, test various ways of stating it, given your audience and purpose:

MAYBE   Parking in the morning before class is annoying.

OR   Parking on campus is a big problem.

Next arrange your ideas and material in a sensible order that clarifies your point. For example, you might group and label the ideas you have generated, make an outline, or analyze the main point, breaking it down into its parts:

> Parking on campus is a problem for students because of the long lines, inefficient entrances, and poorly marked spaces.

But if no clear thesis emerges quickly, don't worry. You may find one while you draft—that is, while you write an early version of your paper.

Drafting. When your ideas first start to flow, you want to welcome them—lure them forth, not tear them apart, so they don't go back into hiding. (For drafting strategies, see Ch. 6.) Don't be afraid to take risks at this stage: you'll probably be surprised and pleased at what happens, even though your first version will be rough. Writing takes time; a paper usually needs several drafts and may need a clearer introduction, a stronger conclusion, more convincing evidence, or a revised plan. Especially when your subject is unfamiliar or complicated, you may decide to throw out your first attempt and start over as a stronger idea evolves.

Developing. As you draft, you'll weave in explanations, examples, details, definitions, and varied evidence to make your ideas clear and persuasive. For example, you may need to define an at-risk student, illustrate the problems faced by a single parent, or supply statistics about hit-and-run accidents. If you lack specific support for your main point, you can use strategies for developing ideas (see Ch. 7) or return to strategies for generating ideas. You'll keep gaining insights and drawing conclusions while you draft. Welcome these ideas, and work them in if they fit.

Revising and Editing

You might want to relax once you have a draft, but for most writers revising begins the work in earnest. (See the visual on p. 7.) After you have a well-developed and well-organized revision, you are ready to edit: to correct errors and improve wording.

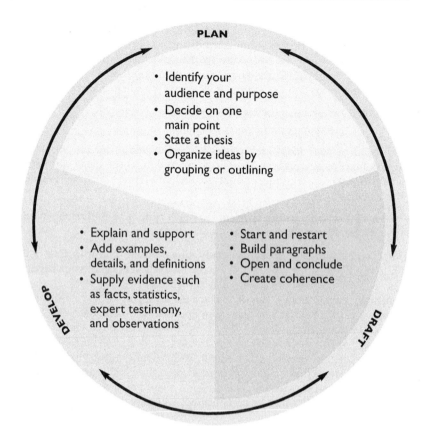

PLAN

- Identify your audience and purpose
- Decide on one main point
- State a thesis
- Organize ideas by grouping or outlining

DEVELOP

- Explain and support
- Add examples, details, and definitions
- Supply evidence such as facts, statistics, expert testimony, and observations

DRAFT

- Start and restart
- Build paragraphs
- Open and conclude
- Create coherence

Revising.   Revision is more than just changing words. It means both reseeing and rewriting, making major changes so that your paper accomplishes what you want it to. You may revise what you know and what you think while you're writing. You can then rework your thesis, reconsider your audience, shift plans, decide what to put in or leave out, rearrange for clarity, move sentences or paragraphs around, connect points differently, or better express ideas. Perhaps you'll add costs to a paper on parking problems or switch to fathers instead of mothers as you consider teen parenthood. (For revising strategies, see Ch. 8.)

If you put aside your draft for a few hours or a day, you can reread it with fresh eyes and a clear mind. Other students can also help you—sometimes more than a textbook or an instructor can—by responding to your drafts as engaged readers.

Editing.   Editing means refining details and correcting flaws that stand in the way of your readers' understanding and enjoyment. (For editing strategies, see Ch. 9.) Don't edit too early, though, because you may waste time on some part that you later revise out. In editing, you usually make these repairs:

- Get rid of unnecessary words.
- Choose livelier and more precise words.
- Replace any incorrect or inappropriate wording.
- Rearrange words in a clearer, more emphatic order.
- Combine short, choppy sentences.
- Break up long, confusing sentences.
- Refine transitions for continuity of thought.
- Check grammar, sentences, punctuation, and mechanics.

Proofreading.   Finally you'll proofread your paper, taking a last look, checking correctness, and catching spelling or word-processing errors. (For more on proofreading, see pp. 167–68.)

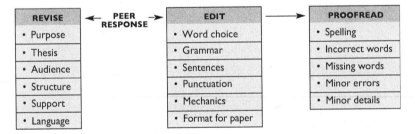

REVISE	← PEER RESPONSE →	EDIT		PROOFREAD
• Purpose		• Word choice		• Spelling
• Thesis		• Grammar		• Incorrect words
• Audience		• Sentences		• Missing words
• Structure		• Punctuation		• Minor errors
• Support		• Mechanics		• Minor details
• Language		• Format for paper		

Discussing Writing Processes

An online class began with an assigned reading about writing processes. The following string of messages starts with the instructor's explanation of the assignment followed by a few responses from students, each responding personally while extending the "thread."

Message no. 2706

Author: Kathleen Beauchene (ENGL1010_600_Beauchene)

Date: Saturday, October 10, 2:37pm

In the attached file, you will read about one author's writing process. In your post, you may either comment on a point he makes or share your own writing process, what works or doesn't work for you.

Message no. 2707

Author: Cristina Berrios

Date: Saturday, October 10, 4:02pm

I find that the author's writing process is similar in many ways to how most write, but I do not always have time to write and rewrite and organize and write and so on. . . . Of course I can see if you are a professional writer rewriting and making sure that your work can be produced to sell, but in my eyes I only need to make sure that my story is interesting, consecutive and progressive, and grammatically correct to the best of my ability. . . . Luckily I work in an office where I can interact closely with colleagues who are willing to listen to my "draft" (some of them are college students as well) and give me feedback.

Message no. 2708

Author: Joshua Tefft

Date: Saturday, October 10, 4:43pm

My writing process, like most people's, is similar to what the author does, given I have a lot of time anyway. I really have trouble with not erasing initial drafts, that is, incomplete drafts. I always find myself too critical of my work before it is anywhere near the final stages. But I've begun to learn to receive outside criticism before I put my own on it; this usually gives me a more open-minded perspective on my writing. But I've realized it's a long process to get the results one wants.

Message no. 2709

Author: Leah Threats

Date: Saturday, October 10, 11:49pm

My writing process includes a lot of thought process before I go anywhere near writing a first draft. Then I begin to write and reread it a few times while in the first paragraph, change wording, cut and paste all over the paper. Then I will move on to the middle of the paper, make sure my introduction has enough to it, and the mid section is full of "beef." Then in the ending, I try to make sure I don't leave the writer thinking, What else? . . . I do take the time to make sure I am not shortchanging my reader. As a person who LOVES to read, I want to be able to draw the reader into whatever it is I am writing to them.

Message no. 2711

Author: Arthur Wasilewski

Date: Sunday, October 11, 1:41pm

I approach the writing process with a shoot-from-the hip mentality. Whatever comes to my head first is usually the right idea. I'll think about the idea throughout the whole day or week, and transcribe it to paper after I've gone through a few mental iterations of my original idea.

Message no. 2713

Author: Joel Torres

Date: Sunday, October 11, 8:21pm

After reading this attachment I realize there are some things I sort of start to do in my own writing process, but stop halfway or do not go through thoroughly. I have used the outline idea from time to time. I should go into more depth and organize the ideas in my papers better in the future though. The whole concept of sleeping between drafts does not sit well with me. I find that when I sit down and write a paper, it is best when I dedicate a couple of hours and get into the "zone" and let the ideas flow through me. If the paper is a research paper, I usually do best when I type it directly onto a word processor. When the assignment is an essay or something along the lines of a written argument or a literary work, I like to handwrite and then go back and type it after. Distractions for me are a huge issue; TV, other websites, and just lack of focus definitely hurt my writing and are obstacles I must overcome every time a written assignment is due.

ACTIVITY 1.1: Describing Your Writing Process

Describe your writing process. How do you get started? How do you keep writing? What process do you go through to reach a final draft? What step or strategy in your writing process would you most like to change?

A SPOTLIGHT ON PURPOSE AND AUDIENCE

At any moment in the writing process, two questions are worth asking:

Why am I writing?   **Who is my audience?**

Writing for a Reason

Most college writing assignments ask you to write for a definite reason. For example, you might be asked to take a stand on an issue and to persuade your readers to respect your position. Be careful not to confuse the sources and strategies you apply in these assignments with your ultimate purpose for writing. "To compare and contrast two things" is not a very interesting purpose; "to compare and contrast two websites *in order to explain their differences*" implies a real reason for writing. In most college writing, your purpose will be to explain something to your readers or to convince them of something.

To sharpen your concentration on your purpose, ask yourself from the start, What do I want to do? And, in revising, Did I do what I meant to do? These practical questions can help you remove irrelevant information and other barriers to getting your paper where you want it to go.

▣ ACTIVITY 1.2: Considering Your Purpose

Imagine that you are in the following writing situations. For each, write a sentence or two summing up your purpose as a writer.

1. The instructor in your psychology course has assigned a paragraph about the meanings of three essential terms in your readings.
2. You're upset about a change in financial aid procedures and plan to write a letter asking the financial aid director to remedy the problem.
3. You're starting a blog about your first year at college so your extended family can visualize the environment and share your experiences.
4. Your supervisor wants you to write an article about the benefits of a new company service for the customer newsletter.
5. Your Facebook profile seemed appropriate last year, but you want to revise it now that you're attending college and have a job with future prospects.

Writing for Readers

Your audience, or your readers, may or may not be defined in your assignment. Consider the following examples:

ASSIGNMENT 1   Discuss the advantages and disadvantages of home schooling.

ASSIGNMENT 2   In a letter to parents of school-age children, discuss the advantages and disadvantages of home schooling.

If your assignment defines an audience, as the second example does, you will need to think about how to approach those readers and what to assume about their relationship to your topic. For example, what points would you direct to parents? How would you organize your ideas? Would you discuss advantages or disadvantages first? On the other hand, how might your approach differ if the assignment read this way?

> ASSIGNMENT 3   In a newsletter article for teachers, discuss the advantages and disadvantages of home schooling.

Some readers you will know personally—friends, classmates, instructors. You will make assumptions about other readers based on your experience and their positions or roles—for example, schoolteachers and parents concerned about home schooling. For a public or civic audience—people motivated by their values and engaged by an issue, a cause, or an election—you'll probably acknowledge their positions and then justify your own with persuasive evidence as you champion action or change. Writers who read widely also can draw on their experience as readers to help decide where to explain, connect, and elaborate. As you analyze what readers know, believe, and value, you can aim your writing toward them with a better chance of hitting your mark. Use these questions to help you write and revise for your audience.

GENERAL AUDIENCE CHECKLIST

☐ Who are your readers? What is their relationship to you?

☐ What do they know about your topic? What do you want them to learn to accomplish your purpose?

☐ How much detail will they want to read about this topic?

☐ What objections are they likely to raise as they read? How can you anticipate and overcome their objections?

☐ What's likely to convince or to offend them?

☐ What tone or style might influence them?

■ ACTIVITY 1.3: Considering Your Audience

Write a short paragraph describing in detail a "worst" event—your worst date, worst dinner, worst car repair, or some similar catastrophe. Then revise that paragraph so your audience is a person involved in the event—the person who went on that date with you, cooked or served the dinner, worked on your car. Now revise again, this time writing to a person you plan to date soon, a cook at a restaurant you want to try, or a repair person from another garage. Compare the three paragraphs. How are they similar? How do they differ?

Targeting Academic Readers

Although you are likely to aim future writing at a specific audience — the marketing team at work or other members of an animal rescue group — many of your college assignments will resemble the sample Assignment 1 (p. 10). Those assignments will assume that you are addressing general academic readers, represented by your instructor and maybe your classmates. General academic readers typically expect clear, logical writing that uses supporting evidence to explain, interpret, or persuade. In addition, their particular expectations may differ by field. For example, biologists might assume you'll supply the findings from your experiment while literature specialists might look for plenty of relevant quotations from the

---

ACADEMIC AUDIENCE CHECKLIST

☐ How has your instructor advised you to write for readers in the field? What criteria will be used for grading your papers?

☐ What do the assigned readings in your course assume about readers and their expectations? Has your instructor recommended useful models or sample readings?

☐ What topics and issues concern readers in the field? What puzzles do they want to solve? How do they want to solve them?

☐ How is writing in the field commonly organized? For example, do writers tend to follow a persuasive pattern: introduce the issue, state their assertion or claim, explain their reasons, acknowledge other views, and conclude? Do they use a series of conventional headings — for example, Abstract, Introduction to the Problem, Methodology, Findings, and Discussion?

☐ What evidence is typically gathered to support ideas or interpretations — facts and statistics, quotations from texts, summaries of research, references to authorities or prior studies, results from experimental research, or field notes from observations or interviews?

☐ What style, tone, and level of formality do writers in the field tend to use and readers tend to expect?

novel you're analyzing. Depending on the field, your readers may expect certain topics, types of evidence, and approaches. Use the questions in the checklist on page 12 to help you pinpoint what they want.

ACTIVITY 1.4: Considering an Academic Audience

Working by yourself or with a small group, use the Academic Audience Checklist to examine several reading or writing assignments in one of your courses. Try to identify prominent features of writing in the field. Which of these characteristics might be expected in student papers? How might you meet those expectations? How would an academic paper differ from writing on the same topic for a general audience—for example, a letter to the editor, newspaper article, consumer brochure, summary for young students, or web page?

2

Reading Processes

What's so special about college reading? Don't you pick up the book, start on the first page, and keep going, just as you have ever since you met *The Cat in the Hat*? Reading from beginning to end works well when you are eager to find out what happens next, as in a thriller, or what to do next, as in a cookbook.

On the other hand, much of what you read in college—textbooks, scholarly articles, research reports, your peers' papers—is complicated and challenging. In addition, when your writing relies on your reading, you not only need to explain what is going on in the reading but also to go further, making your own point based on what you have read. Perhaps you will have to evaluate strengths and weaknesses of essays by professionals and classmates. Perhaps you will have to figure out what complex sources say—and then decide whether they are reliable, what they assume, and how you might use their information. Handling dense academic material often requires close reading and deep thinking—in short, a process for reading critically.

A PROCESS OF CRITICAL READING

Reading critically means approaching whatever you read in an active, questioning manner. This essential college-level skill changes reading from a spectator sport to a contact sport. You no longer sit in the stands, watching skaters glide by. Instead, you charge right into a rough-and-tumble hockey game, gripping your stick and watching out for your teeth.

Critical reading, like critical thinking (see Ch. 3), is not an isolated activity. It is a continuum of strategies that thoughtful people use every day to grapple with new information, to integrate it with existing knowledge, and to apply it to problems in daily life and in academic courses. Many readers use similar strategies:

- They get ready to do their reading.
- They respond as they read.
- They read on literal and analytical levels.

▋ ACTIVITY 2.1: Describing Your Reading Process

How do you read a magazine, newspaper, or popular novel? What are your goals for this kind of reading? What's different about reading material assigned in college? What are your techniques for reading assignments? Which strategies might help classmates, especially in classes with a lot of reading? Sum up how you might read more effectively.

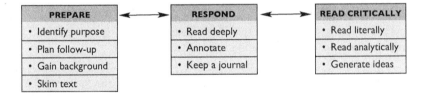

PREPARE	RESPOND	READ CRITICALLY
• Identify purpose	• Read deeply	• Read literally
• Plan follow-up	• Annotate	• Read analytically
• Gain background	• Keep a journal	• Generate ideas
• Skim text		

Preparing to Read

College reading is active reading. Before you read, think ahead about how to approach the reading process, how to make the most of your reading time, and how to assess and apply what you read.

Thinking about Your Purpose.   Naturally, your overall goal for doing most college reading is to succeed in your courses. When you begin to read, ask questions like these about your immediate purpose:

- What are you reading?
- Why are you reading?
- What do you want to do with the reading?
- What does your instructor expect you to learn from the reading?
- Do you need to memorize details, find main points, or connect ideas?
- How does this reading build on, add to, contrast with, or otherwise relate to other reading assignments in the course?

Planning Your Follow-Up.   When you are required to read, ask your-self what your instructor probably expects to follow the reading:

- Do you need to be ready to discuss the reading during class?
- Will you need to mention it or analyze it during an examination?
- Will you need to write about it or its topic?
- Do you need to find its main points? Sum it up? Compare it? Question it? Spot its strengths and weaknesses? Draw details from it?

Skimming the Text.   Before you actively read a text, begin by skimming it, quickly reading only enough to introduce yourself to its content and organization. If the reading has a table of contents or subheadings, read those first to figure out what it covers and how it is organized. Read the first paragraph and then the first (or first and last) sentence of each paragraph that follows. Read the captions for any visuals.

Responding to Reading

You may be used to reading simply for facts or main ideas. However, critical reading is far more active than fact hunting. It requires responding, questioning, and challenging as you read.

Reading Deeply.   Use these questions to dive below the surface of a reading:

- How does the writer begin? What does the opening reveal about the writer's purpose? How does it prepare readers for what follows?
- How might you trace the progression of ideas? How do headings, previews of what's coming up, summaries of what's gone before, and transitions signal the organization?
- Are difficult or technical terms defined in specific ways? How might you highlight, list, or record those terms so that you can master them?
- How might you record or recall the details in the reading? How might you track or diagram interrelated ideas to grasp the connections?
- How do word choice, tone, and style alert you to the complex purpose of a reading that is layered or indirect rather than straightforward?
- Does the reading use figurative or descriptive language, refer to other works, or repeat themes? How do these elements enrich the reading?

- Can you answer any reading questions in your textbook, assignment, study guide, or syllabus? Can you restate headings ("Major Types of X") as questions ("What are the major types of X?") and give the answers?

Keeping a Reading Journal.   A reading journal helps you read actively and build a reservoir of ideas for follow-up writing. You can use a special notebook or computer file to address questions like these:

- What is the subject of the reading? What is the writer's stand?
- What does the writer take for granted? Where are these assumptions stated or suggested?
- What evidence supports the writer's main points?
- Do you agree with what the writer says? Do his or her ideas clash with your ideas or question something you take for granted?
- Has the writer taken account of other views, opinions, or interpretations of evidence?
- What conclusions can you draw from the reading?
- Has the reading opened your eyes to new ways of viewing the subject?

Annotating the Text.   Writing notes on the page (or on a copy if the material is not your own) is a useful way to trace the author's points and to respond to them with your own comments. You can underline key points, add check marks and stars by ideas when you agree or disagree, and jot questions in the margins. (For a Critical Reading Checklist, see p. 23.) When one student investigated the history of women's professional sports, she annotated a key passage from an article called "Why Men Fear Women's Teams" by Kate Rounds from the January–February 1991 issue of *Ms.*

different case from individual sports

By contrast, women's professional (team) sports have failed   *key point—still mostly true?*
spectacularly. Since the mid-seventies, every professional
✔   league—softball, basketball, and volleyball—has gone belly-up.
In 1981, after a four-year struggle, the Women's Basketball   *bitter tone*
1st example backs up point   League (WBL), backed by sports promoter Bill Byrne, folded.   *What*
The league was drawing fans in a number of cities, but the   *women's teams have*
✔   sponsors weren't there, TV wasn't there, and nobody seemed to   *gotten these?*
miss the spectacle of a few good women fighting for a basketball.

Something I know about!

Why does she call it this?

Or a volleyball, for that matter. Despite the success of bikini volleyball, an organization called MLV (Major League Volleyball) bit the dust in March of 1989 after nearly three years of struggling for sponsorship, fan support, and television exposure. [As with pro basketball, there was a man behind women's professional volleyball,] real estate investor Robert (Bat) Batinovich. Batinovich admits that, unlike court volleyball, beach volleyball has a lot of "visual T&A mixed into it."

2nd example

She's suspicious of men

oh, great

credential

Do guys still think we should be weak and prissy?

What court volleyball does have, according to former MLV executive director Lindy Vivas, is strong women athletes. Vivas is assistant volleyball coach at San Jose State University. "The United States in general," she says, "has problems dealing with women athletes and strong, aggressive females. The perception is you have to be more aggressive in team sports than in golf and tennis, which aren't contact sports. Women athletes are looked at as masculine and get the stigma of being gay."

seems like these are only two options

good quote

This student's annotations helped her deepen her reading of the article and generate ideas for her writing.

ACTIVITY 2.2: Annotating a Passage

Annotate the following passage. It opens the summary of findings for the survey "How Mobile Devices Are Changing Community Information Environments" (Pew Internet & American Life Project, *2011 State of the News Media Report*).

Local news is going mobile. Nearly half of all American adults (47%) report that they get at least some local news and information on their cellphone or tablet computer. 1

What they seek out most on mobile platforms is information that is practical and in real time: 42% of mobile device owners report getting weather updates on their phones or tablets; 37% say they get material about restaurants or other local businesses. These consumers are less likely to use their mobile devices for news about local traffic, public transportation, general news alerts or to access retail coupons or discounts. 2

One of the newest forms of on-the-go local news consumption, mobile applications are just beginning to take hold among mobile device owners. 3

Compared with other adults, these mobile local news consumers   4
are younger, live in higher income households, are newer residents
of their communities, live in nonrural areas, and tend to be parents
of minor children. Adults who get local news and information on
mobile devices are more likely than others to feel they can have an
impact on their communities, more likely to use a variety of media
platforms, feel more plugged into the media environment than they
did a few years ago, and are more likely to use social media:

- 35% of mobile local news consumers feel they can have a big
  impact on their community (vs. 27% of other adults)
- 65% feel it is easier today than five years ago to keep up with
  information about their community (vs. 47% of nonmobile
  connectors)
- 51% use six or more different sources or platforms monthly to
  get local news and information (vs. 21%)
- 75% use social network sites (vs. 42%)
- 15% use Twitter (vs. 4%)

Tablets and smartphones have also brought with them news   5
applications or "apps." One-quarter (24%) of mobile local news consumers report having an app that helps them get information or news
about their local community. That equates to 13% of all device owners and 11% of the total American adult population. Thus while
nearly 5 in 10 get local news on mobile devices, just 1 in 10 use apps
to do so. Call it the app gap.

A SPOTLIGHT ON READING LEVELS

Educational expert Benjamin Bloom identified six levels of cognitive
activity: knowledge, comprehension, application, analysis, synthesis, and
evaluation.[1] (A recent update recasts *synthesis* as *creating* and moves it
above evaluation to the highest level.) Each level acts as a foundation for
the next. Each also becomes more complex and demands higher thinking
skills than the previous one. (See Fig. 2.1.) Experienced readers, however, jump among these levels, gathering information and insight as they
occur.

The first three levels are literal skills. When you show that you know
a fact, comprehend its meaning, and can apply it to a new situation, you

[1]Benjamin S. Bloom et al., *Taxonomy of Educational Objectives, Handbook 1: Cognitive Domain.* Copyright © 1956 by David McKay, Inc. Reprinted with the permission of Random House, Inc. Also see the update in David R. Krathwohl, "A
Revision of Bloom's Taxonomy: An Overview," *Theory into Practice* 41.4 (2002):
212–18; print.

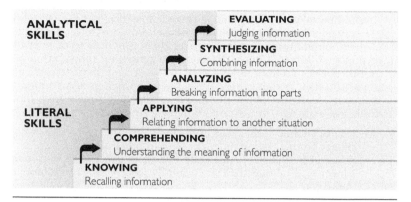

Figure 2.1   Using Literal and Analytical Reading Skills. The information in this figure is adapted from Benjamin S. Bloom et al., *Taxonomy of Educational Objectives, Handbook 1: Cognitive Domain* (New York: McKay, 1956; print).

demonstrate your mastery over building blocks of thought. The last three levels—analysis, synthesis, and evaluation—are critical skills that your instructors especially want you to develop. These skills take you beyond the literal level: you break apart the building blocks to see what makes them work, recombine them in new and useful ways, and judge their worth or significance. To read critically, you must engage with a piece on both literal and analytical levels.

Reading on Literal Levels

As you tackle an unfamiliar reading, you may struggle simply to discover what—exactly—it presents to readers. For example, suppose you read in your history book a passage about Franklin Delano Roosevelt (FDR), the only American president elected to four consecutive terms.

Knowing.   Once you read the passage, even if you have little background in American history, you know and can recall the information it presents about FDR and his four terms in office.

Comprehending.   To comprehend the information, you need to know that a U.S. president's term of office is four years and that *consecutive* means "continuous." Thus, FDR was elected to serve for sixteen years.

Applying.   To apply this knowledge, you think of other presidents—George Washington, who served two terms; Grover Cleveland, who served two terms but not consecutively; Jimmy Carter, who served one term; and George W. Bush, who served two terms. Then you realize that being elected to four terms is unusual. In fact, the Twenty-Second Amendment to the Constitution, ratified in 1951, now limits a president to two terms.

Reading on Analytical Levels

After mastering a passage on the literal levels, you need to probe for meaning beneath the surface. First, you analyze the information, considering its parts and implications from various angles. Then you gather related material and synthesize all of it, combining it to achieve new insights. Finally, you evaluate the significance of the information.

Analyzing.   You can scrutinize FDR's four terms as president from various angles, selecting a principle that suits your purpose to break the information into its components or parts. For example, you might analyze FDR's tenure in office in relation to the political longevity of other presidents. Why has FDR been the only president elected to serve four terms? What circumstances during his terms contributed to three reelections? How is FDR different from other presidents?

Synthesizing.   To answer your questions, you may have to read more or review material you have read in the past. Then you begin synthesizing—creating a new approach or combination by pulling together the facts and opinions, identifying evidence accepted by all or most sources, examining any controversial evidence, and drawing conclusions that reliable evidence seems to support. For example, you might logically conclude that the special circumstances of the Great Depression and World War II contributed to FDR's four terms, not that Americans reelected FDR out of pity because he had polio.

Evaluating.   Finally, you evaluate the significance of your new knowledge for your understanding of Depression-era politics and your assessment of your history book's approach. For instance, you might ask yourself why the book's author has chosen to make this point and how it affects the rest of the discussion. And you may also have formed your own opinion about FDR's reelections, perhaps concluding that FDR's four-term presidency is understandable in light of the events of the 1930s and 1940s, that the author has mentioned this fact to highlight the unique political atmosphere of that era, and that, in your opinion, it is evidence neither for nor against FDR's excellence as a president.

▌ ACTIVITY 2.3: Reading Analytically

Think back to something you have read recently that helped you make a decision, perhaps a newspaper or magazine article, an online posting, or a college brochure. How did you analyze what you read, breaking the information into parts? How did you synthesize it, combining it with what you already knew? How did you evaluate it, judging its contribution to your decision making?

GENERATING IDEAS FROM READING

Like flints that strike each other and cause sparks, writers and readers provoke one another. For example, when your class discusses an essay, you may be surprised by the range of insights your classmates report. If you missed some of their insights during your reading, remember that they may be equally surprised by what you see.

Often you look to other writers—in books or articles—to suggest a topic, provide information about it, or help you explain it or back it up with evidence. Whether you read because you want to understand ideas, test them, or debate with the writer, reading is a dynamic process. It may change your ideas instead of support them. Here are suggestions for unlocking the potential hidden in a good text.

Looking for Meaty Pieces.   Stimulate your thinking about current topics by browsing through essay collections or magazines in the library or online. Try *Atlantic, Harper's, New Republic, Commentary,* or special-interest magazines like *Architectural Digest* or *Scientific American.* Check editorials and op-ed columns in your local newspaper, the *New York Times,* or the *Wall Street Journal.* Also search the Internet on intriguing topics that challenge you to think seriously (for example, film classics or the effects of poverty on children). Look for meaty, not superficial, articles written to inform and convince, not to entertain or amuse.

Logging Your Reading.   For several days keep a log of the articles that you find. Record the author, title, and source for each promising piece so that you can easily find it again. Briefly note the subject and point of view in order to identify a range of possibilities.

Recalling Something You Have Already Read.   What have you read lately that started you thinking? Return to a recent reading—a chapter in a humanities textbook, an article for sociology, a research report for biology.

Capturing Complex Ideas.   When you find a challenging reading, do you feel too overwhelmed to develop ideas from it? If so, read it slowly and carefully. Then try two common methods of recording and integrating ideas from sources into papers. First, try *paraphrasing*, restating the author's ideas fully but in your own words. Then try *summarizing*, reducing the author's main point to essentials. (For examples, see pp. 223–24.) Accurately restating what a reading says can help you grasp its ideas, especially on literal levels. Once you understand what it says, you can agree with, disagree with, or question its points.

Reading Critically.   Read first literally and then analytically. Instead of just soaking up what the reading says, try conversing with the writer. Criticize. Wonder. Argue back. Demand convincing evidence. Use the following checklist to get started as a critical reader.

CRITICAL READING CHECKLIST

☐ What problems and issues does the author raise?

☐ What is the author's purpose? Is it to explain or inform? To persuade? To amuse? In addition to this overall purpose, is the author trying to accomplish some other agenda?

☐ How does the author appeal to you as a reader? Where do you agree, and where do you disagree? Where do you want to say "Yeah, right!" or "I don't think so!"?

☐ How does this piece relate to your own experiences or thoughts? Have you encountered anything similar? Does the topic or approach intrigue you?

☐ Are there any important words or ideas that you don't understand? If so, do you need to reread or turn to a dictionary or reference book?

☐ What is the author's point of view? What does the author assume or take for granted? Where does the author reveal these assumptions? Do they make the selection seem weak or biased?

☐ Which statements are facts that can be verified by observation, firsthand testimony, or research? Which are opinions? Does one or the other dominate the piece?

☐ Is the writer's evidence accurate, relevant, and sufficient? Do you find it persuasive?

Analyzing Writing Strategies.   Reading widely and deeply can reveal not only what others say but also how they say it and how they shape such key features as the introduction, thesis statement or main idea, major points, and supporting evidence. Ask questions to help you identify writing strategies.

WRITING STRATEGIES CHECKLIST

- ☐ How does the author introduce the reading? In what ways does the author try to engage readers?
- ☐ Where does the author state or imply the main idea or thesis?
- ☐ How is the text organized? What main points develop the thesis? What do these points suggest about the author's approach?
- ☐ How does the author supply support—facts, data, statistics, expert opinions, personal experiences, observations, explanations, examples, or other information?
- ☐ How does the author connect or emphasize ideas for readers?
- ☐ How does the author conclude the reading?
- ☐ What is the author's tone? How do the words and examples reveal the author's attitude, biases, or assumptions?

■ ACTIVITY 2.4: Reading Critically

Using the advice in this chapter, critically read the following essay from *Wired* magazine. First, add your own notes and comments in the margin, responding on both literal and analytical levels. Second, add notes about the writer's writing strategies. (Sample annotations are supplied to help you get started.) Finally, write a brief summary of the reading and your own well-reasoned conclusions about the reading.

CLIVE THOMPSON

The New Literacy

Writer starts with complaints and question

As the school year begins, be ready to hear pundits° fretting once again about how kids today can't write—and technology is to blame. Facebook encourages narcissistic°   1

pundits: Critics and commentators.   **narcissistic:** Self-centered.

blabbering, video and PowerPoint have replaced carefully crafted essays, and texting has dehydrated language into "bleak, bald, sad shorthand" (as University College of London English professor John Sutherland has moaned). An age of illiteracy is at hand, right?

Answers with big study

Andrea Lunsford isn't so sure. Lunsford is a professor of writing and rhetoric at Stanford University, where she has organized a mammoth project called the Stanford Study of Writing to scrutinize° college students' prose. From 2001 to 2006, she collected 14,672 student writing samples—everything from in-class assignments, formal essays, and journal entries to e-mails, blog posts, and chat sessions. Her conclusions are stirring.

"I think we're in the midst of a literacy revolution the likes of which we haven't seen since Greek civilization," she says. For Lunsford, technology isn't killing our ability to write. It's reviving it—and pushing our literacy in bold new directions.

And big claim!

The first thing she found is that young people today write far more than any generation before them. That's because so much socializing takes place online, and it almost always involves text. Of all the writing that the Stanford students did, a stunning 38 percent of it took place out of the classroom—life writing, as Lunsford calls it. Those Twitter updates and lists of 25 things about yourself add up.

Is this me?

It's almost hard to remember how big a paradigm shift this is. Before the Internet came along, most Americans never wrote anything, ever, that wasn't a school assignment. Unless they got a job that required producing text (like in law, advertising, or media), they'd leave school and virtually never construct a paragraph again.

But is this explosion of prose good, on a technical level? Yes. Lunsford's team found that the students were remarkably adept at what rhetoricians call *kairos*—assessing their audience and adapting their tone and technique to best get their point across. The modern world of online writing, particularly in chat and on discussion threads, is conversational and public, which makes it closer to the Greek tradition of argument than the asynchronous° letter and essay writing of 50 years ago.

scrutinize: Examine carefully.   **asynchronous:** Not occurring at the same time.

The fact that students today almost always write for an   7
audience (something virtually no one in my generation did)
gives them a different sense of what constitutes good writing. In interviews, they defined good prose as something
that had an effect on the world. For them, writing is about
persuading and organizing and debating, even if it's over
something as quotidian° as what movie to go see. The Stanford students were almost always less enthusiastic about
their in-class writing because it had no audience but the
professor: It didn't serve any purpose other than to get them
a grade. As for those texting short-forms and smileys defil-
ing° *serious* academic writing? Another myth. When Lunsford
examined the work of first-year students, she didn't find a
single example of texting speak in an academic paper.

Of course, good teaching is always going to be crucial,   8
as is the mastering of formal academic prose. But it's also
becoming clear that online media are pushing literacy into
cool directions. The brevity of texting and status updating
teaches young people to deploy haiku°-like concision.° At
the same time, the proliferation° of new forms of online
pop-cultural exegesis°—from sprawling TV-show recaps to
15,000-word videogame walkthroughs—has given them a
chance to write enormously long and complex pieces of
prose, often while working collaboratively with others.

We think of writing as either good or bad. What today's   9
young people know is that knowing who you're writing for
and why you're writing might be the most crucial factor of all.

quotidian: Ordinary, commonplace.   **defiling:** Making dirty;
corrupting.   **haiku:** Japanese form of poetry having three un-
rhymed lines of five, seven, and five syllables.   **concision:** The
quality of being brief; brevity.   **proliferation:** Rapid increase.
exegesis: Explanation or analysis.

Activity 2.5: Responding Critically

Alley Julseth was asked to read "The New Literacy" (pp. 24–26) and to
write a reading response on both literal and analytical levels. Read her
thoughtful personal response. Then write your own critical response,
responding to her, responding in your own way to Thompson's essay,
or both.

ALLEY JULSETH

Analyzing "The New Literacy"

Being part of a generation that spends an immense amount of   1
time online, I find it rather annoying to hear that youth today are
slowly diminishing the art of writing. Because Facebook and Twitter
have limited character space, I do use abbreviations such as s.m.h.
(shaking my head), "abt" (about), and "u" (you). However, my
simplistic way of writing informally for online media has no correlation
with my formal writing. In "The New Literacy" essay, Clive Thompson
indicates that this lack of correlation seems to be the case with many
more students.

Thompson explores the idea that the advancing media is changing   2
the way students write. After citing Professor Sutherland blaming
technology for "bleak, bald, sad shorthand" (qtd. in Thompson 25),
he goes on to describe the Stanford Study of Writing, conducted by
writing professor Andrea Lunsford. She studied over 14,000 examples
of student writing from academic essays to e-mails and chats. From
these samples, she learned that "young people today write far more
than any generation before them" (25). I completely agree with this
point based on the large volume I write socializing on the Internet. I
believe that the time I spend online writing one-dimensional phrases
does not weaken my formal writing as a student.

Thompson goes on to explain that the new way of writing on the   3
Internet is actually more similar to the Greek tradition of argument
than to the essay and letter-writing tradition of the last half century.
Lunsford concluded that "the students were remarkably adept at what
rhetoricians call *kairos* — assessing their audience and adapting their
tone and technique to best get their point across" (25). Their Internet
writing is like a conversation with another person.

I find this conclusion interesting. As I advance in my writing as   4
a student, I remember being taught as a child that there is a distinct
line between writing an essay that is due to a teacher and writing a

letter to a friend. Although the two are different, there are similarities as well. The nice thing about writing on the Internet is that I can choose what I write about and how I say it. When I'm writing to a friend, sticking to the point isn't exactly the goal, but I do get my main point across. However, I never write a formal essay unless it is assigned. Like the Stanford students, I do not look forward to writing an essay simply for the grade. Writing for a prompt I did not choose does not allow me to put my full-hearted passion into the essay. When I was younger, I wrote essays that were more bland and straight to the point. As I write now, I try to think as though I am reading to a room full of people, keeping my essay as interesting as I can.

Thompson ends his piece on the importance of good teaching.   5
This importance is true; teaching is the way students learn how to draw that line between formal and informal writing and how to write depending on audience. I appreciate and completely agree with Thompson's essay. I feel that he describes the younger generation very well. He is pushing away what high-brow critics say, and he is saying we are almost inventing a new way of writing.

Works Cited

Thompson, Clive. "The New Literacy." *Writing and Revising: A Portable Guide.* 2nd ed. Ed. X. J. Kennedy, Dorothy M. Kennedy, and Marcia F. Muth. Boston: Bedford, 2015. 24–26. Print.

READING ONLINE AND MULTIMODAL TEXTS

Traditionally, a literate person was someone who could read and write. That definition remains accurate, but online technologies have vastly increased the complexity of reading and writing. Multimodal texts now combine written words with images, sounds, and motion. Such texts cannot be confined to the fixed form of a printed page in a bound book. In addition, they may be randomly or routinely updated and are often accessed flexibly as readers wander through sites and follow links. More innovations, unimaginable now, might well emerge even before you graduate from college.

Learning to read and write effectively has likewise increased in complexity. Many people simply assume that readers' eyes routinely move from left to right, from one letter or word to the next. However, eye-movement studies show that readers actually jump back and forth, skip letters and words, and guess at what eyes skip over. Online readers also may jump from line to line or chunk to chunk, scanning the page. In addition, images in multimodal texts may draw the eyes to, or from, the typical left-to-right, top-to-bottom path. Analyzing an image's meaning or impact may require "reading" its placement and arrangement.

What might these changes mean for you as a reader and writer? Your critical reading skills are likely to be increasingly necessary and useful. The essential challenge of deep, thoughtful reading applies to web pages, graphic novels, photo essays, and YouTube videos just as it applies to traditional books and articles. In fact, some might argue that multimodal texts appealing to multiple senses require even more thorough scrutiny to grasp what they say and how they say it.

Here are some suggestions for applying your critical reading skills in these new contexts:

- Concentrate on your purpose to stay focused when you read online or multimodal texts, especially if those texts tug you away from your intended search or material.

- Create an online file or a reading journal so you have a handy location for responding to new materials. Bookmark online readings, sites, or multimodal texts so you can easily return to them. Consider what you see or hear, what the material suggests, and how it appeals to you.

- Read the features and effects of visual or multimodal texts as carefully as you read printed words. Observe composition, symmetry, sequence, shape, color, texture, brightness, and other visual components.

- Listen for the presence and impact of audio characteristics such as sound effects (accuracy, clarity, volume, timing, emotional power), speech (pitch, tone, dialect, accent, pace), and music (instrumentation, vocals, melody, rhythm, harmony, musical roots, cuts, remix decisions).

- Critically examine visual or multimodal materials—analyzing components, synthesizing varied information, and evaluating effects.

- Go beyond the immediate impact of a text to consider its foundation: Who wrote, prepared, or presented it? What audience does it address? What is its purpose or goal? How does it try to appeal logically, emotionally, or ethically?

- Carefully assess multimodal evidence that might support your points or challenge other views to ensure that you rely on trustworthy sources.

- Secure any necessary permission to add someone else's visual or audio material to your text and credit your source appropriately.

- Generate even more ideas by rereading this chapter and thinking about how you could apply the skills presented here in new situations.

ACTIVITY 2.6: Reading a Website

Work with a classmate or small group to examine a website about a topic you might want to investigate. Critically "read" and discuss the site's text, images, organization, and other features that might persuade you that it is or isn't a reliable source. Briefly sum up your conclusions.

3

Critical Thinking
Processes

Critic, from the Greek word *kritikos*, means "one who can judge and discern"—in short, someone who thinks critically. College will have given you your money's worth if it leaves you better able to judge and discern—to determine what is more and less important, to make distinctions and recognize differences, to generalize from specifics, to draw conclusions from evidence, to grasp complex concepts, to choose wisely. The effective thinking that you will need in college, on the job, and in your daily life is active and purposeful, not passive and ambling. It is critical thinking.

A PROCESS OF CRITICAL THINKING

You use critical thinking every day to solve problems and make decisions. Suppose you don't have enough money both to pay your tuition and to buy the car you need to get to campus and to work. First, you might pin down the causes of your financial problem. Next, you might examine your options to find the best solution, as shown in the graphic on page 32.

■ ACTIVITY 3.1: Thinking Critically to Solve a Campus Problem

With classmates, identify a common problem for students at your college—juggling a busy schedule, parking on campus, changing a class, joining a social group, getting a job, or some other issue. Working together, use critical thinking to explore the problem and identify possible solutions.

? **Problem**

You can't afford both your college tuition and the car you need.

SOLUTION

1 **IDENTIFY CAUSES**

Causes in your control:
Expensive vacation?
Credit card debt?

Causes out of your control:
Medical emergency?
Job loss?
Tuition increase?
Financial aid policy change?

2 **ANALYZE, SYNTHESIZE, AND EVALUATE OPTIONS**

Do without a car	(how?)	• Get rides with family or friends?
		• Take public transportation?
Decrease your tuition	(how?)	• Take fewer courses?
Get more money	(how?)	• Get a loan from the college?
		• Get a loan from a family member?
		• Get another job?

3 **REACH A LOGICAL CONCLUSION**

Apply for a short-term loan through the college for tuition.

Building Critical Thinking Skills

Using critical thinking, you can explore many problems step-by-step and reach reasonable solutions. Although you need to think hard—taking time to concentrate, consider alternatives, and allow deeper ideas to evolve—you may also need to think differently. Critical thinking, like critical reading, draws on a cluster of intellectual strategies and skills (see p. 20). Three activities—analysis, synthesis, and evaluation—are the core of critical thinking:

- Analysis—identifying crucial parts, phases, components, or other elements of a situation, problem, or issue.
- Synthesis—pulling together thought and investigation to form a new idea, propose an alternative, or support a different conclusion that

combines your own ideas, considerations, and possible solutions with other relevant, alternative, or competing ideas.

- Evaluation—judging in terms of significance, value, importance, practicality, or other criteria.

These activities are not new to you, but applying them rigorously may be. When you approach college-level reading and writing tasks, instructors will expect you (and you should expect yourself) to think, read, write, and think some more as the graphic below illustrates.

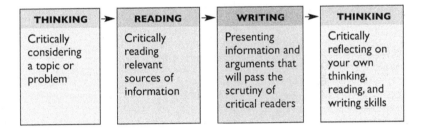

THINKING	READING	WRITING	THINKING
Critically considering a topic or problem	Critically reading relevant sources of information	Presenting information and arguments that will pass the scrutiny of critical readers	Critically reflecting on your own thinking, reading, and writing skills

■ ACTIVITY 3.2: Thinking Critically to Explore an Issue

You have worked hard on a group presentation that will be a major part of your grade—and each member of the group will get the same grade. Two days before the project is due, you discover that one group member has plagiarized heavily from various sources well known to your instructor. Working together with classmates, use critical thinking to explore your problem and determine what you might do. Analyze to identify the crucial parts of the issue; synthesize to combine the group's views and possible solutions with any other relevant ideas (such as the campus honor code or your instructor's policies); and evaluate to judge your conclusions in terms of significance, value, importance, practicality, or other criteria.

Applying Critical Thinking to Academic Problems

Your college assignments will pose academic problems to help you gain experience grappling with them. As you do so, you'll be expected to use your critical thinking skills—analyzing, synthesizing, and evaluating—in your reading and writing. Although you could simply dive in, using each skill as needed, sometimes the very wording of an assignment or exam question will alert you to a skill that your instructor expects to assess as Table 3.1 illustrates.

TABLE 3.1   Using Critical Thinking for Academic Assignments

Critical Thinking Skill	Sample Academic Assignments
Analysis: Breaking into parts and elements based on a principle **Applications:** Identifying parts of information as you read; explaining parts of events, ideas, processes, and structures as you write	• Describe the immediate causes of the 1929 stock market crash. • Trace the stages through which a bill becomes federal law. • Explain and illustrate the three dominant styles of parenting. • Define romanticism, identifying and illustrating its major characteristics.
Synthesis: Combining parts and elements to form new wholes **Applications:** Pulling information and implications together as you read; merging ideas from sources with your own ideas to write about the unique combination	• Discuss the following statement: High-minded opposition to slavery was only one cause, and not a very important one, of the animosity between North and South that in 1861 escalated into civil war. • Imagine that you are a trial lawyer in 1921, charged with defending Nicola Sacco and Bartolomeo Vanzetti, two anarchists accused of murder. Argue for their acquittal on whatever grounds you can justify.
Evaluation: Judging according to standards or criteria **Applications:** Using standards to judge the significance or value of what you read; convincing readers that your criteria for judging are reasonable	• Present and evaluate the most widely accepted theories that explain the disappearance of the dinosaurs. • Defend or show weaknesses in the idea that houses and public buildings should be constructed to last no longer than twenty years. • Contrast the models of the solar system advanced by Copernicus and by Kepler, showing how the latter improved on the former.

ACTIVITY 3.3: Thinking Critically to Respond to an Academic Problem

Working with a partner or in a small group, bring in an assignment from one of your classes or select one of the sample assignments in Table 3.1. Does the assignment indicate what is expected? Does it suggest how to meet expectations? Explain how you would approach the assignment in order to demonstrate your critical thinking. Share your explanations and strategies for figuring out how to tackle academic assignments.

A SPOTLIGHT ON EVIDENCE

As you write a college paper, you try to figure out your purpose, the position you want to take, and ways to get readers to follow and accept your logic. Your challenge is not just to think clearly but to demonstrate your thinking to others, to persuade them to pay attention to what you say. And sound evidence is what critical readers want to see.

Sound evidence supports your main idea or thesis, substantiating your points for readers. It also bolsters your credibility as a writer, demonstrating the merit of your position. Without evidence, thoughtful readers have no reason to agree with your position or believe what you claim. When you write, you need to marshal enough appropriate evidence to clarify, explain, and support your ideas. You need to weave claims, evidence, and your own interpretations together into a clearly reasoned explanation or argument. And as you do so, you need to select and test your evidence so that it will convince your readers.

Using Different Types of Evidence

What is evidence? It is anything that demonstrates the soundness of a claim. Facts, statistics, expert testimony, and firsthand observations are four reliable forms of evidence (see Table 3.2 on p. 39). Other evidence might include examples, illustrations, details, and authoritative opinions. Depending on the purpose of your assignment, some kinds of evidence weigh more heavily than others. For example, readers might appreciate your memories of caring for animals on the farm in an essay recalling your childhood summers. However, they would probably discount your memories in an explanatory or argumentative paper about methods of livestock care unless you could show that your memories are representative or that you are an expert on the subject. Personal experience may strengthen an argument but generally is not sufficient as its sole support. If you are in doubt about the type of evidence an assignment requires, ask your instructor whether you should use sources or rely on personal experience and examples.

Facts.   Facts are statements that can be verified objectively, by observation or by reading a reliable account. They are usually stated dispassionately: "If you pump the air out of a five-gallon varnish can, the can will collapse." Of course, we accept many of our facts based on the testimony of others. For example, we believe that the Great Wall of China exists although we may never have seen it with our own eyes.

Sometimes people say facts are true statements, but truth and sound evidence can be confused. Consider the truth of these statements:

The tree in my yard is an oak.	*True* because it can be verified
A kilometer is 1,000 meters.	*True* using the metric system
The highway speed limit is sixty-five miles per hour.	*True* according to law
Fewer fatal highway accidents have occurred since the new exit ramp was built.	*True* according to research studies
My favorite food is pizza.	*True* as an opinion
More violent criminals should receive the death penalty.	*True* as a belief
Murder is wrong.	*True* as a value judgment

Some might claim that each statement is true. When you think critically, however, you should avoid treating opinions, beliefs, judgments, and personal experience as true in the same sense that verifiable facts and events are true.

▌ ACTIVITY 3.4: Separating Facts and Opinions

Bring to class a letter to the editor, editorial, or opinion piece from a print or online newspaper or magazine. Working with a partner or in a small group, analyze your selection to identify which statements are facts and which are opinions. Then trade selections and do the same. Discuss your responses to see where you agree, disagree, or are unsure about what is fact or opinion.

Statistics.   Statistics are facts expressed in numbers. What portion of American children are poor? According to statistics from the U.S. Census Bureau, 12.9 million children (or 17.6 percent of all American children) lived in poverty in 2003 compared with 15.7 million (or 21.6 percent) in 2010. Clear as such figures seem, they can raise complex questions. For example, how significant is the increase in the poverty rate over seven years? What percentage of children were poor over longer terms, twenty years, for example?

Most writers, without trying to be dishonest, interpret statistics to help their causes. The statement "Fifty percent of the population have incomes above the poverty level" might substantiate the fine job done by the government of a developing nation. Putting the statement another way—"Fifty percent of the population have incomes below the poverty level"—might use the same statistic to show the inadequacy of the government's efforts.

Even though a writer is free to interpret a statistic, statistics should not be used to mislead. On the wrapper of a peanut candy bar, we read that a one-ounce serving contains only 150 calories. The claim is true, but the bar weighs 1.6 ounces. Gobble it all—more likely than eating exactly 62 percent of it—and you'll ingest 240 calories, making the candy bar a heftier snack than the innocent statistic on the wrapper suggests. Because abuses make some readers automatically distrustful, use figures fairly when you write, and make sure they are accurate. If you doubt a statistic, compare it with figures reported by several other sources. Distrust a statistical report that differs from every other report unless it is backed by further evidence.

ACTIVITY 3.5: Interpreting Statistics

Working in a small group, go to the government website for the U.S. Census Bureau or for your state's population information (probably .gov or your state's abbreviation). Select topics of interest to your group—population groups, ethnicity, businesses, languages, family composition, housing, education, poverty, and so forth. Figure out what the relevant statistics do—and don't—state or imply about each topic.

Expert Testimony.   By *experts*, we mean people with knowledge gained from study and experience in a particular field. The test of an expert is whether his or her expertise stands up to the scrutiny of others who are knowledgeable in that field. The views of Peyton Manning on how to play offense in football carry authority. So do the views of economist and former Federal Reserve chairman Alan Greenspan on what causes inflation. However, Manning's take on the economy or Greenspan's thoughts on football might not be authoritative. Also consider whether the expert's reliability might be affected by any bias or special interest. Statistics on cases of lung cancer attributed to smoking might be better taken from government sources than from the tobacco industry.

ACTIVITY 3.6: Checking Expertise

By yourself or with a classmate, conduct several web searches, looking for reliable information about a politician, corporate CEO, best-selling author, Oscar winner, sports figure, fashion designer, scientist, war hero, local celebrity, or other notable person. Work together to evaluate the accuracy and relevance of the credentials you find. What background or experience would establish each person as an expert in some area? How would you define the limits of the person's expertise?

Firsthand Observation. Firsthand observation is persuasive. It can add concrete reality to abstract or complex points. You might support the claim "The Meadowfield waste recycling plant fails to meet state guidelines" by recalling your own observations: "When I visited the plant last January, I was struck by the number of open waste canisters and by the lack of protective gear for the workers who handle these toxic materials daily."

As readers, most of us tend to trust a writer who declares, "I was there. This is what I saw." Sometimes that trust is misplaced, however, so always be wary of a writer's claim to have seen something that no other evidence supports. Ask yourself, Is this writer biased? Might the writer have (intentionally or unintentionally) misinterpreted what he or she saw? Of course, your readers will scrutinize your firsthand observations too. Take care to reassure them that your observations are unbiased and accurate.

ACTIVITY 3.7: Looking for Evidence

Using the issue you explored with classmates for Activity 3.1 on page 31, what would you need to support your identification, explanation, or solution of the problem? Working with classmates, identify the kinds of evidence that would be most useful. Where or how might you find such evidence?

Testing Evidence

Perhaps you've heard that germs can't contaminate dropped food—if you pick it up fast enough. Your own critical thinking might encourage your skepticism about this claim. After all, you can think of plenty of places where a food rescue couldn't possibly be fast enough to avoid germs. In fact, you might wonder if this claim is an urban legend, debunked or confirmed at Snopes.com. For other issues, you might visit FactCheck.org (sponsored by the Annenberg Public Policy Center), which evaluates the accuracy of political ads and news; Charity Navigator, which evaluates charities that appeal for contributions; Consumer Reports, which rates products; or similar reliable and unbiased sources that can help you assess evidence.

As both a reader and a writer, you should also question evidence to see whether it is strong enough to carry the weight of an author's claims. Use the Evidence Checklist on pages 39–40 to determine whether evidence is useful and trustworthy.

TABLE 3.2   Drawing on Varied Evidence

Type of Evidence	Definition	Example and Source Identification
Facts	Information that can be confirmed or substantiated by an objective person	When employment drops, college enrollment tends to go up because people are motivated to increase their skills (Colorado Commission on Higher Education, "Governor's Task Force to Strengthen and Improve the Community College System. Final Report, April 5, 2004," p. 16, at <http://highered.colorado.gov/Publications/Studies/Taskforce/CCCS/20040405_rpt_final.pdf).
Statistics	Factual information presented in numerical form	According to the U.S. Census Bureau's *American Fact Finder*, 23.6 percent of Aurora, Colorado, residents are enrolled in postsecondary education, more than 5 percent below the national rate of 28.8 percent. Compared to the country as a whole, Aurora also has more veterans and more households with children under age eighteen. All these groups may need job-oriented educational opportunities.
Expert Testimony	Information from a knowledgeable person whose study, research, or experience is respected by others in the field	According to a press release from Daniela Higgins, director of the Center for Workforce Development, the Career Enrichment Program at Community College of Aurora, Colorado, wants to attract people looking for career advancement to improve their family resources.
Firsthand Observation	Your own accurate, unbiased eyewitness account	During my visit to Community College of Aurora to interview a workforce specialist, I collected campus publicity for programs in computer skills, paramedic and firefighter training, criminal justice, law enforcement, and early childhood education.

EVIDENCE CHECKLIST

☐ Is it accurate?
- Do the facts and figures seem accurate based on what you have found in published sources, reports by others, or reference works?
- Are figures or quoted facts copied correctly?

☐ Is it reliable?
- Is the source trustworthy and well regarded?
- Does the source acknowledge any commercial, political, advocacy, or other bias that might affect the quality of its information?
- Does the writer supplying the evidence have appropriate credentials or experience? Is the writer respected as an expert in the field?
- Do other sources agree with the information?

☐ Is it up-to-date?
- Are facts and statistics current?
- Is the information from the latest sources?

☐ Is it to the point?
- Does the evidence back the exact claim made?
- Is the evidence all pertinent? Does any of it drift from the point to interesting but irrelevant information?

☐ Is it representative?
- Are examples typical of all the things included in the writer's position?
- Are examples balanced? Do they present the topic or issue fairly?
- Are contrary examples acknowledged?

☐ Is it appropriately complex?
- Is the evidence sufficient to account for the claim made?
- Does it avoid treating complex things superficially?
- Does it avoid needlessly complicating simple things?

☐ Is it sufficient to back the claim and persuade readers?
- Are the amount and quality of the evidence appropriate for the claim and for the readers?
- Is the evidence aligned with the existing knowledge of readers?
- Does the evidence answer the questions readers are likely to ask?
- Is the evidence vivid and significant?

Selecting Persuasive Supporting Evidence

Although supporting evidence can come from many sources—your experience, observation, imagination, or interaction with others—college instructors often expect you to turn to the writings of others. This expectation reflects the view that academic ideas develop through exchange: each writer reads and responds to the writing of others, building on earlier discussion while expanding the conversation. In books, articles, and reports, you can find pertinent examples, illustrations, details, and expert testimony—in short, reliable information that shows your claims and statements are sound. You'll be more likely to find and use persuasive evidence that supports your thinking if you try to define what you need as a writer, considering questions such as those in the Purpose Checklist.

PURPOSE CHECKLIST

- ☐ What is the thesis you want to support or the point you want to demonstrate?
- ☐ Does the assignment require or suggest certain kinds of supporting evidence, sources, or presentations of material?
- ☐ Which ideas do you want to support with good evidence?
- ☐ Which ideas might you want to check, clarify, or change?
- ☐ Which ideas or opinions of others do you want to verify or counter?
- ☐ Do you want to analyze material yourself (for example, by comparing articles or websites) or to find someone else's analysis?
- ☐ What kinds of evidence do you want to use—for example, facts, statistics, or expert testimony? Do you also want to add your own firsthand observation?

Although your evidence should satisfy you as a writer, it also needs to meet the criteria of your college readers—your instructors and possibly your classmates—as the following graphic illustrates.

TWO VIEWS OF SUPPORTING EVIDENCE

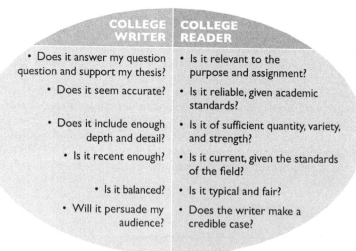

COLLEGE WRITER	COLLEGE READER
• Does it answer my question question and support my thesis?	• Is it relevant to the purpose and assignment?
• Does it seem accurate?	• Is it reliable, given academic standards?
• Does it include enough depth and detail?	• Is it of sufficient quantity, variety, and strength?
• Is it recent enough?	• Is it current, given the standards of the field?
• Is it balanced?	• Is it typical and fair?
• Will it persuade my audience?	• Does the writer make a credible case?

Using the Statement-Support Pattern

As you plan or write a draft, you may tuck in notes to yourself—find this, look that up, add some numbers here. Other times, you may not know exactly what or where to add information. One way to determine where you need to supply supporting evidence is to examine your plan or draft, sentence by sentence.

- What does each statement claim or promise to a reader?
- Where do you provide supporting evidence to demonstrate the claim or fulfill the promise?

The answers to these questions—your statements and your supporting evidence—often fall into a common alternating pattern:

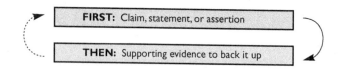

FIRST: Claim, statement, or assertion

THEN: Supporting evidence to back it up

When you spot a string of assertions without much support, you have found a place where you might need more evidence. Select reliable evidence so that it substantiates the exact statement, claim, or assertion that precedes it. Likewise, if you spot a string of examples, details, facts, quotations, or other evidence, introduce or conclude it with an interpretive statement that explains the point the evidence supports. Make sure your general statement connects and pulls together all of the particular evidence. (See also pp. 123–25 on reasoning inductively and deductively.)

When Carrie Williamson introduced her cause-and-effect paper, "Rain Forest Destruction," she made a general statement and then supported it by quoting facts from a source. Then she repeated this statement-support pattern, backing up her next statement in turn. By using this pattern from the very beginning, Carrie reassured her readers that she was a trustworthy writer who would try to supply convincing evidence throughout her paper.

The tropical rain forests are among the most biologically diverse communities in the world. According to the Rainforest Alliance, "The forests of the Neotropics are the habitat for tens of thousands of plant and wildlife species," as in "a single square mile of tropical forest in Rondonia, Brazil," which is home to "1,200 species of butterflies—twice the total number found in the United States and Canada" ("Conservation"). These amazing communities depend on each part being intact in order to function properly but are being destroyed at an alarming rate. Over several decades, even in protected areas, only 2% increased while 85% "suffered declines in surrounding forest cover" (Laurance et al. 291). Many rain forest conservationists debate the leading cause of deforestation. Regardless of which is the major cause, logging, slash-and-burn farming, and resource exploitation are destroying more of the rain forests each year.

Statement

Supporting evidence: Information and statistics about species

Statement

Supporting evidence: Facts about destruction

Statement identifying cause-and-effect debate

Statement previewing points to come

Carrie further strengthened this impression of reliability by following the conventions of MLA style (see Ch. 12) to credit her sources in her list of works cited:

"Conservation in the Neotropics." *Rainforest-alliance.org*. Rainforest Alliance, 2012. Web. 6 Dec. 2012.

Laurance, William F., et al. "Averting Biodiversity Collapse in Tropical Forest Protected Areas." *Nature* 489.7415 (13 Sept. 2012): 290–94. *Academic OneFile*. Web. 6 Dec. 2012.

TABLE 3.3   Supporting Statements with Evidence

Function of Statement	Possible Supporting Evidence
Introduce a topic	Facts or statistics to justify the importance or significance of the topic
Describe a situation	Factual examples or illustrations to convey the reality or urgency of the situation
Introduce an event	Accurate firsthand observations to describe an event that you have witnessed
Present a problem	Expert testimony or firsthand observation to establish the necessity or urgency of a solution
Explain an issue	Facts and details to clarify the significance of the issue
State your point	Facts, statistics, or examples to support your viewpoint or position
Interpret and prepare readers for evidence that follows	Facts, examples, observations, or research findings to define and develop your case
Conclude with your recommendation or evaluation	Facts, examples, or expert testimony to persuade readers to accept your conclusion

Besides checking for the statement-support pattern, consider your paper's overall purpose, organization, and line of reasoning. Persuasive evidence may help you define key terms, justify the significance of a problem, back up your stand on an issue, or support your solution to a problem. Table 3.3 above shows some of the many ways the pattern can be used to clarify and substantiate your ideas.

Use the Statement-Support Checklist to help you decide whether—and where—you might need evidence to support your critical thinking.

STATEMENT-SUPPORT CHECKLIST

☐ What does each statement promise that you'll deliver? What additional evidence would ensure that you have effectively kept this promise?

☐ Are your statements, claims, and assertions backed up with supporting evidence? If not, what evidence might you add?

☐ Which criteria for evidence matter most for your assignment or readers? What evidence would best meet the criteria? How much evidence would readers expect?

- ☐ Which parts of your paper seem weak or incomplete to you?
- ☐ What facts or statistics would clarify your topic or substantiate your statements?
- ☐ What examples or illustrations would make the background or the current circumstances clearer and more compelling for readers?
- ☐ What does a reliable expert say about your topic or the situation that it involves?
- ☐ What firsthand observation would add authenticity?
- ☐ Where have peer readers or your instructor suggested adding more or stronger evidence?

ACTIVITY 3.8: Supporting Critical Thinking

Working with a classmate, analyze one of your assigned readings, the essay on pages 24–26, or one of your own papers. Where does the writer use the statement-support pattern? How does the statement-support pattern affect the essay's persuasiveness? Where might the writer have stated a claim or assertion more clearly? Where might the writer have added supporting evidence?

PART TWO

Strategies

4

Strategies for Generating Ideas

No matter how much you read or think, neither activity replaces the task of writing down the words. For most writers, the hardest part of writing comes first—confronting an empty screen or a blank sheet of paper. Fortunately, you can prepare for that moment, both for finding ideas and for getting ready to write. All of the techniques that follow have worked for some writers—both professionals and students—and some may work for you.

DISCOVERING IDEAS

When you begin to write, you need to start the ideas flowing. Sometimes they appear effortlessly, perhaps triggered by the opportunities and resources around you—something you read, see, hear, discuss, or think about. (See the top half of the graphic on p. 49.) At other times you need an arsenal of idea generators, strategies you can use at any point in the writing process, whenever your ideas dry up or you need more examples or evidence. If one strategy doesn't work for a particular writing task, try another. (See the strategies in the lower half of the graphic, all detailed in the following pages.)

Building from Your Assignment

Learning to write is learning what questions to ask yourself. Sometimes your assignment triggers this process by raising certain questions and

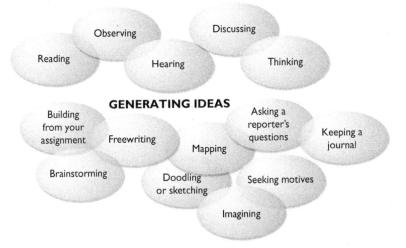

answering others. For example, Ben Martinez jotted notes on the hand-out as his instructor and classmates discussed the first assignment for his composition class—recalling a personal experience.

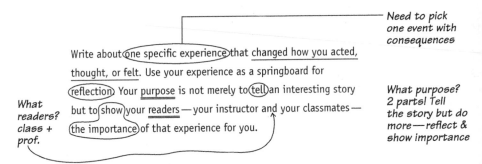

The assignment clarified what audience to address and what purpose to try to accomplish. It also raised three big questions for Ben: Which experience should I pick? How did it change me? Why was it so important for me? His classmates asked the instructor other questions about the length, format, and due date for the essay. As class ended, Ben didn't know what he'd write about, but he had figured out which questions to tackle first, and he had several other strategies in mind for generating ideas.

Sometimes an assignment will assume that you already understand something critical—how to address a particular audience, for example, or what to include in a certain type of writing. When Amalia Blackhawk read her argument assignment, she jotted down several questions about its assumptions to ask her instructor.

Anything OK? Or only newspaper type of issue?

Editor of what?

Select a campus or local issue that matters to you, and write a letter to the editor about it. Be certain to tell readers what the issue is, why it is important, and how you propose to address it. Assume that your letter will appear in a special opinion feature that allows letters longer than the usual word-count limits.

My classmates? The publication's readers?

How long is the usual letter? How long should mine be? Anything else letters like this should do?

What's my purpose? Persuading readers to respect my view or to agree?

Try these steps as you examine an assignment:

1. *Read through the assignment once* to discover its overall direction.
2. *Read it again*, highlighting or marking information about your situation as a writer. Does the assignment identify or suggest the readers you should address, your purpose in writing, the type of paper expected, the parts usually included in that kind of writing, or the format required? Does it specify the types of supporting evidence or the line of reasoning you should use?
3. *Jot down the questions that the assignment raises for you.* Exactly what do you need to decide—the type of topic to pick, the focus to develop, the issues or aspects to consider, or other guidelines to follow?
4. *List any questions that the assignment doesn't answer or ask you to answer.* Ask your instructor about these questions.

■ ACTIVITY 4.1: Building from Your Assignment

Select an assignment from this class, another course, or a textbook, and jot down some notes about it. What questions does the assignment answer for you? Which questions or decisions does it direct to you? What other questions might you want to ask your instructor? When you finish your notes, exchange assignments with a classmate, and make notes about that assignment too. Working with your partner, compare your responses to both.

Brainstorming

A *brainstorm* is a sudden insight or inspiration. As a writing strategy, brainstorming uses free association to stimulate a chain of ideas, often to personalize a topic and break it down into specifics. When you brainstorm, start with a word or phrase and spend a set amount of time scribbling a list of ideas as rapidly as possible, writing down whatever comes to mind with no editing or going back. Record ideas in a brainstorming or mapping app, in a new file, or on paper.

Brainstorming can be a group activity. In the business world, it is commonly used to fill a specific need—finding a name for a product, a corporate emblem, a slogan for an advertising campaign. In college, you can try brainstorming with a few other students or your entire class. Have your group sit facing one another. Designate one person to record on screen, paper, or chalkboard whatever the others suggest or the best idea in the air at a busy moment. After several minutes of calling out ideas, the group can look over the recorder's list to identify useful results. Online, toss out ideas during a chat or post them for all to consider.

On your own, brainstorm to define a topic, generate an example, or find a title for a finished paper. Angie Ortiz brainstormed after her instructor assigned a paper ("Demonstrate from your experience how electronic technology is changing our lives"). She wrote *electronic technology* on the page, set her alarm for fifteen minutes, and began to scribble.

> *Electronic technology*
> *iPod, cell phone, laptop, tablet. Plus TV, cable, DVDs. Too much?!*
> *Always on call—at home, in car, at school. Always something playing.*
> *Spend so much time in electronic world—phone calls, texting, tunes.*
> *Cuts into time really hanging with friends—face-to-face time.*
> *Less aware of my surroundings outside of the electronic world?*

When her alarm went off, Angie took a break. After returning to her list, she crossed out ideas that did not interest her and circled her final promising question. A focus began to emerge: the capacity of the electronic world to expand information but reduce awareness.

When you want to brainstorm, try this advice:

1. *Launch your thoughts with a key word or phrase.* If you need a topic, try a general term (*computer*); if you need an example for a paragraph in progress, try specifics (*financial errors computers make*).
2. *Set a time limit.* Ten minutes (or so) is enough for strenuous thinking.

3. *Rapidly list brief items.* Stick to words, phrases, or short sentences that you can quickly scan later.

4. *Don't stop.* Don't worry about spelling, repetition, or relevance. Don't judge, and don't arrange: just produce. Record whatever comes to mind, as fast as you can. If your mind goes blank, keep moving, even if you only repeat what you've just written.

When you finish, circle or check anything that suggests a provocative direction. Scratch out whatever looks useless or dull. Then try some conscious organizing: Are any thoughts related? Can you group them? If so, does the group suggest a topic?

▪ ACTIVITY 4.2: Brainstorming

From the following list, choose a subject that interests you, that you know something about, and that you'd like to learn more about—in other words, that you might like to write on. Then brainstorm for ten minutes.

travel	fear	exercise
dieting	dreams	automobiles
family	technology	sports
advertisements	animals	education

Now look over your brainstorming list, and circle any potential topic for a paper. How well did this brainstorming exercise work for you? Can you think of any variations that would make it more useful?

▪ ACTIVITY 4.3: Brainstorming with a Group

Working with a small group of classmates—or the entire class—choose one subject listed in the brainstorming activity that each person knows about. Brainstorm about it individually for ten minutes. Then compare and contrast the brainstorming lists of everyone in the group. Although the group began with the same subject, each writer's treatment will be unique because of differences in experience and perspective. What does this activity tell you about group brainstorming as a strategy for generating topics for writing?

Freewriting

To tap your unconscious by *freewriting*, you simply write a series of sentences without stopping for fifteen or twenty minutes. The sentences don't have to be grammatical or coherent or stylish; just keep them flowing to unlock an idea's potential.

Generally, freewriting is most productive if it has a goal—for example, finding a topic, a purpose, or a question you want to answer. Angie Ortiz wrote her topic at the top of a page and then explored her rough ideas.

> *Electronic devices—do they isolate us? I chat all day online and by phone, but that's quick communication, not in-depth conversation. I don't really spend much time hanging with friends and getting to know what's going on with them. I love listening to my iPod on campus, but maybe I'm not as aware of my surroundings as I could be. I miss seeing things, like the new art gallery that I walk by every day. I didn't even notice the new sculpture park in front! Then, at night, I do assignments on my computer, browse the web, and watch some cable. I'm in my own little electronic world most of the time. I love technology, but what else am I missing?*

The result, as you can see, wasn't polished prose. It was full of false starts and little asides. Still, in a short time Angie produced a paragraph to serve as a springboard for her essay.

If you want to try freewriting, here's what you do:

1. *Write a sentence or two at the top of your page*—the idea you plan to develop by freewriting.
2. *Write steadily without stopping for at least ten minutes.* Record whatever comes to mind, even "My mind is blank," until some new thought occurs to you.
3. *Don't censor yourself.* Don't cross out false starts, misspellings, or grammar errors. Don't worry about connecting ideas or finding perfect words.
4. *Feel free to explore.* Your initial sentences may be a rough guide, but they shouldn't be a straitjacket. If you find yourself straying from your original idea, a change in direction may be valuable.
5. *Prepare yourself*—if you want to. While you wait for your ideas to start racing, you may want to ask yourself some of these questions:

What interests you about the topic? What do you care most about?

What do you recall about this topic from your own experience? What do you know about it that the next person doesn't?

What have you read, observed, or heard about the topic?

How might you feel about this topic if you were someone else—say a parent, an instructor, or a person from another country?

6. *Repeat the process, looping back to expand a good idea if you want.* Poke at the most interesting parts to see if they will further unfold:

What does that mean? If that's true, what then? So what?

What other examples or evidence does this statement call to mind?

What objections might a reader raise? How might they be answered?

▇ ACTIVITY 4.4: Freewriting

Choose an idea you've been thinking about or a thought from a brainstorming list. Write it at the top of a page or file, and then freewrite about it for fifteen minutes. Share your freewriting with your classmates. If you wish, repeat this process, looping back to explore a provocative idea from your freewriting.

Doodling or Sketching

If you like to fill the margins of your notebooks with doodles, harness that artistic energy to generate ideas for writing. As Elena Lopez started thinking about her collision with a teammate during a soccer tournament, she began to sketch the accident (Fig. 4.1). She added stick figures, notes, symbols, and color as she outlined a series of events and their consequences.

Try this advice as you develop ideas by doodling or sketching:

1. *Give your ideas room to grow.* Open a new file using a drawing program, doodle in pencil on a blank page, or sketch on a series of pages to capture a sequence of events.

2. *Concentrate on your topic, but welcome new ideas.* Begin with a key visual in the center or at the top of a page. Add new sketches or doodles as they occur to you; you may find that they embellish, expand, define, or redirect your initial topic.

3. *Add icons, symbols, colors, figures, labels, notes, or questions.* Freely mix visual materials and text, recording ideas without stopping to refine them.

4. *Follow up on your discoveries.* After a break, return to your pages to see how your ideas have evolved. Jot notes by your doodles, making connections, identifying sequences, noting details, or converting visual concepts into descriptive sentences.

▇ ACTIVITY 4.5: Doodling or Sketching

Start with a doodle or sketch that illustrates your topic. Add related events, ideas, or details to develop your topic visually. Share your material with classmates, and then use their observations or questions to help you refine your direction as a writer.

Mapping

Mapping taps your visual and spatial creativity as you generate ideas. When you use mapping, you position ideas on a page or in a file or app to show their relationships or relative importance—radiating outward from a key term in the center, dropping down from a key word at the top, sprouting upward from a root idea, branching out from a trunk, flowing across the page or screen in chronological or causal sequence, or following a circular, spiral, sequential, or other familiar form.

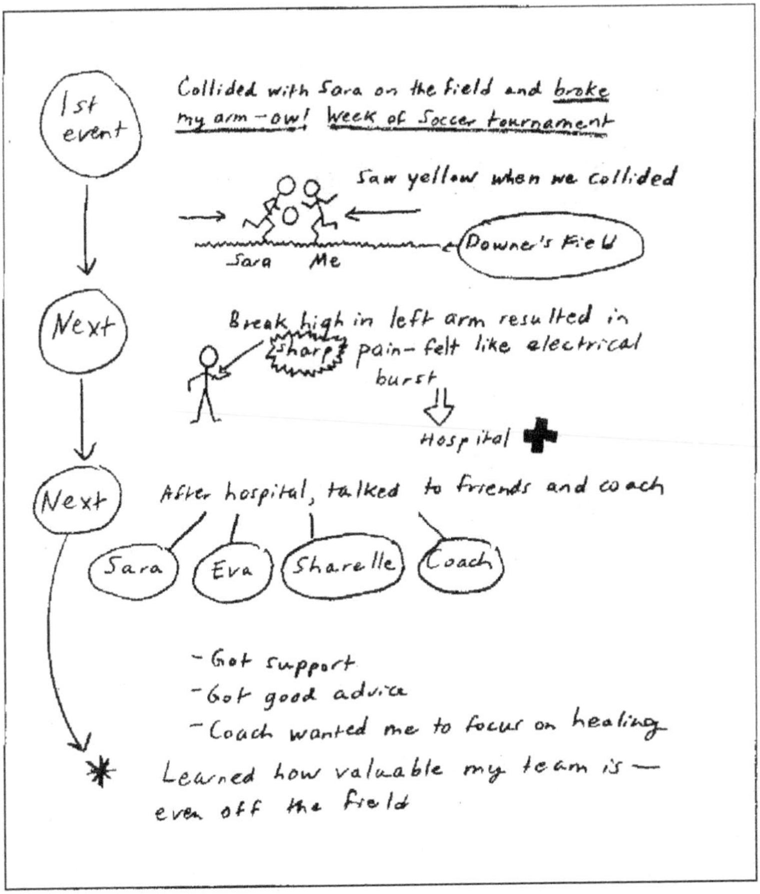

Figure 4.1   Doodling or Sketching to Generate Ideas

Andrew Choi used mapping to gather ideas for his proposal for revitalizing the campus radio station (Fig. 4.2). He noted ideas on differently shaped sticky notes—ovals for problems, rectangles for solutions, and

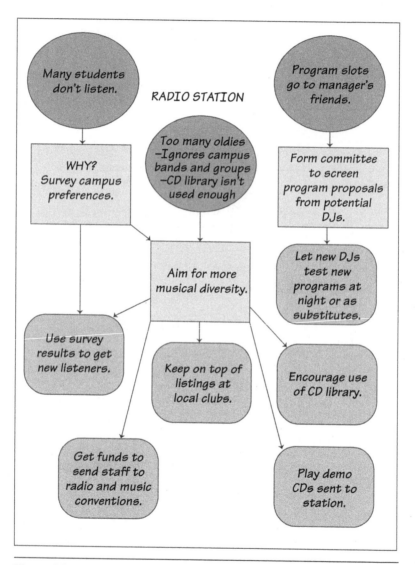

Figure 4.2   Mapping to Generate Ideas

rounded rectangles for implementation details. Then he moved the sticky notes around on a blank page, arranging them as he connected ideas.

Here are some suggestions for mapping:

1. *Allow space for your map to develop.* Open a new computer file, find some posterboard for arranging sticky notes or cards, or use a large page or dry-erase board for jotting notes.
2. *Begin with your topic or a key idea.* Drawing on your imagination, memory, class notes, or reading, place a key word at the center or top of a screen, page, or board.
3. *Add related ideas, examples, issues, or questions.* Quickly and spontaneously place these points above, below, or beside your key word.
4. *Refine the connections.* As your map evolves, use lines or arrows to connect ideas; box or circle them to focus attention; add colors or use different shapes to relate comparable points or to distinguish source materials from your own ideas.

After a break, continue mapping to probe one part more deeply, refine the structure, add detail, or build an alternate map from a different viewpoint. Because mapping is so versatile, you can also use it to develop graphics that present ideas in visual form.

▌ ACTIVITY 4.6: Mapping

Start with a key word or idea that you know something about. Map related ideas, using visual elements to show how they connect. Share your map with classmates, and then use their questions or comments to refine your mapping.

▌ ACTIVITY 4.7: Mapping with a Group

Working with a group of three to five classmates, write on a notecard or sticky note the word or phrase your instructor assigns to the entire class—for example, *campus dining* or *balancing work and college.* Then spend ten or fifteen minutes writing other ideas on new notes or cards and arranging them around the center. Move the cards or notes around, and draw lines or arrows to help connect your ideas. Share each group's ideas with the entire class.

Imagining

Your imagination is a valuable resource for exploring possibilities and discovering surprising ideas, original examples, striking expressions, and unexpected relationships. Suppose your instructor asks, "What if the average North American lived more than a century?" No doubt many more people would be old. How would that shift affect doctors, nurses, hospitals, and other medical facilities? How might city planners respond to the needs of so many more old people? What would the change mean for shopping centers? For TV programming? For leisure activities? For Social Security? For taxes?

Use some of the following strategies to unleash your imagination:

1. *Speculate about changes, alternatives, and options.* What common assumption—something most people take for granted—might you question or deny? What problem or deplorable condition would you like to remedy? What changes in policy, practice, or attitude might avoid problems you foresee for the future? What different paths in life—each with challenges and opportunities—might you take?

2. *Shift your perspective.* Experiment by taking a different point of view. How would someone on the opposite side of the issue respond? How would a plant respond? An animal? A Martian? Try shifting the debate: What happens when the issue is whether people over sixty-five, not teenagers, should be allowed to drink? What happens when the time frame changes from the present to the past or future?

3. *Envision what might be.* Join the many other writers who have imagined a utopia (an ideal state) or an antiutopia. By envisioning, you can conceive of possible alternatives—a better way of treating illness, electing a president, or finding meaning in chaos.

4. *Synthesize.* Synthesizing (generating new ideas by combining previously separate ideas) is the opposite of analyzing (breaking ideas down into component parts). Synthesize to make fresh connections, fusing ideas—perhaps old or familiar—into something new.

■ ACTIVITY 4.8: Imagining

Begin with a problem that cries out for a solution, a condition that requires a remedy, or a situation that calls for change. Ask "What if?" or use "Suppose that . . ." to trigger your imagination. Speculate about what might be, record your ideas, and share them with classmates.

Asking a Reporter's Questions

Journalists assembling facts to write a news story ask themselves six simple questions—the five *W*s and an *H:*

Who?	Where?	Why?
What?	When?	How?

In the lead, or opening paragraph, of a good news story, the writer tries to condense the whole story into a sentence or two that answer all six questions.

> A giant homemade fire balloon [*what*] startled residents of Costa Mesa [*where*] last night [*when*] as Ambrose Barker, 79, [*who*] zigzagged across the sky at nearly 300 miles per hour [*how*] in an attempt to set a new altitude record [*why*].

Later in the story, the reporter will add details, using the six basic questions to generate more about what happened and why.

For your college papers, use these six helpful questions to generate specific details. The questions can help you explore the significance of a childhood experience, analyze what happened at some moment in history, or investigate a campus problem. Their purpose is to help you gather ideas. Don't worry if some of them go nowhere or lead to repetitious answers. Later you'll weed out irrelevant points, keeping only those that look promising for your topic.

For a topic that is not based on your personal experience, you may need to read or conduct interviews to answer some of the questions. For example, take the topic of the assassination of President John F. Kennedy. Notice how each question can lead to further questions.

- *Who* was John F. Kennedy? What was his background? What kind of person was he? What kind of president? Who was with him when he was killed? Who was nearby? Who do most people believe shot him?

- *What* happened to Kennedy—exactly? What events led up to the assassination? What happened during the assassination? What did the people around the president do? What did the media representatives do? What did everyone across the country do? Ask someone who remembers the event what he or she did on hearing about it.

- *Where* was Kennedy assassinated? In what city? On what street? Where was he going? What was he riding in? Where was he sitting? Where did the shots likely come from? Where did the shots hit him? Where did he die?

- *When* was he assassinated—what day, month, year, time? When did Kennedy decide to go to this city? When—precisely—were the shots fired? When did he die? When was a suspect arrested?

- *Why* was Kennedy assassinated? What are some of the theories of the assassination? What solid evidence is available to explain it? Why has this event caused so much controversy?

- *How* was Kennedy assassinated? What kind of weapon was used? How many shots were fired? What specifically caused his death? How can we get at the truth of this event?

■ **ACTIVITY 4.9**: Asking a Reporter's Questions

Choose one of the following topics, or use one of your own:

A memorable event in history or in your life
A concert or other performance you have attended
An accomplishment on campus
An occurrence in your city
An important speech
A proposal for change
A questionable stand someone has taken

Answer the six reporter's questions about the topic. Then write a sentence or two synthesizing the answers to the six questions. Incorporate that sentence into an introductory paragraph for an essay you might write later.

Seeking Motives

In a surprisingly large part of your college writing, you will try to explain the motives behind human behavior. In a history paper, you might consider how George Washington's conduct shaped the U.S. presidency. In a psychology report, you might try to explain the behavior of participants in an experiment. In a literature essay, you might analyze the motives of Hester Prynne in *The Scarlet Letter*. Because people, including characters in fiction, are so complex, identifying their motives is challenging.

According to philosopher-critic Kenneth Burke, if you want to understand any human act, you can break it down into a set of five basic components, a *pentad,* and ask questions about each one. While covering much the same ground as the reporter's questions, Burke's pentad differs in that it can show how the components of a human act affect one another. This line of thought can take you deeper into the motives for human behavior than most reporters' investigations ever go.

Suppose that you are preparing to write a political science paper on President Lyndon Baines Johnson (LBJ). Right after John Kennedy's assassination in 1963, Vice President Johnson was sworn in as president. A year later he was elected to the office by a landslide. By 1968, however, Johnson had decided not to run for a second term as president. You decide to use Burke's pentad to investigate why he made that decision.

1. *The act:* What was done?
   Announcing the decision to leave office without standing for reelection.
2. *The actor:* Who did it?
   President Johnson.

3. *The agency:* What means did the person use to make it happen?
   A televised address to the nation.
4. *The scene:* Where, when, and in what circumstances did the act happen?
   Washington, DC, March 31, 1968. Protesters against the Vietnam war were gaining numbers and influence. The press was increasingly critical of the escalating war. Senator Eugene McCarthy, an antiwar candidate for president, had made a strong showing against LBJ in the New Hampshire primary election.
5. *The purpose or motive for acting:* What could have made the person do it?
   LBJ's motives might have included wanting to avoid a probable defeat, escape further personal attacks, spare his family, make it easier for his successor to pull the country out of the war, and ease bitter dissension among Americans.

To carry Burke's method further, you can pair each component with another—act to actor, agency, scene, and purpose, for example—and begin fruitful lines of inquiry by asking questions about the pairs:

PAIR   actor to agency

QUESTION   What did LBJ [actor] have to do with his televised address [agency]?

ANSWER   Commanding the attention of a vast audience, LBJ must have felt he was in control, even though his ability to control the situation in Vietnam was slipping.

Not all paired questions prove fruitful; some may not even apply. But one or two might reveal valuable connections and start you writing.

▮ ACTIVITY 4.10: Seeking Motives

Choose an action that puzzles you—something you, a family member, or a friend has done; a decision of a historical or current political figure; or something in a movie, on television, in a book, or online. Apply Burke's pentad to seek motives for the action. You can also pair up components to perceive deeper relationships. When you believe you understand the motivation behind the action, write a paragraph explaining the action, and share it with classmates.

Keeping a Journal

Journal writing richly rewards anyone who faithfully engages in it every day or several times a week. You can write anywhere or anytime; all you need is a few minutes to record an entry and the willingness to set down what you genuinely think and feel. Your journal will become a mine studded with priceless nuggets—thoughts and observations, reactions and revelations that are yours for the taking.

Reflective Journal Writing.   When you write in your journal, put less emphasis on recording what happened, as you would in a diary, than on reflecting about what you do or see, hear or read, learn or believe. An entry can be a list or an outline, a paragraph or an essay, a poem or a letter you don't intend to send. Describe a person or a place, set down a conversation, or record insights into your actions or those of others. Consider your pet peeves, fears, dreams, or moral dilemmas. Use your experience as a writer to nourish and inspire your writing, recording what worked, what didn't, and how you reacted to each.

Responsive Journal Writing.   Sometimes you respond to something in particular—to reading, classroom discussions, a movie, a conversation, or an observation. Faced with a long paper to write, you might assign *yourself* a response journal so you will have plenty of material ready to use.

Warm-up Journal Writing.   To prepare for an assignment, you can group ideas, scribble outlines, sketch beginnings, capture stray thoughts, record relevant material. Of course, a quick comment may turn into a draft.

E-Journals.   Once you create a file and make entries by date or subject, you can record ideas, feelings, images, memories, and quotations. You will find it easy to copy and paste inspiring e-mail, quotations from web pages, or images and sounds. Always identify the source of copied material so that you won't later confuse it with your original writing.

Blogs.   Like traditional journals, "web logs" aim for frank, honest, immediate entries. Unlike journals, they often explore a specific topic and may be available publicly on the web or privately by invitation. Especially in an online class, you might blog about your writing or research processes.

ACTIVITY 4.11: Keeping a Journal

Keep a journal for at least a week. Each day—on paper or in a file—record your thoughts, feelings, observations, and reactions. Reflect on what happens, and respond to what you read. At the end of the week, bring your journal to class or open the file. Share the entry you like best with your classmates.

GETTING READY TO WRITE

Once you have generated a suitable topic and some ideas about it, you are ready to get down to the job of actual writing.

Setting Up Circumstances

If you can write only with your shoes off or with a snack nearby, set yourself up that way. Some writers need a radio blaring; others need quiet. Create an environment that puts you in the mood to write.

Devoting a Special Place to Writing. Your place should have good lighting and space to spread out. It may be a desk in your room, the dining room table, or a quiet library cubicle — someplace where no one will bother you and where your mind and body will be ready to settle in for work. Try to make it a place where you can leave your projects and keep your materials handy.

Establishing a Ritual. Some writers find that a ritual relaxes them and helps them get started. You might open a soda, straighten your desk, turn the radio on (or off), and create a new file on the computer.

Reducing Distractions. Most of us can't prevent interruptions, but we can reduce them. If you are expecting your boyfriend to call, call him before you start writing. If you have small children, write when they are asleep or at school. Ignore social calls and messages until later. Let people around you know you are serious about writing, and then give it your full attention. Learn to block out the noises around you and concentrate on your writing.

Exhausting Your Excuses. If you, like most writers, are an expert procrastinator, help yourself run out of reasons not to write. Is your room annoyingly jumbled? Straighten it. Sharpen those pencils, format that file, throw out that trash, and make that call. Then, with your room, your desk, and your mind in order, sit down and write.

Relocating. If you're not getting anywhere, look for a new place to write. Move from the library to home or from the kitchen to your room. Or try an unfamiliar place — a park, a coffee shop, or a crowded spot like an airport.

Choosing the Best Time to Write. Some people think best early in the morning; others favor the small hours, when the world — and their stern self-critic—is still. Writing at dawn or in the wee hours also reduces the distraction of other people.

Writing on a Schedule.   Many writers find that it helps to write at a regular time each day. This method worked marvels for English novelist Anthony Trollope, who would start at 5:30 A.M., write 2,500 words before 8:30 A.M., and then go to his job at the post office. (He wrote more than sixty books.) Even if you can't set aside the same time every day, it may help to decide that you're going to sit down at four this afternoon and write for an hour. Or if you get stuck, vary your schedule.

Preparing Your Mind

Ideas, images, or powerful urges to write may arrive like sudden miracles. Even if you're taking a shower or getting ready to go to a movie, yield to impulse and write. Encourage your ideas and words to flow by talking and thinking about your writing.

Talking about Your Writing.   Discuss your ideas with a classmate or friend, encouraging questions, comments, and suggestions. Talk in person, by phone, or through e-mail. Or talk to yourself, using an audio app or a voice-activated recorder, while you sit in a traffic jam or walk your dog.

Keeping a Notebook or Journal Handy.   Always have some paper in your pocket or backpack or on the night table to write down good ideas that pop into your mind. Imagination can strike in the checkout line, in a doctor's waiting room, or during a lull on the job.

Reading.   The step from reading to writing is a short one. Even when you're just reading for fun, you start to involve yourself with words. Who knows? You might also hit on something useful for your paper. Or read purposefully: set out to read and take notes.

Use the questions in the Discovery Checklist to help you get ready to write.

DISCOVERY CHECKLIST

- ☐ Is your environment organized for writing? What changes might help you reduce distractions and procrastination?
- ☐ Have you scheduled enough time to get ready to write? How might you adjust your schedule or your expectations to encourage productivity?

□ Is your assignment clear? What additional questions might you want to ask about what you are expected to do?

□ Have you generated enough ideas that interest you? What other strategies for generating ideas might help you expand, focus, or deepen your ideas?

5

Strategies for Planning

Starting to write often seems a chaotic activity, but you can use the strategies in this chapter to help create order. For most papers, you first consider your audience and purpose and then focus on a central point or thesis. To help you arrange your material sensibly, the chapter also includes advice on grouping ideas and on outlining. Although no strategy appeals to every writer or fits every situation, the ideas here can expand your options as a writer.

SHAPING YOUR TOPIC FOR YOUR PURPOSE
AND YOUR AUDIENCE

As you work on your college papers, you may feel as if you're juggling—selecting weighty points and lively details, tossing them into the air, catching each one as it falls, deftly keeping them all moving in sequence. Busy as you are simply keeping points and details in the air, your performance almost always draws a crowd. Your instructor, your classmates, or other readers expect you to attend to their concerns as you try to achieve your purpose—probably informing, explaining, or persuading.

Thinking carefully about your audience and purpose can help you plan a paper more effectively. If you want to show your classmates and instructor the importance of an event, you'll have to decide how much detail about the event your readers need. Those who have gotten speeding tickets, for instance, will need less information about the experience than those who haven't. However, to achieve your purpose, you'll need to

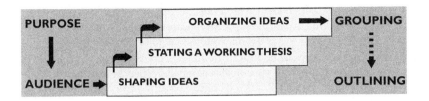

go beyond what happened to why the event mattered to you. No matter how many tickets your readers have gotten, they won't know exactly how that experience changed you unless you share that information with them. They might assume that you were worried about being late to class or paying higher insurance rates when, in fact, you had suddenly realized how narrowly you escaped having an accident like your cousin's and how that recognition motivated you to change your driving habits.

Similarly, if you want to persuade county officials to adopt your proposal for changing the way absentee ballots are distributed to college students, you'll need to support your idea with reasons and evidence — drawing on state election laws and legal precedents familiar to those readers as well as on the experiences of student voters. You may need to show how your proposal would solve existing problems and also why it would do so more effectively than other proposals.

Although your assignment may help you begin to define your purpose and audience, you can refine your understanding using the Planning Checklist.

PLANNING CHECKLIST

- ☐ What is your purpose? What would you like to accomplish in your paper? How would you like your readers to react to your paper? Do you want them to smile, think, or agree? To understand, learn, accept, respect, care, change, or reply? How might you plan your writing to accomplish your aims?

- ☐ Who are your readers? If they are not clearly identified in your assignment or by your situation, what do you assume about them? What do they know or want to know? What opinions do they hold? What do they find informative or persuasive? How might you plan your writing to appeal to them?

- ☐ How might you narrow and focus your ideas about the topic, given what you know or assume about your audience and purpose? Which slant would best accomplish your purpose? What points about the topic would appeal most strongly to your readers? What details would engage or persuade them?

□ What qualities of good writing have been discussed in your class, explained in your syllabus, or identified in assigned readings? What criteria for college writing have emerged from exchanges of drafts with classmates or comments from your instructor? How might you shape your writing to demonstrate desirable qualities to your readers?

ACTIVITY 5.1: Considering Purpose and Audience

Think back to a recent writing task—a college essay, a job application, a report or memo at work, a message to a relative, a letter to a campus office, or some other text. Write a brief description of your situation as a writer at that time. What was your purpose? Who—exactly—were your readers? How did you account for both as you planned your writing? How might you have made your writing more effective?

STATING AND USING A THESIS

Most pieces of effective writing are unified around one main point. That is, all the subpoints and details are relevant to that point. Generally, after you have read an essay, you can sum up the writer's main point in a sentence, even if the author has not stated it explicitly. We call this summary statement a *thesis.*

Often a thesis is *explicit*, plainly stated in the writing itself. In "The Myth of the Latin Woman: I Just Met a Girl Named María," an essay from *The Latin Deli* (Athens: University of Georgia Press, 1993), Judith Ortiz Cofer states her thesis in the last sentence of the first paragraph: "You can leave the Island, master the English language, and travel as far as you can, but if you are a Latina, especially one like me who so obviously belongs to Rita Moreno's gene pool, the Island travels with you." This clear statement, strategically placed, helps readers see her main point.

Sometimes a thesis is *implicit*, clearly indicated rather than directly stated. In "The Niceness Solution," a selection from Bruce Bawer's *Beyond Queer* (New York: Free Press, 1996), Paul Varnell describes an ordinance "banning rude behavior, including rude speech," passed in Raritan, New Jersey. After discussing a 1580 code of conduct, he identifies four objections to such attempts to limit free speech. He concludes with this sentence: "Sensibly, Raritan Police Chief Joseph Sferro said he would not enforce the new ordinance." Although Varnell does not state his main point in one concise sentence, readers know that he opposes the New Jersey law and any other attempts to legislate "niceness."

The purpose of most academic and workplace writing is to inform, to explain, or to convince. To achieve any of these purposes, you must make your main point crystal clear. A thesis sentence helps you clarify that idea in your own mind and stay on track as you write. It also helps your readers see your point and follow your discussion. Sometimes you may want to imply your thesis, but if you state it explicitly, you ensure that readers cannot miss it.

■ **ACTIVITY 5.2**: Identifying Theses with a Group

Working in a small group, select and carefully read several essays assigned in your class. Then, individually, write out the thesis for each essay. Of course, some thesis sentences are stated outright (explicit), while others are indicated (implicit). Compare and contrast the thesis statements that you identified with those your classmates found, and discuss the similarities and differences. How can you account for the differences? Try to agree on a thesis statement for each essay.

Discovering Your Working Thesis

It's rare for a writer to develop a perfect thesis statement early in the writing process and then to write an effective essay that fits the thesis exactly. What you should aim for is a *working thesis*—a statement that can guide you but that you will ultimately refine. Ideas for a working thesis are probably all around you.

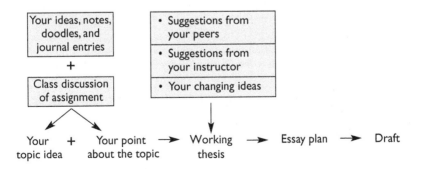

A useful thesis contains not only the key words that identify your topic but also the point you want to make or the attitude you intend to express. Your topic identifies the area you want to explore. To convert a topic to a thesis, you need to add your own slant, attitude, or point.

Topic   +   Slant or attitude or point   =   Working thesis

Suppose your instructor has asked you to identify and write about a specific societal change. After listening to discussion in class and thinking about the topic, you decide to focus on changes in formal courtesy.

TOPIC IDEA   Old-fashioned formal courtesy

Now you experiment, testing ideas to make the topic your own.

TRIAL   Old-fashioned formal courtesy is a thing of the past.

Although your trial sentence emphasizes change, it's still a circular statement, repeating rather than advancing a workable point. It doesn't say anything new about old-fashioned formal courtesy; it simply defines *old-fashioned*. You still need to find and state your own slant—maybe examining why things have changed.

TOPIC IDEA + SLANT   Old-fashioned formal courtesy + its decline as gender roles have changed

WORKING THESIS   As the roles of men and women have changed in our society, old-fashioned formal courtesy has declined.

Beginning with this working thesis, you could focus on how changing attitudes toward gender roles have caused changes in courtesy. Later, when you revise, you may refine your thesis further, perhaps restricting it to courtesy toward the elderly, toward women, or, despite stereotypes, toward men. Figure 5.1 suggests ways of developing a thesis. (For advice about revising a thesis, see pp. 144–46.)

Once you have a working thesis, be sure its point accomplishes the purpose of your assignment. For example, suppose your assignment asks you to compare and contrast two local newspapers' coverage of a Senate election. Ask yourself what the point of that comparison and contrast is. Simply noting a difference won't be enough to satisfy most readers.

NO SPECIFIC POINT   The *Herald*'s coverage of the Senate elections was different from the *Courier*'s.

WORKING THESIS   *The Herald*'s coverage of the Senate elections was more thorough than the *Courier*'s.

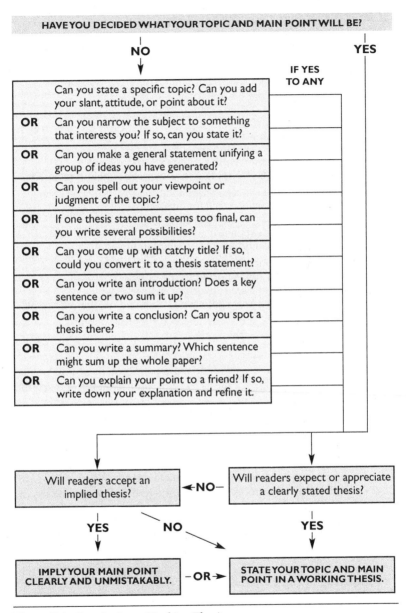

Figure 5.1   Developing a Working Thesis

▤ **ACTIVITY 5.3**: Discovering a Thesis

Write a sentence, a working thesis, that unifies each of the following groups of details. Then compare and contrast your theses with those of your classmates. What other information would you need to write a good paper on each topic? How might the thesis statement change as you write the paper?

1. Cigarettes are expensive.
   Cigarettes can cause fires.
   Cigarettes cause unpleasant odors.
   Cigarettes can cause health problems for smokers.
   Secondhand smoke from cigarettes can cause health problems.

2. Clinger College has a highly qualified faculty.
   Clinger College has an excellent curriculum in my field.
   Clinger College has a beautiful campus.
   Clinger College is expensive.
   Clinger College has offered me a scholarship.

3. Crisis centers report that date rape is increasing.
   Most date rape is not reported to the police.
   Often the victim of date rape is not believed.
   Sometimes the victim of date rape is blamed or blames herself.
   The effects of date rape stay with a woman for years.

Stating a Thesis

Once you have a notion of a topic and main point, use these four pointers to help you state or improve a thesis to guide your planning and drafting.

1. *State the thesis sentence exactly.* Replace vague or general wording with concise, detailed, and down-to-earth language.

   TOO GENERAL   There are a lot of troubles with chemical wastes.

   Are you going to deal with all chemical wastes, all over the world, throughout all of history? Are you going to list all the problems they can possibly cause?

   MORE SPECIFIC   Careless dumping of leftover paint is to blame for a
                      recent outbreak of skin rashes in Atlanta.

   For an argument, you need to take a stand on a debatable issue that would allow others to take different positions. State yours exactly.

   SPECIFIC STAND   The recent health consequences of carelessly dump-
                       ing leftover paint require Atlanta officials both to
                       regulate and to educate.

2. *State just one central idea in the thesis sentence.* If your paper is going to focus on one point, your thesis should state only one main idea.

> TOO MANY IDEAS
>
> Careless dumping of leftover paint has caused a serious problem in Atlanta, and a new kind of biodegradable paint has been developed, and it offers a promising solution to one chemical waste dilemma.
>
> ONE CENTRAL IDEA
>
> Careless dumping of leftover paint has caused a serious problem in Atlanta.
>
> OR
>
> A new kind of biodegradable paint offers a promising solution to one chemical waste dilemma.

3. *State your thesis positively.* You can usually find evidence to support a positive statement, but you'd have to rule out every possible exception to prove a negative one. Negative statements also may sound halfhearted and seem to lead nowhere.

> NEGATIVE   Researchers do not know what causes breast cancer.
>
> POSITIVE   The causes of breast cancer still challenge researchers.

Presenting the topic positively as a "challenge" could lead to a paper about an exciting quest. Besides, showing that researchers are working on the problem would be relatively easy, given an hour of online research.

4. *Limit your thesis to a statement that you can demonstrate.* A workable thesis is limited so that you can support it with sufficient convincing evidence. It should stake out just the territory that you can cover thoroughly within the length assigned and the time available, and no more.

> DIFFICULT TO SHOW   For centuries, popular music has announced vital trends in Western society.
>
> DIFFICULT TO SHOW   My favorite piece of music is Handel's *Messiah*.

The first thesis above could inform a whole encyclopedia of music; the second would require you to explain why that selection is your favorite, contrasting it with all the other musical compositions you know. The following thesis sounds far more workable for a brief essay.

> POSSIBLE TO SHOW   In the past two years, an increase in the number of teenagers has resulted in a comeback for pop dance music on the local scene.

Unlike a vague statement or broad claim, a limited thesis statement narrows and refines your topic, restricting your essay to a reasonable scope.

TOO VAGUE	Native American blankets are very beautiful.
TOO BROAD	Native Americans have adapted to many cultural shifts.
POSSIBLE TO SHOW	For some members of the Apache tribe, working in high-rise construction has enabled both economic stability and cultural integrity.

ACTIVITY 5.4: Examining Thesis Statements

Discuss each of the following thesis sentences with your classmates. Answer these questions for each:

Is the thesis stated exactly?
Does the thesis state just one idea?
Is the thesis stated positively?
Is the thesis sufficiently limited for a short essay?
How might the thesis be improved?

1. Teenagers should not get married.
2. Cutting classes is like a disease.
3. Students have developed a variety of techniques to conceal inadequate study from their instructors.
4. Older people often imitate teenagers.
5. Violence on television can be harmful to children.
6. I don't know how to change the oil in my car.

Using a Thesis to Organize

Often a good, clear thesis suggests an organization for your ideas.

WORKING THESIS	Despite the disadvantages of living in a downtown business district, I wouldn't live anywhere else.
FIRST ¶S	Disadvantages of living in the business district
NEXT ¶S	Advantages of living there
LAST ¶	Affirmation of your preference for downtown life

Just putting your working thesis into words can stake out your territory. A clear thesis can direct you as you select details and connect sections of the essay.

In addition, your thesis can prepare your readers for the pattern of development or sequence of ideas that you plan to present. As a writer, you look for key words (such as *compare, propose,* or *evaluate*) when you size up an assignment. Such words alert you to what's expected. When you write or revise your thesis, you can use such terms or their equivalents (such as *benefit* or *consequence* instead of *effect*) to preview the likely direction of your paper for readers. Then they, too, will know what to expect.

WORKING THESIS	Expanding energy conservation on campus would bring welcome financial and environmental benefits.
FIRST ¶S	Explanation of the campus energy situation
NEXT ¶S	Justification of the need for the proposed expansion
NEXT ¶S	Financial benefits for the college and students
NEXT ¶S	Environmental benefits for the region and beyond
LAST ¶	Concluding assertion of the value of the expansion

As you write, however, you don't have to cling to a thesis for dear life. If further investigation changes your thinking, you can change your thesis.

WORKING THESIS	Because wolves are a menace to people and farm animals, they ought to be exterminated.
REVISED THESIS	The wolf, a relatively peaceful animal useful in nature's scheme of things, ought to be protected.

You can restate a thesis any time—as you write, revise, or revise again.

▨ Activity 5.5: Using a Thesis to Preview

Each of the following thesis statements is from a student paper in a different field. With your classmates, consider how each one previews the essay to come and how you would expect the essay to be organized.

1. Although the intent of inclusion is to provide the best care for all children by treating both special- and general-education students equally, some people in the field believe that the full inclusion of disabled children in mainstream classrooms may not be in the best interest of either type of student. (From "Is Inclusion the Answer?" by Sarah E. Goers)

2. With ancient Asian roots and contemporary European influences, the Japanese language has continued to change and to reflect cultural change as well. (From "Japanese: Linguistic Diversity" by Stephanie Hawkins)

3. *Manifest destiny* was an expression by leaders and politicians in the 1840s to clarify continental extension and expansion and in a sense revitalize the mission and national destiny for Americans. (From ethnic studies examination answer by Angela Mendy)

4. By comparing the *Aeneid* with *Troilus and Criseyde*, one can easily see the effects of the code of courtly love on literature. (From "The Effect of the Code of Courtly Love: A Comparison of Virgil's *Aeneid* and Chaucer's *Troilus and Criseyde*" by Cindy Keeler)

5. The effects of pollutants on the endangered Least Tern entering the Upper Newport Bay should be quantified so that necessary action can be taken to further protect and encourage the species. (From "Contaminant Residues in Least Tern [*Sterna antillarum*] Eggs Nesting in Upper Newport Bay" by Susanna Olsen)

ORGANIZING YOUR IDEAS

When you organize an essay, you choose a sensible order for the parts, an order that shows your readers how the ideas are connected. Often your organization will both help readers follow your points and reinforce your emphases by moving from beginning to end or from least to most significant, as Table 5.1 illustrates.

Grouping Your Ideas

As you explore a topic, some ideas may seem to belong together. For a paper about driving in Manhattan, for example, you might have two facts on city traffic jams, four actions of city drivers, and three problems with city streets. But similar ideas seldom appear together in your notes because you did not discover them all at the same time. To identify an effective order, you'll need to sort them into groups and arrange them in sequences. Here are five ways to work:

1. *Rainbow connections.* List all the main points you want to express. Highlight points that go together with the same color. When you write, follow the color code to integrate related ideas at the same time.

TABLE 5.1   Using Spatial, Chronological, and Logical Organization

Organization	Movement	Typical Use	Example
Spatial	Left to right, right to left, bottom to top, top to bottom, front to back, outside to inside	• Describing a place or a scene • Describing a person's physical appearance	Describe an ocean vista, moving from the tidepools on a rocky beach to the buoys floating offshore and then to the sparkling water meeting the sunset.
Chronological	What happens first, second, and next, continuing until the end	• Narrating an event • Explaining steps in a procedure	Narrate the events that led up to an accident: leaving home late, stopping to do an errand, checking messages while speeding along the highway, racing up to the intersection.
Logical	General to specific (or the reverse), least important to most, cause to effect, problem to solution	• Explaining an idea • Persuading readers to accept a stand, a proposal, or an evaluation	Analyze the effects of last year's storms by selecting four major consequences, placing the most important one last for emphasis

2. *Linking.* List major points, and then draw lines (in color if you like) to link related ideas. Figure 5.2 illustrates a linked list for an essay on Manhattan driving. The writer has connected related points and supplied each linked group with a heading. Each heading will probably inspire a topic sentence to introduce a major division of the essay, and each could be numbered in sequence. Because one point, "chauffeured luxury cars," failed to relate to any other, the writer has a choice: drop it or develop it.

3. *Solitaire.* Collect ideas on sticky notes or roomy (5-by-8-inch) note cards, especially to write about literature or research. To organize, spread out the notes or cards, and then arrange and rearrange them, as you would the cards in a game of solitaire. When each idea seems to lead to the next, gather the cards into a deck in that order. As you write, deal yourself a card at a time and translate its contents into sentences.

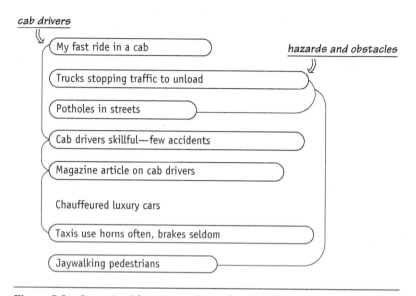

Figure 5.2   Grouping Ideas Using the Linking Method

4. *Slide show.* Use presentation software to write your notes and ideas on "slides." When you're done, view your slides one by one or as a collection. Sort your slides into a logical order.

5. *Clustering.* Like mapping (see pp. 55–57), clustering is a visual method useful for generating as well as grouping ideas. In the middle of a page, write your topic in a word or a phrase. Then think of the topic's major divisions. For an essay on Manhattan drivers, the major divisions might be *types* of drivers: (1) taxi drivers, (2) bus drivers, (3) truck drivers, (4) New York drivers of private cars, and (5) out-of-town drivers of private cars. Arrange these divisions around your topic, circle them, and draw lines out from the major topic (Fig. 5.3). You now have a rough plan for an essay.

Around each division, make another cluster of details you might include—examples, illustrations, facts, statistics, opinions. Circle each specific item, and connect it to the appropriate type of driver. When you write your paper, you can expand the details into one paragraph for each type of driver.

This technique lets you know where you have enough specific information to make your paper clear and interesting and where you don't. If one subtopic has no small circles around it—like "bus drivers" in Figure 5.3—add some specifics to expand it or drop it.

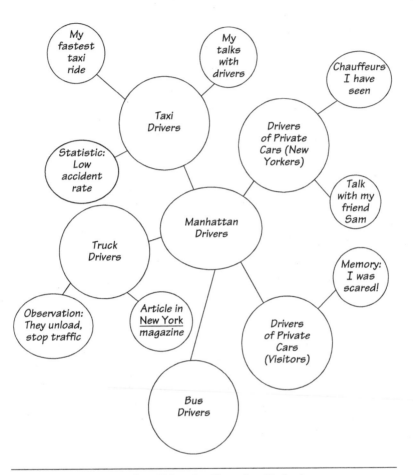

Figure 5.3   Grouping Ideas Using the Clustering Method

■ ACTIVITY 5.6: Clustering

Generate clusters for three of the following topics. With your classmates, discuss which one of the three would probably help you write
the best paper.

classes	fast food	civil rights
Internet sites	leisure activities	substance abuse
favorite restaurants	musicians	technology

ACTIVITY 5.7: Grouping Ideas on the Computer

Here are some easy computer tools you can use to highlight, catego-
rize, and shape your thinking by distinguishing your points on a
screen:

Highlighting

Boxing

Showing color

Using **bold**, *italics*, or underlining

- Adding bullets

1. Numbering

Changing fonts

Varying print sizes

Try these features by clicking on your toolbar or menu. You can also
experiment with organization by using a function like Track Changes
or by creating a table or column of ideas in a separate window next
to your text.

Outlining

A familiar way to organize is to outline. Whether brief or detailed, a written outline acts like a map. It shows you where to start, where to stop
along the way, and where to end up. If you get lost, you can consult it to
get back on track.

Some writers begin with a working thesis. A clear thesis can suggest
how to develop an outline, allowing the plan for the paper to grow naturally from the idea behind it. Others start with a loose informal outline—
perhaps just a list of points to make. Still others, especially those laying
out a research paper or complicated argument, like to follow a detailed
formal outline. Those who freeze up when they try to outline might make
a *revision outline,* an outline prepared after writing to identify what actually appears in a draft and to diagnose what might need to be added or
changed (see pp. 147–48).

An outline discussed during a peer exchange or submitted with your
essay can also act as a map or skeletal summary for your readers. Sometimes it can even help you respond to readers' suggestions. For example,
if readers find your writing mechanical, a loose informal outline may free
up your ideas. On the other hand, if readers find your writing disorga-
nized and hard to follow, a more detailed plan might be especially useful.
Experiment with the various types and uses of outlines to learn what
helps you plan effectively.

Making a Thesis-Guided Outline.   Your working thesis may identify
points that you can use to organize your paper. (If it doesn't, you may
want to revise your thesis and then return to your outline, or vice versa.)

For example, suppose you are assigned an anthropology paper on the people of Melanesia. You decide to focus on the following idea:

> *Working thesis: Although the Melanesian pattern of family life may look strange to Westerners, it fosters a degree of independence that rivals our own.*

Laying out ideas in the same order they follow in the two parts of this thesis statement, you might make a simple outline like this:

> 1. *Features that appear strange to Westerners*
>   — *A woman supported by her brother, not her husband*
>   — *Trial marriages common*
>   — *Divorce from her children possible for any mother*
>
> 2. *Admirable results of system*
>   — *Wives not dependent on husbands for support*
>   — *Divorce between mates uncommon*
>   — *Greater freedom for parents and children*

This informal outline suggests an essay that naturally falls into two parts: (1) features that seem strange and (2) admirable results of the system. When you are creating a thesis-guided outline, look for the key element of your working thesis that can suggest a logical outline, as Table 5.2 illustrates (p. 82).

Developing an Informal Outline.   For in-class writing, brief essays, and familiar topics, a short or informal outline, also called a *scratch outline,* may serve your needs. Jot down a list of points in the order you plan to make them. Use this outline, for your eyes only, to help you get organized, stick to the point, and remember good ideas under pressure. The following example outlines a short paper explaining how outdoor enthusiasts can avoid illnesses carried by unsafe drinking water. It simply lists each of the methods for treating potentially unsafe water that the writer plans to explain in the paper.

> *Working thesis: Campers and hikers need to ensure the safety of the water they drink from rivers or streams.*
>
> *Introduction: Treatments for potentially unsafe drinking water*
>
> 1. *Small commercial filter*
>   — *Remove bacteria and protozoa including salmonella and E. coli*
>   — *Use brands convenient for campers and hikers*

TABLE 5.2   Organizing by Questioning the Key Element of Your Thesis

Key Element of Thesis with Examples	Sample Thesis Statement	Question You Might Ask	Possible Organization of Outline
Plural word Examples: *benefits, advantages, teenagers,* or *reasons*	A varied personal exercise program has four main *advantages.*	What are the types, kinds, or examples of this word?	List outline headings based on the categories or cases you identify.
Key word identifying an approach or vantage point Examples: *argument, position, interpretation,* or *point of view*	Wylie's *interpretation* of Van Gogh's last paintings unifies aesthetics and psychology.	What are the parts, aspects, or elements of this approach?	List outline headings based on the components you identify.
Key word identifying an activity Examples: *preparing, harming,* or *improving*	*Preparing* a pasta dinner for surprise guests can be easy.	How is this activity accomplished, or how does it happen?	Supply a heading for each step, stage, or element that the activity involves.
One part of the sentence subordinate to another Examples: qualifiers such as *because, although,* or *despite*	*Although* the new wetland preserve will protect only some wildlife, it will bring long-term benefits to the region.	What does the qualification include, and what does the main statement include?	Use a major heading for the qualification and another for the main statement.
General evaluation that assigns a quality or value to someone or something Examples: *typical, unusual, valuable,* or *notable*	When Sandie Burns arrives at the field in her wheelchair, other parents soon see that she is a *typical* soccer mom.	What examples, illustrations, or clusters of details will show this quality?	Add a heading for each extended example or each group of examples or details you want to use.
Claim or argument advocating a certain decision, action, or solution Examples: *should, could, might, ought to, need to,* or *must.*	Due to the tough economic times, the student Senate *should* support extended hours for the computer lab.	Which reasons and evidence will justify this opinion? Which will counter the opinions of others who disagree with it?	Provide a heading for each major justification or defensive point; add headings for countering reasons.

2. Chemicals
   — Use bleach, chlorine, or iodine
   — Follow general rule: 12 drops per gallon of water

3. Boiling
   — Boil for 5 minutes (Red Cross) to 15 minutes (National Safety Council)
   — Store in a clean, covered container

Conclusion: Using one of three methods of treating water, campers and hikers can enjoy safe water from natural sources.

This simple outline could easily fall into a five-paragraph essay or grow to eight paragraphs: introduction, conclusion, and three paragraphs or pairs of paragraphs in between. You probably won't know until you write the paper exactly how many paragraphs you'll need.

An informal outline can be even briefer than the preceding one. To answer an exam question or prepare a very short paper, your outline might be no more than an *outer plan*—three or four phrases jotted in a list:

Isolation of region
Tradition of family businesses
Growth of electronic commuting

Making an informal outline also can help you develop your ideas. Say you plan a how-to essay analyzing the process of buying a used car, beginning with this thesis:

Working thesis: Despite traps that await the unwary, preparing yourself before you shop can help you find a good used car.

The key word here is *preparing*. Considering how the buyer should prepare before shopping for a used car, you're likely to outline several ideas:

— Read car sites, car magazines, and Consumer Reports.
— Check seller or dealer ads online or in newspapers.
— Make phone calls to several dealers.
— Talk to friends who have bought used cars.
— Know what to look and listen for when you test-drive.
— Have a mechanic check out any car before you buy.

After some horror stories about people who got taken by car sharks, you can discuss, point by point, your advice. Of course, you can always change the sequence, add or drop an idea, or revise your thesis as you go along.

▌ ACTIVITY 5.8: Organizing an Informal Outline

Begin with a working thesis or a few points you might make in an essay. Develop your own informal outline, like those in the previous section, that could help you develop an essay.

Preparing a Formal Outline.   A *formal outline* is an elaborate guide, built with time and care, for a long, complex paper. Because major reports, research papers, and senior theses require so much work, some professors and departments ask a writer to submit a formal outline at an early stage and to include one in the final draft. A formal outline shows how ideas relate to one another—which ones are equal and important (coordinate) and which are less important (subordinate). It clearly and logically spells out where you are going. If you outline again after writing a draft, you can use the revised outline to check your logic and perhaps reveal where to revise.

When you make a full formal outline, follow these steps:

1. Place your thesis statement at the beginning.
2. List the major points that support and develop your thesis, labeling them with roman numerals (I, II, III).
3. Break down the major points into divisions with capital letters (A, B, C), subdivide those using arabic numerals (1, 2, 3), and subdivide those using lowercase letters (a, b, c). Continue until your outline is fully developed. If a very complex project requires further subdivision, use arabic numerals and lowercase letters in parentheses.
4. Indent each level of division in turn: the deeper the indentation, the more specific the ideas. Align like-numbered or -lettered headings under one another.
5. Cast all headings in parallel grammatical form. (See pp. 183–84 on parallelism.) Use phrases or sentences but not both in the same outline.

Because an outline divides or analyzes ideas, some instructors and other readers disapprove of categories with only one subpoint, reasoning that you can't divide anything into one part. Let's say that your outline on earthquakes lists a 1 without a 2:

> D. Probable results of an earthquake include structural damage.
> 1. Houses are stripped of their paint.

Logically, if you are going to discuss the probable results of an earthquake, you need to include more than one result:

D. Probable results of an earthquake include structural damage.

   1. Houses are stripped of their paint.

   2. Foundations crack.

   3. Road surfaces are damaged.

   4. Water mains break.

Not only have you now come up with more points, but you have also placed the most important last for emphasis.

A *formal topic outline* for a long paper might include several levels of ideas, as this outline for Linn Bourgeau's research paper illustrates. Such an outline can help you work out both a persuasive sequence for the parts of a paper and a logical order for any information from sources.

Crucial Choices: Who Will Save the Wetlands If Everyone Is at the Mall?

Working Thesis: Federal regulations need to foster state laws and educational requirements that will help protect the few wetlands that are left, restore as many as possible of those that have been destroyed, and take measures to improve the damage from overdevelopment.

  I. Nature's ecosystem

    A. Loss of wetlands nationally

    B. Loss of wetlands in Illinois

      1. More flooding and poorer water quality

      2. Lost ability to prevent floods, clean water, and store water

    C. Need to protect humankind

  II. Dramatic floods

    A. Midwestern floods in 1993 and 2011

      1. Lost wetlands in Illinois and other states

      2. Devastation in some states

    B. Cost in dollars and lives

      1. Deaths during recent flooding

      2. Costs in millions of dollars a year

    C. Flood prevention

      1. Plants and soil

      2. Floodplain overflow

III. Wetland laws

    A. Inadequately informed legislators

        1. Watersheds

        2. Interconnections in natural water systems

    B. Water purification

        1. Wetlands and water

        2. Pavement and lawns

IV. Need to save wetlands

    A. New federal laws

    B. Re-education about interconnectedness

        1. Ecology at every grade level

        2. Education for politicians, developers, and legislators

    C. Choices in schools, legislature, and people's daily lives

■ ACTIVITY 5.9: Responding to a Topic

Discuss the formal topic outline on pages 85–86 with some of your classmates or the entire class, considering the following questions:

- Would this outline be useful in organizing an essay?
- How is the organization logical? Is it easy to follow? What are other possible arrangements for the ideas?
- Is this outline sufficiently detailed for a paper? Can you spot any gaps?
- What possible pitfalls would the writer using this outline need to avoid?

A topic outline may help you work out a clear sequence of ideas but may not elaborate or connect them. Although you may not be sure how everything will fit together until you write a draft, you may find that a *formal sentence outline* clarifies what you want to say. To develop one, simply turn topics and headings into sentences—specifying ideas, changing wording, or even reworking your thesis as needed. A sentence outline can clarify what you intend to say and help you draft topic sentences and paragraphs, but you cannot be sure how everything fits together until you write the draft itself. Notice how this sentence outline for Linn Bourgeau's research paper expands her ideas.

Crucial Choices: Who Will Save the Wetlands If Everyone Is at the Mall?

Working Thesis: Federal regulations need to foster state laws and educational requirements that will help protect the few wetlands that are left, restore as many as possible of those that have been destroyed, and take measures to improve the damage from overdevelopment.

I. Each person, as part of nature's ecosystem, chooses how to interact with nature, including wetlands.

    A. The nation has lost over half its wetlands since Columbus arrived.

    B. Illinois has lost even more by legislating and draining them away.

        1. Destroying wetlands creates more flooding and poorer water quality.

        2. The wetlands could prevent floods, clean the water supply, and store water.

    C. The wetlands need to be protected because they protect and serve humankind.

II. Floods are dramatic and visible consequences of not protecting wetlands.

    A. The midwestern floods of 1993 and 2011 were disastrous.

        1. Illinois and other states had lost their wetlands.

        2. Those states also suffered the most devastation.

    B. The cost of flooding can be tallied in dollars spent and in lives lost.

        1. Nearly thirty people died in floods between 1995 and 2011.

        2. Flooding in 2011 cost Illinois about $216 million.

    C. Preventing floods is a valuable role of wetlands.

        1. Plants and soil manage excess water.

        2. The Mississippi River floodplain was reduced from 60 days of water overflow to 12.

III. The laws misinterpret or ignore the basic understanding of wetlands.

    A. Legislators need to know that an "isolated wetland" does not exist.

        1. Water travels within an area called a watershed.

        2. The law needs to consider interconnections in water systems.

    B. Wetlands naturally purify water.

        1. Water filters and flows in wetlands.

        2. Pavement and lawns carry water over, not through, the soil.

IV. Who will save the wetlands if everyone is at the mall?

    A. Federal laws should require implementing what we know.

    B. The vital concept of interconnectedness means reeducating everyone from legislators to fourth graders.

     1. Ecology must be incorporated into the curriculum for every grade.

     2. Educating politicians, developers, and legislators is more difficult.

  C. The choices people make in their schools, legislative systems, and daily lives will determine the future of water quality and flooding.

Reviewing Your Outline

Whether your outline is informal or formal, short or long, what matters is how well it will guide and stimulate your writing. Let your outline rest for a while—even a day or so if time allows. Then return to it, asking these planning questions again (see the Planning Checklist on pages 67–68).

- Does your outline sketch out a paper that will accomplish your purpose?
- Will the paper outlined speak to your readers?
- Does your outline identify enough appropriate ideas, examples, or arguments to support your thesis and inform or persuade your readers?
- Does your plan meet any other criteria for your specific assignment?

If you aren't sure your current plan would produce the paper assigned and expected, try to strengthen your outline. Add, revise, or simply jot notes to yourself. And don't panic—time to think and rethink can be a writer's best friend.

Now take one more close look at your outline. Ask yourself how to sharpen it so that your paper will be as effective as possible.

- Can you strengthen your thesis to make it more exact, focused, and demonstrable?
- Does your outline block out the structure you'd like your paper to follow: your engaging introduction, your compelling middle sections with the evidence to support your thesis, and your clear conclusion?
- Does your outline suggest an orderly and persuasive flow of information and ideas, making your point or building your case as it moves along?
- Does your outline lay out a statement-support structure? Does it show where you'll back up claims and assertions with evidence? Does it pin down the main points that details, examples, and reasons will support?

Once more, note the ideas or changes that occur to you. If you can't think of further refinements now, don't worry. Below the surface, you'll be thinking about where to go next, and you'll probably surprise yourself with new insights when you write.

■ ACTIVITY 5.10: Building a Sentence Outline

1. Using one of your groups of ideas from the activities in Chapter 4 or your informal outline from Activity 5.8, construct a formal topic outline that might serve as a guide for an essay.

2. Now turn that topic outline into a formal sentence outline.

3. Discuss both outlines with your classmates and your instructor, bringing up any difficulties you encountered. If you come up with a better way to organize your ideas, change the outline.

6

Strategies for Drafting

Learning to write well involves learning key questions to ask yourself: How can I begin this draft? What should I do if I get stuck? How can I flesh out the bones of my paper? How can I end effectively? How can I keep my readers with me? In this chapter we offer advice to get you going and keep you going, drafting the first paragraph to the last.

STARTING AND RESTARTING

A playful start may get you hard at work before you know it.

- **Time yourself.** Set your watch, alarm, or egg timer, and vow to draft a page before the buzzer sounds. Don't stop for anything. If you're writing drivel, just push on. You can cross out later.
- **Slow to a crawl.** If speed quotas don't work, time yourself to write with exaggerated laziness, maybe a sentence every fifteen minutes.
- **Open your app.** Jot down ideas, details, lists, audio notes, images, or video notes.
- **Scribble on a scrap.** If you dread the blank screen or page, try starting on scrap paper, the back of a list, or a small notebook.
- **Begin writing the most appetizing part.** Start in the middle or at the end, wherever the thoughts come easily to mind. As novelist Bill Downey observes, "Writers are allowed to have their dessert first."

- **State your purpose.** Set forth what you want to achieve: to tell a story? to explain something? to win a reader over to your way of thinking?
- **Slip into the reader's shoes.** Put yourself in your reader's place. Start writing what you'd like to find out from the paper.
- **Nutshell it.** Sum up the paper you want to write. Condense your ideas into one small, terse paragraph. Later you can expand each sentence until the meaning is clear and all points are well supported.
- **Shrink your job.** Break the writing task into small parts, and do only the first, perhaps just two paragraphs.
- **Seek a provocative title.** Write down a dozen possible titles for your paper. If one sounds strikingly good, don't let it go to waste!
- **Record yourself.** Talk a first draft into your voice mail, app, or recorder. Play it back, then write. Even if you find it hard to transcribe spoken words, this technique may get you thinking.
- **Speak up.** On your feet, before an imaginary cheering crowd, state your opening paragraph. Then—quick!—write it or record it.
- **Take short breaks.** Even if you don't feel tired, take a break every half hour or so. Get up, walk around the room, stretch, or drink some water. Two or three minutes should be enough to refresh your mind.

When you can't finish a long or demanding essay in one sitting, you may return to it only to find yourself stalled. You crank your starter, and nothing happens. Your engine seems reluctant to turn over. Try the following suggestions for getting back on the road.

- **Leave hints for how to continue.** If you're ready to quit, jot down what might come next, or write the first sentence of the next section. When you return, you will face not a blank wall but rich and suggestive graffiti.
- **Pause in midstream.** Try breaking off in midsentence or midparagraph. Just leave a sentence trailing off into space, even if you know how it should end. When you return, you can start writing again immediately.
- **Repeat.** If the next sentence refuses to appear, simply recopy the last one until that shy creature emerges on the page.
- **Reread.** When you return to work, spend just a few minutes rereading what you have already written or what you have planned.
- **Switch instruments.** Do you write on a tablet or laptop? Try longhand. Or trade your pen for a green pencil. Try writing on note cards or colored paper.

- **Change activities.** When words won't come, run, walk your dog, cook a meal, or nap. Or reward yourself—after you reach a certain point—with a trip to the vending machine, a text message to a friend, or a game. All the while, your unconscious mind will work on your writing task.

ACTIVITY 6.1: Organizing Your Drafts

Use your menu options to format a template for your papers. Set the margin widths, line spacing, print size, and other aspects of your paper's layout. If your instructor has not specified formatting, customize your files to produce pages with 1-inch margins and double-spacing, using 12-point type.

Next, figure out a simple file-naming convention and folder system to make it easy for you to store and keep track of your work. Some students prefer file names that identify the course, term, assignment, and draft number, while others note the paper topic or activity with the draft number—Eng101F2014-1-1 or Argument-1. When you revise a draft, be sure to duplicate and rename the file—Eng101F2014-1-2 or Argument-2—instead of simply reworking the original file. Then all the versions of your paper will be available in case you want to retrieve writing from an early draft or your instructor wants to review the stages of your writing process. Use the menu or the help screen to create a folder for each course, and store all your drafts there.

PARAGRAPHING

An essay is written not in large, indigestible lumps but in *paragraphs*—small units, each more or less self-contained, each contributing some new idea in support of the thesis or main point of the essay. Writers focus on one idea at a time, stating it, developing it, illustrating it with examples or a few facts—showing readers, with plenty of detailed evidence, exactly what they mean. (For more on developing ideas within paragraphs, see Ch. 7.)

Paragraphs can be as short as one sentence or as long as a page. Sometimes length is governed by audience, purpose, or medium. Journalists expect newspaper readers to gobble up facts like popcorn, quickly skimming articles with short one- or two-sentence paragraphs. College writers, in contrast, should assume their readers expect to read well-developed paragraphs.

When readers see a paragraph indentation, they interpret it as a pause, a chance for a deep breath. After that signpost, they expect you to concentrate on a new aspect of your thesis for the rest of that paragraph. In this way, your sequence of paragraphs guides readers through your writing: your opening paragraph draws them in, your body paragraphs focus their attention, and your concluding paragraph wraps up the discussion.

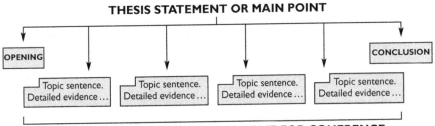

Using Topic Sentences

A *topic sentence* spells out the main idea of a paragraph in the body of an essay. It guides you as you write, and it hooks your readers as they discover what to expect and how to interpret the rest of the paragraph. As the topic sentence establishes the focus of the paragraph, it also relates the paragraph to the thesis of the essay, supporting the topic and main point of the essay as a whole. (For this reason, much of the advice on writing topic sentences for paragraphs also extends to writing thesis statements for essays.) To convert an idea to a topic sentence, you need to add your own slant, attitude, or point.

Main idea   +   Slant or attitude or point   =   Topic sentence

How do you write a good topic sentence? Make it interesting, accurate, and limited. The more pointed and lively your topic sentence, the more it will interest your readers. Even a dull and vague start can be enlivened once you zero in on a specific point:

MAIN IDEA + SLANT	Television + Everything that's wrong with it
DULL START	There are many things wrong with television.
POINTED TOPIC SENTENCE	Of all the shoddy television programming, what I dislike most is melodramatic news.
¶ PLAN	Illustrate the point with two or three melodramatic news stories.

A topic sentence also should be an accurate guide to the rest of the paragraph so that readers expect just what the paragraph delivers:

INACCURATE GUIDE	All types of household emergencies can catch people off guard. [The paragraph explains types of household emergencies, not preparedness.]
ACCURATE TOPIC SENTENCE	Although an emergency may not be a common event, emergency preparedness should be routine at home.
¶ PLAN	Explain how a household can prepare for an emergency with a medical kit, a well-stocked pantry, and a communication plan.

Finally, a topic sentence should be limited so you don't mislead or frustrate readers about what the paragraph covers.

MISLEADING SENTENCE	Seven factors have contributed to the increasing obesity of the average American. [The paragraph discusses only one.]
LIMITED TOPIC SENTENCE	Portion size is a major factor that contributes to the increasing obesity of average Americans.
¶ PLAN	Define healthy portion sizes, contrasting them with the large portions common in restaurants and packaged foods.

Opening with a Topic Sentence

Usually the topic sentence appears first in the paragraph, followed by sentences that clarify, illustrate, and support what it says. It is typically a statement but can be a question, alerting the reader to the topic without giving away the punchline. The following example comes from "The Virtues of the Quiet Hero," Senator John McCain's essay about "honor, faith, and service," presented on October 17, 2005, as part of the "This I Believe" series on National Public Radio's *All Things Considered*. Here and in all the following examples, we have put the topic sentence in *italics*.

> *Years later, I saw an example of honor in the most surprising of places.* As a scared American prisoner of war in Vietnam, I was tied in torture ropes by my tormentors and left alone in an empty room to suffer through the night. Later in the evening, a guard I had never spoken to entered the room and silently loosened the ropes to relieve my suffering. Just before morning, that same guard came back and re-tightened

the ropes before his less humanitarian comrades returned. He never said a word to me. Some months later on a Christmas morning, as I stood alone in the prison courtyard, that same guard walked up to me and stood next to me for a few moments. Then with his sandal, the guard drew a cross in the dirt. We stood wordlessly there for a minute or two, venerating the cross, until the guard rubbed it out and walked away.

This paragraph moves from a general statement to specific examples. The topic sentence clearly states at the outset what the paragraph is about. The second sentence introduces the situation that McCain recalls. Then the next half dozen sentences supply two concrete, yet concise, illustrations of his central point.

Placing a Topic Sentence Near the Beginning

Sometimes the first sentence of a paragraph acts as a transition, linking what has gone before with what is to come. Then the second sentence might be the topic sentence. This pattern is illustrated in the following paragraph from *Tim Gunn's Fashion Bible: The Fascinating History of Everything in Your Closet* by Tim Gunn with Ada Calhoun (New York: Gallery Books, 2012, p. 190). The paragraph immediately before this one summarizes how the early history of shoe design often tried to balance competing desires for modesty, alluring beauty, and practicality.

> Heel height has fluctuated ever since, as have platforms. *One goal of a high shoe is to elevate the wearer out of the muck.* Before there was pavement (asphalt didn't even appear until 1824, in Paris), streets were very muddy. People often wore one kind of shoe indoors, like a satin slipper, and another outside, perhaps with some kind of overshoe. One type of overshoe was called pattens, which were made of leather, wood, or iron, and lifted the wearer up a couple of inches or more from the sidewalk to protect the sole of the shoe from grime. Men and women wore these from the fourteenth- to the mid-nineteenth century, when street conditions started to become slightly less disgusting.

Ending with a Topic Sentence

Occasionally a writer, especially one trying to persuade the reader to agree with an argument, piles detail on detail. Then, with a dramatic flourish, the writer concludes with the topic sentence, as student Heidi Kessler does in this paragraph:

A fourteen-year-old writes to an advice columnist in my hometown newspaper that she has "done it" lots of times and sex is "no big deal." At the neighborhood clinic where my aunt works, a hardened sixteen-year-old requests her third abortion. A girl-child I know has two children of her own, but no husband. A college student in my dorm now finds herself sterile from a "social disease" picked up during casual sexual encounters. Multiply these examples by thousands. *It seems clear to me that women, who fought so hard for sexual freedom equal to that of men, have emerged from the battle not as joyous free spirits but as the sexual revolution's walking wounded.*

This paragraph moves from particular to general—from four examples about individuals to one large statement about American women. By the time you finish, you might be ready to accept the paragraph's conclusion.

Implying a Topic Sentence

It is also possible to find a perfectly unified, well-organized paragraph that has no topic sentence at all, like the following from "New York" by Gay Talese (*Esquire*, July 1960):

Each afternoon in New York a rather seedy saxophone player, his cheeks blown out like a spinnaker, stands on the sidewalk playing "Danny Boy" in such a sad, sensitive way that he soon has half the neighborhood peeking out of windows tossing nickels, dimes, and quarters at his feet. Some of the coins roll under parked cars, but most of them are caught in his outstretched hand. The saxophone player is a street musician named Joe Gabler; for the past thirty years he has serenaded every block in New York and has sometimes been tossed as much as $100 a day in coins. He is also hit with buckets of water, empty beer cans and eggs, and chased by wild dogs. He is believed to be the last of New York's ancient street musicians.

No one sentence neatly sums up the writer's idea. Like most effective paragraphs that do not state a topic sentence, this one contains something just as good—a *topic idea*. The author doesn't wander aimlessly. He knows exactly what he wants to achieve—a description of how Joe Gabler, a famous New York street musician, plies his trade. Because Talese keeps this purpose firmly in mind, the main point—that Gabler meets both reward and abuse—is clear to the reader as well.

■ ACTIVITY 6.2: Shaping Topic Sentences

Discuss each of the following topic sentences with classmates, answering these questions:

Will it catch readers' attention?
Is it accurate?
Is it limited?
How might you develop the idea in the rest of the paragraph?
Can you improve it?

1. Television commercials stereotype people.
2. Living away from home for the first time is hard.
3. It's good for a child to have a pet.
4. A flea market is a good place to buy jewelry.
5. Pollution should be controlled.
6. Everybody should recycle waste.

WRITING AN OPENING

Even writers with something to say may find it hard to begin. Often they are so intent on writing a brilliant opening that they freeze, unable to write at all. They forget even the essentials—setting up the topic, sticking to what's relevant, and establishing a thesis. If your first page makes you feel like a deer paralyzed by headlights, try these ways of tackling the opening.

- Start with your thesis statement, with or without a full opening paragraph. You can fill in the rest later.
- Write your thesis statement—the one you planned or one you'd now like to develop—in the middle of the page. Then go back to the top of the page, and concisely add the background a reader needs to see where you're going.
- Write a long beginning for your first draft; then cut it down to the most dramatic, exciting, or interesting essentials.
- Simply set down words—any words—on paper, without trying to write an arresting opening. Then rewrite later.
- Write the first paragraph last, after you know exactly where your essay goes.
- Move your conclusion to the beginning, and write a new ending.
- Write a summary for yourself and your readers.

Your opening paragraph should intrigue readers—engaging their minds and hearts, exciting their curiosity, drawing them away from their preoccupations into the world you create in your writing. Use the Opener Checklist as you hunt for an effective opening that fits your paper. Then read the sample opening paragraphs that follow.

OPENER CHECKLIST

☐ What vital background might readers need?

☐ What general situation might help you narrow your focus?

☐ What facts or statistics might make your issue compelling?

☐ What powerful anecdote or incident might introduce your point?

☐ What striking example or comparison would engage a reader?

☐ What question will your thesis—and your essay—answer?

☐ What lively quotation would set the scene for your essay?

☐ What assertion or claim might be the necessary prelude for your essay?

☐ What points should you preview to prepare readers for what will come?

☐ What would compel someone to keep on reading?

Beginning with a Story

Often a simple anecdote can capture your readers' interest and make a good beginning. Here is how Dan Leeth opens his essay "Trails of Treasure" (*Encompass*, November/December 2013).

> It was my first ever hike. I was 9 years old when my father's friend, Scotty, invited us to join him on a trek into the Superstition Mountains, a rugged jumble of bluffs, buttes, crags, cliffs and canyons rising 35 miles east of Phoenix. Naturally, I wore my Roy Rogers cowboy boots. Six blisters later, I realized why Roy rode and seldom walked. Only Scotty's tales of treasure kept me going.

Leeth continues, explaining that the hike introduced him to the territory of the long-lost—and long-sought—golden treasure trove known as the Lost Dutchman Mine. Most of us, after an anecdote, want to read on. What will the writer say next? What does the anecdote have to do with the essay as a whole?

Commenting on a Topic

Sometimes a writer expands on a topic, bringing in vital details to clarify it, as does David Morris to open his article "Rootlessness" (*Utne*, May/June 1990):

> Americans are a rootless people. Each year one in six of us changes residences; one in four changes jobs. We see nothing troubling in these statistics. For most of us, they merely reflect the restless energy that made America great. A nation of immigrants, unsurprisingly, celebrates those willing to pick up stakes and move on: the frontiersman, the cowboy, the entrepreneur, the corporate raider.

After baldly stating his point, Morris supplies statistics to support his contention and briefly explains the phenomenon. This same strategy can be used to present a controversial opinion: open with the opinion, and then back it up with examples.

Asking a Question

An essay can begin with a question and answer, as James H. Austin begins "Four Kinds of Chance," in *Chase, Chance, and Creativity: The Lucky Art of Novelty* (New York: Columbia UP, 1978):

> What is chance? Dictionaries define it as something fortuitous that happens unpredictably without discernible human intention. Chance is unintentional and capricious, but we needn't conclude that chance is immune from human intervention. Indeed, chance plays several distinct roles when humans react creatively with one another and with their environment.

By beginning to answer the question in the first paragraph, Austin leads readers to expect the answer to continue in the rest of the essay.

Ending with the Thesis Statement

Opening paragraphs often end by stating the essay's main point. After capturing readers' attention with an anecdote, gripping details, or pertinent examples, you lead readers in exactly the direction you want your essay to go. In his response to the question "Should Washington stem the tide of both legal and illegal immigration?" ("Symposium," *Insight on the News*, March 11, 2002), Daniel T. Griswold uses this strategy to begin his answer:

> Immigration always has been controversial in the United States. More than two centuries ago, Benjamin Franklin worried that too many German immigrants would swamp America's predominantly British culture.

In the mid-1800s, Irish immigrants were scorned as lazy drunks, not to mention Roman Catholics. At the turn of the century a wave of "new immigrants"—Poles, Italians, Russian Jews—were believed to be too different ever to assimilate into American life. *Today the same fears are raised about immigrants from Latin America and Asia, but current critics of immigration are as wrong as their counterparts were in previous eras.*

■ ACTIVITY 6.3: Exchanging Openings

Working with a classmate or in a small group, exchange the drafts of your opening paragraphs for your current assignment or an essay you might write. As you read each draft paragraph, highlight the part that you find most interesting. Then point out anything that might be stronger or clearer for you as a reader. After the exchanges are complete, discuss the observations of both writers and readers.

WRITING A CONCLUSION

The final paragraphs of an essay linger longest in readers' minds. Consider E. B. White's conclusion to "Once More to the Lake" in *One Man's Meat* (Gardiner, ME: Tilbury House, 1941). In the essay, White describes returning with his young son to a vacation spot White had loved as a child. At the end of the essay, in an unforgettable image, he recalls how old he really is and realizes the inevitable passing of generations:

> When the others went swimming my son said he was going in, too. He pulled his dripping trunks from the line where they had hung all through the shower and wrung them out. Languidly, and with no thought of going in, I watched him, his hard little body, skinny and bare, saw him wince slightly as he pulled up around his vitals the small, soggy, icy garment. As he buckled the swollen belt, suddenly my groin felt the chill of death.

White's classic ending opens with a sentence that points back to the previous paragraph but also looks ahead. Then White leads us quickly to his final chilling insight. And then he stops.

It's easy to say what not to do at the end of an essay. Don't leave your readers half expecting you to go on. Don't restate everything you've already said. Don't introduce a brand-new topic that leads away from your point. And don't signal that the end is near with an obvious phrase like "As I have said. . . ."

How do you write an ending, then? Use the Conclusion Checklist as you tackle your ending. Then read the sample concluding paragraphs that follow.

CONCLUSION CHECKLIST

☐ What restatement of your thesis would give readers a satisfying sense of closure?

☐ What provocative implications of your thesis might answer "What now?" or "What's the significance of what I've said?"

☐ What snappy quotation or statement would wrap up your point?

☐ What closing facts or statistics might confirm the merit of your point?

☐ What final anecdote, incident, or example might round out your ideas?

☐ What question has your essay answered?

☐ What assertion or claim might you want to restate?

☐ What summary might help a reader pull together what you've said?

☐ What would make a reader sorry to finish such a satisfying essay?

Ending with a Quotation

An apt quotation can neatly round out an essay, as literary critic Malcolm Cowley shows in *The View from Eighty* (New York: Viking, 1980), his discussion of the pitfalls and compensations of old age:

> "Eighty years old!" the great Catholic poet Paul Claudel wrote in his journal. "No eyes left, no ears, no teeth, no legs, no wind! And when all is said and done, how astonishingly well one does without them!"

Stating or Restating Your Thesis

In a sharp criticism of American schools, humorist Russell Baker in "School vs. Education" ends by stating his main point, that schools do not educate:

> Afterward, the former student's destiny fulfilled, his life rich with Oriental carpets, rare porcelain, and full bank accounts, he may one day find himself with the leisure and the inclination to open a book with a curious mind, and start to become educated.

Ending with a Brief Emphatic Sentence

For an essay that traces causes or effects, evaluates, or argues, a deft concluding thought can reinforce the main idea. In "How to Be a Climate Hero" (*Orion*, May/June 2008), Audrey Schulman explains the bystander effect, a term used by psychologists to describe the likelihood that witnesses to emergencies do not act if others are present. She relates this effect to the absence of public response to global climate changes, concluding with a succinct call to action:

> Scientists tell us we have ten years, if that, to make significant changes. Every indication, from ice caps to defrosting tundra, seems to show this is the tipping point. This is our moment. Perhaps you never thought you'd get a chance to play hero. Here it is. The kid on the train is screaming out for help. The weather is convulsing. It doesn't matter if you aren't sure what to do. Make your best guess. Call 9-1-1.

Stopping When the Story Is Over

Even a quiet ending can be effective, as long as it signals clearly that the essay is finished. When *Smithsonian* (November 2013) featured articles on "101 Objects That Made America," space-age historian Andrew Chaikin prepared the selection on "Neil Armstrong's Spacesuit." His engaging account of the suit's model number, cost, construction, technical qualities, and wearability describes the essential features that protected Armstrong as he took his famous first step on the moon. Then Chaikin concludes his article with this succinct paragraph:

> "Its true beauty, however," said Armstrong, "was that it worked."

■ ACTIVITY 6.4: Opening and Concluding

Openings and conclusions frame an essay, contributing to its unity. The opening sets up the topic and main idea; the conclusion reaffirms the thesis and rounds off the ideas. Discuss the following with your classmates.

1. Here are two possible opening paragraphs for a student essay on the importance of teaching children how to swim.

   A. Humans inhabit a world made up of over 70 percent water. In addition to these great bodies of water, we have built millions of swimming pools for sports and leisure activities. At one time or another most people will be faced with either the danger of drowning or the challenge of aquatic recreation. For these reasons, it is essential that we learn to swim. Being a competitive swimmer and a swimming instructor, I fully realize the importance of knowing how to swim.

B. Four-year-old Carl, curious like most children, last spring ventured out onto his pool patio. He fell into the pool and, not knowing how to swim, helplessly sank to the bottom. Minutes later his uncle found the child and brought him to the surface. Because Carl had no pulse, his uncle administered CPR until the paramedics arrived. Eventually the child was revived. During his stay in the hospital, his mother signed him up for beginning swimming classes. Carl was a lucky one. Unlike thousands of other children and adults, he got a second chance.

  a. Which introduction is more effective? Why?
  b. What would the body of this essay consist of? What kinds of evidence would be included?
  c. Write a suitable conclusion for this essay.

2. Here are possible introductions and conclusions for two student essays. How effective are they? Could they be improved? If so, how? If they are satisfactory, explain why. What would be a catchy yet informative title for each essay?

A. Recently a friend down from New York astonished me with stories of several people infected—some with AIDS—by stepping on needles washed up on the New Jersey beaches. This is just one incident of pollution, a devastating problem in our society today. Pollution is increasing in our world because of greed, apathy, and Congress's inability to control this problem. . . .

   Wouldn't it be nice to have a pollution-free world without medical wastes floating in the water and washing up on our beaches? Without garbage scattered on the streets? With every corporation abiding by the laws set by Congress? In the future we can have a pollution-free world, but it is going to take the cooperation of everyone, including Congress, to ensure our survival on this Planet Earth.

B. The divorce rate rose 700 percent in the last century and continues to rise. More than one out of every two couples who are married end up in divorce. Over one million children a year are affected by divorce in the family. From these statistics it is clear that one of the greatest problems concerning the family today is divorce and the adverse effects it has on our society. . . .

   Divorce causes problems that change people for life. The number of divorces will continue to exceed the 700 percent figure unless married couples learn to communicate, to accept their mates unconditionally, and to sacrificially give of themselves.

ACHIEVING COHERENCE

Effective writing proceeds in some sensible order, each sentence follow-ing naturally from the one before it. Yet even well-organized prose can be hard to read unless it is *coherent* and effectively integrates its ele-ments. Readers need cues and connections—devices that tie together words in a sentence, sentences in a paragraph, paragraphs in an essay.

Adding Transitional Words and Sentences

You use transitions every day to help the people around you follow your train of thought. For example, you might say to a friend, "Well, *on the one hand,* a second job would help me save money for tuition. *On the other hand,* I'd have less time to study." But some writers rush through, omitting links between thoughts or mistakenly assuming that connec-tions they see will automatically be clear to readers.

Often a transitional word, phrase, or sentence inserted in the right place can transform a disconnected passage into a coherent one. Many words and phrases can signal connections between or within sentences. In Table 6.1, examples of these *transitional markers* are grouped by pur-pose or the kind of relationship or connection they establish.

Occasionally a whole sentence serves as a transition. The opening of one paragraph may hark back to the last one while revealing a new or narrower direction. The next excerpt came from "Preservation Basics: Why Preserve Film?" a web page of the National Film Preservation Foun-dation (NFPF) at filmpreservation.org. The first paragraph introduces the organization's mission; the next two each open with transitional sen-tences (italics ours) that introduce major challenges to that mission.

Since Thomas Edison's invention of the kinetoscope in 1893, Ameri-cans have traveled the world using motion pictures to tell stories, docu-ment traditions, and capture current events. Their work stands as the collective memory of the first century witnessed by the moving image. By saving and sharing these motion pictures, we can illuminate our common heritage with a power and immediacy unique to film.

Preservationists are working against the clock. Made on perishable plastic, film decays within years if not properly stored.

Already the losses are high. The Library of Congress has documented that fewer than 20 percent of U.S. feature films from the 1920s survive in complete form in American archives; of the American features pro-duced before 1950, only half still exist. For shorts, documentaries, and independently produced works, we have no way of knowing how much has been lost.

TABLE 6.1   Using Transitional Markers

	Common Transitions
To Mark Time	then, soon, first, second, next, recently, the following day, in a little while, meanwhile, after, later, in the past, still, finally
To Mark Place or Direction	in the distance, close by, near, far away, above, below, to the right, on the other side, opposite, to the west, next door
To Summarize or Restate	in other words, to put it another way, in brief, in simpler terms, on the whole, in fact, in a word, to sum up, in short, in conclusion, to conclude, finally, therefore
To Relate Cause and Effect or Result	therefore, accordingly, hence, thus, for, so, consequently, as a result, because of, due to, eventually, inevitably
To Add, Amplify, or List	and, also, too, besides, as well, moreover, in addition, furthermore, in effect, second, in the second place, again, next
To Compare	similarly, likewise, in like manner, in the same way
To Concede	whereas, on the other hand, with that in mind, still, and yet, even so, in spite of, despite, at least, of course
To Contrast	on the other hand, but, or, however, unlike, nevertheless, on the contrary, conversely, in contrast, instead
To Indicate Purpose	to this end, for this purpose, with this aim
To Express Condition	although, though
To Give Examples or Specify	for example, for instance, in this case, in particular, to illustrate
To Qualify	for the most part, by and large, with few exceptions, mainly, in most cases, generally, some, sometimes, typically, frequently, rarely
To Emphasize	it is true, truly, indeed, of course, to be sure, obviously, without doubt, evidently, clearly, understandably

The first paragraph establishes the value of "saving and sharing" the American film legacy. The next two paragraphs use key words related to preservation and its absence (*perishable, decays, losses, lost*) to clarify that what follows builds on what has gone before. Each also opens with a short, dramatic transition to one of the major problems: time and existing loss.

Supplying Transitional Paragraphs

Transitions may be even longer than sentences. In a long, complicated essay, moving clearly from one idea to the next sometimes requires a short transition paragraph.

> So far, the physical and psychological effects of driving nonstop for hundreds of miles seem clear. The next consideration is why drivers do this. What causes people to become addicted to their steering wheels?

Use a transition paragraph only when you sense that your readers might get lost if you don't patiently lead them by the hand. If your essay is short, one question or statement beginning a new paragraph will be enough.

A transition paragraph also can help you move between one branch of argument and your main trunk or between a digression and your main direction. In this excerpt from *The Film Preservation Guide: The Basics for Archives, Libraries, and Museums* (San Francisco: NFPF, 2004; http:// www.filmpreservation.org/userfiles/image/PDFs/fpg_3.pdf), the writer introduces the importance of inspecting film and devotes the next paragraph to a digression—referring readers to an inspection sheet in the appendix.

> Inspection is the single most important way to date a film, identify its technical characteristics, and detect damage and decay. Much can be learned by examining your film carefully, from start to finish.
>
> A standardized inspection work sheet (see appendix B) lists things to check and helps organize notes. This type of written report is the foundation for future preservation actions. Collecting the information during inspection will help you make informed decisions and enable you to document any changes in film condition over time.
>
> Signs of decay and damage may vary across the length of the film. . . .

The second paragraph acts as a transition, guiding readers to specialized information in the appendix and then drawing them back to the overall purpose of inspection: assessing the extent of damage to a film.

Using Repetition

Another way to clarify the relationship between two sentences, paragraphs, or ideas is to repeat a key word or phrase. Such purposeful repetition almost guarantees that readers will understand how all the parts of a passage fit together. Notice the repetition of the word *anger* in the following paragraph (the italics are ours) from *Of Woman Born* (New York: Norton, 1976) by poet Adrienne Rich. In this complex paragraph, the writer explores her relationship with her mother. The repetition holds all the parts together, making the paragraph's ideas coherent.

> And I know there must be deep reservoirs of *anger* in her; every mother has known overwhelming, unacceptable *anger* at her children. When I think of the conditions under which my mother became a mother, the impossible expectations, my father's distaste for pregnant women, his hatred of all that he could not control, my *anger* at her dissolves into grief and *anger* for her, and then dissolves back again into *anger* at her: the ancient, unpurged *anger* of the child.

Strengthening Pronouns

Because they always refer back to nouns or other pronouns, pronouns serve as transitions by making readers refer back as well. Notice how certain pronouns (in italics) hold together the following paragraph from "Misunderstood Michelle" by columnist Ellen Goodman in *At Large* (New York: Summit Books, 1981):

> I have two friends who moved in together many years ago. *He* looked upon this step as a trial marriage. *She* looked upon it as, well, moving in together. *He* was sure that in a matter of time, after *they* had built up trust and confidence, *she* would agree that marriage was the next logical step. *She*, on the other hand, was thrilled that here at last was a man *who* would never push *her* back to the altar.

The paragraph contains other transitions, too: time markers like *many years ago*, *in a matter of time*, and *after*; *on the other hand*, which indicates contrast; and the repetition of words related to marriage—*trial marriage*, *marriage*, and *the altar*. All serve the main purpose of transitions: keeping readers on track.

■ ACTIVITY 6.5: Identifying Transitions

Go over one of the papers you have already written for this or another course, and circle all the transitional devices you find. Then share your paper with a classmate. Can the classmate find additional transitions? Does the classmate think you need transitions where you don't have any?

7

Strategies for Developing

How can you spice up your general ideas with the stuff of real life? How can you tug your readers deeper and deeper into your essays until they say, "I see just what you mean"? Well-developed essays have that power because they back up general points with evidence that comes alive for readers. In this chapter we cover more than a dozen strategies for developing your writing. (Also see Ch. 10 for resources for arguing.) Although you may choose to use only one method within a single paragraph, a strong essay almost always requires a combination of developmental strategies.

Whenever you develop a piece of writing or return to it to revise, you face a challenge: How do you figure out what to do? Sometimes you may suspect that you've wandered into the buffet line at the Writer's Grill. You watch others load their plates, but you still hesitate. What will taste best? How much will fit on your plate? What will create a memorable experience? For you as a writer, the answers depend on your situation, the clarity of your main idea or thesis, and the state of your draft, as the Development Checklist on page 109 suggests.

GIVING EXAMPLES

An example—the word comes from the Latin *exemplum*, "one thing chosen from among many"—is a typical instance that illustrates a whole type or kind. Giving examples to support a generalization is probably

DEVELOPMENT CHECKLIST

Purpose

☐ Does your assignment recommend or require any specific methods of development?

☐ Which developmental strategies might be most useful to explain, inform, or persuade?

☐ What type of development might best achieve your specific purpose?

Audience

☐ Which developmental strategies will best clarify your topic for your readers?

☐ Which will best demonstrate your thesis to your readers?

☐ What kinds of evidence will your specific readers prefer? Which developmental strategies might present this evidence most effectively?

Thesis

☐ What kinds of development does your thesis promise or imply you will supply?

☐ What sequence of developmental strategies will best support your thesis?

Essay Development

☐ Has a reader or peer editor pointed out ideas in your draft that need fuller or more effective development?

☐ Where might your readers have trouble following or understanding without more or better development?

Paragraph Development

☐ Should any paragraphs with one or two sentences be developed more fully?

☐ Should any long paragraphs with generalizations, repetition, and wordy phrasing be developed differently so that they are richer, deeper, and more compelling for readers?

the most common means of development. This example from *In Search of Excellence* (New York: Harper & Row, 1982) by Thomas J. Peters and Robert H. Waterman Jr. explains the success of America's top corporations.

> Although he's not a company, our favorite illustration of closeness to the customer is car salesman Joe Girard. He sold more new cars and trucks, each year, for eleven years running, than any other human being. In fact, in a typical year, Joe sold more than twice as many units as whoever was in second place. In explaining his secret of success, Joe said: "I sent out over thirteen thousand cards every month."
>
> Why start with Joe? Because his magic is the magic of IBM and many of the rest of the excellent companies. It is simply service, overpowering service, especially after-sales service. Joe noted, "There's one thing that I do that a lot of salesmen don't, and that's believe the sale really begins *after* the sale—not before. . . . The customer ain't out the door, and my son has made up a thank-you note." Joe would intercede personally, a year later, with the service manager on behalf of his customer. Meanwhile he would keep the communications flowing.

Notice how Peters and Waterman focus on the specific, Joe Girard. They don't write *corporation employees* or even *car salespeople*. Instead, they zero in on one particular man to make the point come alive. The specific example of Joe Girard makes closeness to the customer *concrete* to readers: he is someone readers can relate to.

Joe Girard	Level 4: Specific example
Car salespeople	Level 3: Even more specific group
Corporation employees	Level 2: More specific group
America's top corporations	Level 1: General group or category

The ladder of abstraction shown here moves up from the general—America's top corporations—to a specific person—Joe Girard. To check the level of specificity in one of your paragraphs or outlines, draw a ladder of abstraction for it. Do the same to restrict a broad subject to a topic you can manage in a short essay. If you haven't climbed up to the fourth or fifth level, you are probably being too general and need to add specifics.

An example doesn't always have to be a specific individual. Sometimes you can create a picture of something readers have never encountered or give an abstraction a recognizable personality and identity.

Using this strategy, Jonathan Kozol makes real the plight of illiterate people in our health-care system in this paragraph from *Prisoners of Silence: Breaking the Bonds of Adult Illiteracy in the United States* (New York: Continuum, 1980):

> Illiterates live, in more than literal ways, an uninsured existence. They cannot understand the written details on a health insurance form. They cannot read waivers that they sign preceding surgical procedures. Several women I have known in Boston have entered a slum hospital with the intention of obtaining a tubal ligation and have emerged a few days later after having been subjected to a hysterectomy. Unaware of their rights, incognizant of jargon, intimidated by the unfamiliar air of fear and atmosphere of ether that so many of us find oppressive in the confines even of the most attractive and expensive medical facilities, they have signed their names to documents they could not read and which nobody, in the hectic situation that prevails so often in those overcrowded hospitals that serve the urban poor, had ever bothered to explain.

Examples aren't trivial doodads you add to a paragraph for decoration; they both hold your readers' attention and make your ideas more concrete and tangible. Giving plenty of examples is one of the writer's chief tasks, and you can generate more at any point in the writing process. Begin with your own experience, even with a topic about which you know little, or try conversing with others, reading, digging in the library, or browsing on the web. (For ways to generate ideas, see Ch. 4.)

Consider the questions in the following checklist when you use examples in your writing.

EXAMPLE CHECKLIST

- ☐ Are your examples relevant to your main idea or thesis?
- ☐ Are your examples the best ones you can think of? Will readers find them strong and appropriate?
- ☐ Are your examples truly specific? Or do they just repeat generalities?
- ☐ From each paragraph, can you draw a ladder of abstraction to at least the fourth level?

▓ ACTIVITY 7.1: Giving Examples

To help you get in the habit of thinking specifically, fill in a ladder of abstraction for five of the following general subjects. Then share your ladders with classmates, and compare and contrast your specifics with theirs. Here are two examples:

```
Iceberg
 Lettuce
  Vegetables
   Food
```

```
Prius
 Toyota
  Hybrids
   Automobiles
    Land vehicles
     Transportation
```

colleges	fast foods	jewelry
college courses	music	books
clothes	movies	buildings
diseases	machines	television

PROVIDING DETAILS

A *detail* is any specific, concrete piece of information—a fact, a bit of the historical record, your own observation. Details make scenes and images more realistic and vivid for readers. They also back up generalizations, convincing readers that the writer can make broad assertions with authority.

Mary Harris "Mother" Jones tells the story of her life as a labor organizer in *The Autobiography of Mother Jones* (Chicago: Kerr, 1925, 1980). She lends conviction to her general statement about a coal miner's lot at the end of the nineteenth century with ample evidence from her own experience and observations.

> Mining at its best is wretched work, and the life and surroundings of the miner are hard and ugly. His work is down in the black depths of the earth. He works alone in a drift. There can be little friendly companionship as there is in the factory; as there is among men who build bridges and houses, working together in groups. The work is dirty. Coal dust grinds itself into the skin, never to be removed. The miner must stoop as he works in the drift. He becomes bent like a gnome.
>
> His work is utterly fatiguing. Muscles and bones ache. His lungs breathe coal dust and the strange, damp air of places that are never

filled with sunlight. His house is a poor makeshift and there is little to encourage him to make it attractive. The company owns the ground it stands on, and the miner feels the precariousness of his hold. Around his house is mud and slush. Great mounds of culm [the refuse left after coal is screened], black and sullen, surround him. His children are perpetually grimy from playing on the culm mounds. The wife struggles with dirt, with inadequate water supply, with small wages, with overcrowded shacks.

Although Mother Jones, not a learned writer, relies on short, simple sentences, her writing is clear and powerful because of the specific details she uses. Her opening makes two general statements: (1) mining "is wretched work," and (2) the miner's "life and surroundings" are "hard and ugly." She supports these generalizations with a barrage of factual evidence and detail, including well-chosen verbs: "Coal dust *grinds* itself into the skin." The result is a moving, convincingly detailed portrait of the miner and his family.

In *Lipstick Jihad: A Memoir of Growing Up Iranian in America and American in Iran* (New York: Public Affairs, 2005), Azadeh Moaveni uses details to evoke the "drama and magic" she experienced during a childhood visit to Iran.

To my five-year-old suburban American sensibilities, exposed to nothing more mystical than the Smurfs, Iran was suffused with drama and magic. After Friday lunch at my grandfather's, once the last plates of sliced cantaloupe were cleared away, everyone retired to the bedrooms to nap. Inevitably there was a willing aunt or cousin on hand to scratch my back as I fell asleep. Unused to the siesta ritual, I woke up after half an hour to find the bed I was sharing with my cousin swathed in a tower of creamy gauze that stretched high up to the ceiling. "Wake up," I nudged him, "we're surrounded!" "It's for the mosquitoes, *khareh*, ass, go back to sleep." To me it was like a fairy tale, and I peered through the netting to the living room, to the table heaped with plump dates and the dense, aromatic baklava we would nibble on later with tea. The day before I had helped my grandmother, Razi joon, make *ash-e gooshvareh*, "earring stew"; we made hoops out of the fresh pasta, and dropped them into the vat of simmering herbs and lamb. Here even the ordinary had charm, even the names of stews.

To guide readers through her details, Moaveni uses transitions—chronological (*After Friday lunch, after half an hour, The day before*), spatial (*through the netting to the living room*), and thematic (*To me it was like a fairy tale*). (For more on transitions, see pp. 104–7.)

Quite different from Moaveni's personal, descriptive details are the comparative statistics in *Families and Faith: How Religion Is Passed Down Across Generations* by Vern L. Bengtson with Norella M. Putney and Susan Harris (New York: Oxford University Press, 2013). Before reporting his current findings, Bengtson sums up societal changes during his ongoing research project, begun over thirty-five years ago, surveying grandparents, parents, participants, and now their offspring.

> Since World War II, there has been unprecedented change at the most intimate level of American society: family life. The rate of divorce increased slowly through the first half of the twentieth century and then rose dramatically over the next few decades. By 1990, one out of every two marriages ended in divorce, and by the end of the century, almost as many children lived in single-parent households—most headed by mothers—as in dual-parent households. Of those children in two-parent households, one-quarter lived in "blended" families with stepparents and stepsiblings.

Providing details is one of the simplest yet most effective ways of developing ideas. All it takes on your part is close attention and precise wording to communicate details to readers. If readers were on the scene, what would they see? What would they hear, smell, or feel? Which small details from your reading are most meaningful to you? Would a bit of research turn up just the right fact or statistic? Remember that, to be effective, details must have a specific purpose: they must make your images more evocative or your point more convincing. Every detail should in some way support your main idea.

The Details Checklist offers questions to consider when you use specific information.

DETAILS CHECKLIST

☐ Do all your details support your point of view, main idea, or thesis?

☐ Do you have details of sight? sound? taste? touch? smell?

☐ Have you included enough details to make your writing clear?

☐ Have you selected details that will engage and inform your readers?

☐ Have you arranged your details in an order that is easy to follow?

◾ ACTIVITY 7.2: Providing Details

To practice generating and using specific details, brainstorm (see pp. 51–52) with classmates or alone on one of the following subjects. Be sure to include details that appeal to all five senses. Group the details in your list (see pp. 76–80), and write a paragraph or two using them. Begin by stating a main idea that conveys an engaging impression of your subject (not "My grandmother's house was in Topeka, Kansas" but "My grandmother's house was my childhood haven").

the things in my room	a memorable event	my job
my grandmother's house	an unusual person	a classroom
a haunted house	my favorite pet	the cafeteria
a special possession	a hospital room	an incident

DRAWING ON EXPERIENCE

Your experience includes whatever has happened to or around you. As you tell, or narrate, that story, you share its significance with your readers. Your experience can supply evidence to support a statement, illustrate a point, establish the rationale for your point of view, or enhance your credibility as a writer. Even a brief account can bring the authenticity of a real event and the power of personal testimony to your writing.

As you recall experience, you draw on memory, a writer's richest—and handiest—resource. All by itself, memory may not give you enough to write about, and in some situations, readers will expect evidence other than experience. However, you will rarely go wrong if you start by jotting down something you remember, even if it serves primarily as the platform on which you build a research scaffold. As you think back, you're likely to recall an event or a person that is part of a tale you might tell—something memorable that happened, an encounter with someone notable, a situation that provoked a decision, or the struggle necessary to overcome an obstacle.

In "Cheers for Tears" (*Salon.com*, October 18, 2005), Cecelie S. Berry demonstrates how to convey experience powerfully yet briefly. She supports her opening assertion with three experiences, each sketched in a single sentence.

I discovered early on that crying was controversial. "People will think you're weak," my older sister said, when I came home from a schoolyard fight in tears. "People will think you're unstable," I was told as a summer associate in a big city law firm, when I went crying to a female lawyer after a senior partner obliterated one of my memos. "People will think you're unhappy," my mother warned when I cried at my son's brilliant performance as Charlie Brown in the kindergarten play.

On the other hand, in "Deporting Resident Aliens: No Compassion, No Sense" (*America,* February 27, 1999), attorney Ann Carr takes two paragraphs to recount her meeting with a client.

> The young man fidgets as he sits across from me in the prison consulting room. As his immigration lawyer, I have just finished telling him that he is going to have to leave the country and go back to Mexico. The reason: He was guilty of the "crime" of working in the United States without permission, doing work that most Americans won't do, so that he could support his American wife and child. Earning one's living and supporting one's family used to be considered a virtue, last time I checked.
>
> "But my wife is expecting her baby in a few weeks. How is she going to live if I can't work to support her?" His face quivers with the anxiety and stress this thought provokes. I am at a complete loss to explain to him the rationale of the law that mandates such a result—a young American family being deprived of the husband and father figure, and almost certainly being forced onto the welfare rolls to boot. The young man has fallen afoul of the recent legislation that sends people back to their country of origin to apply for an immigrant visa. They usually experience delays of a year or more before they can return. When he asks if there is anything he can do, I suggest that his wife, a U.S. citizen with a vote, call her Congressional representatives to ask them for a solution.

Carr pares her experience down to the essentials that convey to readers its significance to her. She could have begun her account with her walk into the building; instead, she zeroes in on the exchange with her client. She might have described what he wore; instead, she focuses on his quivering face and his concern for his family.

When you recount your experience, you'll need to dig deeply but select carefully so that you stick to what matters. Consider the questions in the Experience Checklist when you recall and write about experience.

EXPERIENCE CHECKLIST

☐ What is your purpose in recalling your experience? Given your writing task, what role would be appropriate for personal experience?

☐ What do you want your readers to grasp? How might you engage their interest?

☐ Have you deepened your account of events by asking the reporter's questions: Who? What? Where? When? Why? How?

☐ Do you plan to present events in chronological order, from beginning to end, or with flashbacks, jumping from the middle or end back to earlier events?

☐ Have you brought your story to life by supplying details that appeal to the senses—sight, sound, taste, touch, and smell?

☐ Have you selected what's necessary for your purpose and left out what's not?

■ ACTIVITY 7.3: Drawing on Experience

Think back to an experience that you'd like to share with readers. Answer the reporter's questions or list events chronologically to establish what happened during the event. Then highlight what's relevant to the particular point you want to make. Finally, sum up the impact you'd like your story to have.

OBSERVING A SCENE

Sometimes you can develop your writing simply by observing, using your senses to notice what's around you. Formal observation is a valuable research method in education and the social sciences. Informal observation is a handy resource for compelling eyewitness evidence and concrete details about a scene, activity, or event. Observe with all of your senses—sight, sound, taste, touch, smell—and record the details accurately.

Generally you notice and record far more than you'll be able to use in your writing, so you'll need to select and group the details. If you want to share an overall impression of the scene with readers, you might arrange details in spatial or chronological order, using movement through space or time to draw readers into the scene. For example, you might begin with the outermost details and then move closer to the central activity. Or you might move around a crowded urban classroom, across a polluted skyline, or up a hiking trail. You might also wish to generalize or summarize, perhaps based on typical or representative scenes you have observed. Then you might group your details thematically, clustering them to support each of your points. (See also pp. 76–80.)

In "To the Singing, to the Drums" (*Natural History,* February 1975), N. Scott Momaday describes his observations at the Kiowa celebration of the Gourd Dance on the Fourth of July in Carnegie, Oklahoma.

> The celebration is on the north side. We turn down into a dark depression, a large hollow among trees. It is full of camps and cars and people. At first there are children. According to some centrifugal social force, children function on the periphery. They run about, making festival noises. Firecrackers are snapping all around. We park and I make ready; the girls help me with my regalia. I am already wearing white trousers and moccasins. Now I tie the black velvet sash around my waist, placing the beaded tassels at my right leg. The bandoleer of red beans, which was my grandfather's, goes over my left shoulder, the V at my right hip. I decide to carry the blanket over my arm until I join the dancers; no sense in wrapping up in this heat. There is deep, brick-red dust on the ground. The grass is pale and brittle here and there. We make our way through the camps, stepping carefully to avoid the pegs and guy lines that reach about the tents. Old people, imperturbable, are lying down on cots and benches in the shadows. Smoke hangs in the air. We smell hamburgers, popcorn, gunpowder. Later there will be fried bread, boiled meat, Indian corn.

Momaday arranges his vivid details both spatially and chronologically. Notice his spatial transitions: *on the north side, turn down, on the periphery, all around, on the ground, here and there, through the camps, in the shadows, in the air.* Look also at the time markers: *At first, Now, until, Later.* These transitions guide readers through the experience, helping them approach the celebration alongside Momaday.

Use the following checklist to help you strengthen your observations.

OBSERVATION CHECKLIST

☐ What did you see—landmarks, structures, objects, people, animals, activities, colors, shapes, or sizes?

☐ What did you hear—conversations, music, other sounds, tones, pitches, rhythms, or silence?

☐ What did you taste—sweet, salty, spicy, or other flavors?

☐ What did you touch and feel—shapes, textures, movements, or sensations?

☐ What did you smell—aromas, fragrances, or odors?

☐ Have you selected and organized the details needed to support the overall impression that you want to share with your audience?

☐ Do you need to sharpen either your overall impression of the scene or your selection of supporting details?

▚ ACTIVITY 7.4: Observing a Scene

Practice observing by positioning yourself in a rich environment full of activity or sensory detail. Watch carefully, using all of your senses, and record what you notice. Conclude by writing a sentence that sums up your overall impression of the scene highlighting or listing details to support that impression.

CONVERSING AND INTERVIEWING

When you need fresh or timely information to develop your writing, try talking with someone. A simple conversation with a friend can suggest new ideas or details, challenge assumptions, or introduce alternative views. A more formal interview with the right person can supply expert testimony, a valuable form of evidence in either verbal or written form. Select your expert carefully, looking for someone with the appropriate background or professional credentials to convince your readers that his or her knowledge is credible. As reporters know, interviews often capture the flavor of the moment, the passion behind the topic, or the insight of those personally engaged in a situation.

Student Dawn Kortz interviewed Emmett Sherwood, a regular customer at the cafe where she worked and a longtime resident of her community. Early in her essay, "Listen," Kortz introduces him to her readers:

> As we begin to talk, I notice the far-off look in his eyes, as if he is trying to remember the old days, his youth, and how the city he loves looked when he first arrived. Over a cup of steaming coffee, Emmett begins by telling me he was born in Oklahoma but grew up in St. Johns, Kansas. As a young man of fourteen, he became attracted to the big city and in 1920 moved to Dodge City, Kansas, where he was married, raised a family, and continues to live.

As their conversation continues, he recalls Dodge City from the carefree 1920s with the popular Harvey House restaurant and its short-skirted waitresses, the fire that destroyed the majestic O'Neal Hotel, the Great

Depression with many hungry families, and World War II when women first commonly entered the workforce. Kortz concludes the essay with her own observations:

> Today, when I look around the city in which I live, I realize that what I see is not what Dodge City has always been. Emmett has given me a new appreciation of the past. He has instilled in me the importance of history — my family history, my town's history, my country's history, and my world's history. Every day when he comes into Mic-Leo's and I serve him coffee, I remember our talk, and I can only hope that others like Emmett are sharing their life stories with people of another generation. I also hope that more people of my generation are willing to take the time to listen.

When you want to interview someone, plan ahead: schedule the meeting, write out questions in advance, and gather supplies for recording the conversation. Be prepared to jot down and label direct quotations during the interview and to add notes about your impressions immediately afterward. Then evaluate your material before adding it to your writing. For example, if the person you interviewed is the focus of your paper, you'd select and organize comments that reveal the person's character, passion, or impact. On the other hand, to support your assertions about an issue, you'd integrate information from your interview as it logically fits.

Use the Interview Checklist to help you get started.

INTERVIEW CHECKLIST

- ☐ Have you selected an appropriate expert for the interview? Have you researched his or her background, experience, publications, or other professional activities?
- ☐ Have you scheduled the interview at a convenient time and location?
- ☐ Have you prepared questions, perhaps moving from general background to specifics?
- ☐ Have you revised your questions, making sure each is clear, relevant, and sufficiently open-ended to stimulate a valuable response?
- ☐ Are you prepared to record the interview (with your subject's permission) and jot notes on paper (as a backup in all cases)?

☐ Did you thank your expert after the interview? If necessary, have you confirmed the accuracy of direct quotations or specific information?

☐ Have you selected and organized your material to speak meaningfully to your readers and to achieve your writing purpose?

■ ACTIVITY 7.5: Interviewing

Schedule a practice interview with a classmate or friend. In advance, develop a list of questions to help you discover and learn about something at which that person is expert. (That expertise might fall in any area—academic, social, work, sports, hobbies, or activities.) Take notes during the interview, and then evaluate your notes afterward to learn how you might strengthen your interviewing skills.

DEFINING

Define, from the Latin, means "to set bounds to." You define a thing, a word, or a concept by describing it so that it is distinguished from all similar things. If people don't agree on the meaning of a word or an idea, they can't share knowledge about it. Scientists in particular take special care to define their terms precisely. "Climate Engineering," a 2012 *State of the Science Fact Sheet* from the National Oceanic and Atmospheric Administration, opens with a definition:

> Climate engineering, also called geoengineering, refers to deliberate, large-scale manipulation of Earth's climate intended to counteract human-caused climate change.

After outlining why this topic needs study, the fact sheet identifies its two main subdivisions:

> Two different climate engineering approaches are commonly considered:
> * Removing some CO_2 from the atmosphere to reduce its greenhouse effect.
> * Increasing the reflection of sunlight away from Earth back to space, thus cooling the planet.

If you use a word in a special sense or coin a word, you have to explain it or your readers will be lost. In his article "When Past Disasters Are Prologue" (*Nautilus*, Issue 4, 2013), David Ropeik examines the utility of past disasters for predicting future ones, improving preparedness and survival rates, and increasing risk awareness. For instance, after video of a comet colliding with Jupiter and several movies on the same theme, the public became aware of objects that might collide with the earth. Ropeik identifies and defines the term for this behavior.

> What happened with asteroids is an example of what cognitive psychologists call the Availability Heuristic, a phenomenon whereby we tend to pay more attention to, and worry more about, matters that readily come to mind. Here's an example: Does the letter *r* appear more frequently as the first letter in words, or the third? As you search through the words you know to figure this out, the first letter is the first thing that comes to mind. As a result, most people say *r* is more common as a first letter in words, but in fact it is more common as the third. The effect is compounded when strong emotions, like fear, are brought into play. Emotionally powerful experiences burn more deeply into our memories and are more readily summoned, and the speed and power of that recall give those memories disproportionate influence on our perceptions.

Sometimes you will define an unfamiliar word to save your readers a trip to the dictionary or a familiar but often misunderstood concept to clarify the meaning you intend. For example, what would you mean by *guerilla, liberal,* or *minimum wage*? The more complex or ambiguous an idea, a thing, a movement, a phenomenon, or an organization, the more detailed the definition you will need to clarify the term for your readers.

The Definition Checklist includes questions to consider when you explain a term.

DEFINITION CHECKLIST

- ☐ Have you used definitions to help your readers understand the subject matter (not to show off your knowledge)?
- ☐ Have you tailored your definition to the needs of your audience?
- ☐ Is your definition specific, clear, and accurate?
- ☐ Would your definition benefit from an example or from details?

■ ACTIVITY 7.6: Defining

Write an extended definition (a paragraph or so) of one of the following words. Begin with a one-sentence definition of the word. Then, instead of turning to a dictionary or textbook, expand and clarify your ideas using some of the strategies explained in this chapter—examples, details, analysis, and so forth. You may also use *negation,* explaining what something is by stating what it is not. Share your definition with your classmates.

education	abuse	exercise	literacy
privacy	jazz	dieting	success
taboo	hip-hop	gossip	fear
prejudice	bird flu	security	gender

REASONING INDUCTIVELY AND DEDUCTIVELY

As you develop a typical paragraph in a paper, you are likely to rely on both generalizations and particulars. A *generalization* is a broad statement that establishes the point you want to make, the viewpoint you hold, or the conclusion you have reached. A *particular* is an instance, a detail, or an example—specific evidence that a general statement is reasonable. Your particulars support your generalizations; compelling instances, details, and examples back up your broader point. At the same time, your generalizations pull together your particulars, identifying patterns or connections that relate individual cases. (See also pp. 42–45 on the statement-support pattern and Ch. 10 on argument.)

To relate particulars and generalizations, you can use an inductive or deductive process. An *inductive process* begins with the particulars—a convincing number of instances, examples, tests, or experiments. Taken together, these particulars substantiate a larger generalization. In this way a number of long-term studies of weight loss can eventually lead to a consensus about the benefits of walking or eating low-fat foods or of some other variable. Less formal inductive reasoning is common as people *infer* or conclude that particulars do or do not support a generalization. For example, if your sister ate strawberries three times and got a rash each time, she might infer that she is allergic to strawberries. Induction breaks down when the particulars are too weak or too few to support a generalization: for example, not enough weight-loss studies have comparable results or not enough clear instances occur when strawberries—and nothing else—trigger a reaction.

A *deductive process* begins with a generalization and applies it to another case. When your sister says no to a piece of strawberry pie, she does so because, based on her assumptions, she *deduces* that it, too, will trigger a rash. Deduction breaks down when the initial generalization is flawed or when a particular case doesn't fit the generalization. Suppose that each time your sister ate strawberries she drizzled them with lemon juice, the real culprit. Or suppose that the various weight-loss studies defined low-fat food so differently that no one could determine how their findings might be related.

Once you have reached your conclusions as a writer—either by using particulars to reach generalizations or by applying reliable generalizations to other particulars—you still need to decide how to present your reasoning to your readers. Do you want your readers to follow your own process, perhaps examining numerous cases before reaching a conclusion about them? Or do you want them to learn what you've concluded first and then review the evidence? Because audiences for academic writing tend to expect conclusions first, many writers begin essays with thesis statements and paragraphs with topic sentences. On the other hand, if your readers are likely to reject an unexpected thesis initially, you may need to show them the evidence first and then lead them gently but purposefully to your point.

In "Disaster Planning for Libraries: Lessons from California State University, Northridge," librarian Mary M. Finley opened her presentation at the Eighth Annual Federal Depository Library Conference with a broad generalization and then supported it with specifics from her campus:

> In Northridge we learned that a university with facilities for over 25,000 students can be changed in less than thirty seconds into a university with no usable buildings, no electrical power, no water, and no telephone service. California State University, Northridge (CSUN) is about a mile from the epicenter of the Northridge Earthquake of January 17, 1994, and the damage total for the campus stands at over 400 million dollars. The earthquake happened at 4:31 a.m. on a holiday during semester break, so only a few people were in university buildings during the quake. Fortunately, no one was seriously injured on campus. All of the buildings on campus were damaged, some beyond repair.

At the end of her presentation, she reversed her approach. She detailed several extensive action plans, listing specific procedures, issues, and questions that fellow librarians might consider to prepare for disasters on their own campuses. Based on these particulars, she personalized her broad concluding generalization:

> Please understand that a disaster can happen to your library and that the time it chooses to happen could be in the next minute. An earthquake, hurricane, tornado, flood, fire, or explosion will not ask for your

permission in advance. But you can choose to be well prepared. Think about what would make your library a safer place to be during a disaster. Think about what you can do to make it easier for your library to recover from a disaster.

Use the following questions to help you present your reasoning clearly and persuasively.

INDUCTION AND DEDUCTION CHECKLIST

☐ Do your generalizations follow logically from your particulars? Can you substantiate what and how much you claim?

☐ Are your particulars typical, numerous, and relevant enough to support your generalizations? Are your particulars substantial enough to warrant the conclusion you have drawn?

☐ Are both your generalizations and your particulars presented clearly? Have you identified your assumptions for your readers?

☐ How do you expect your reasoning patterns to affect your readers? What are your reasons for opening with generalizations or reserving them until the end of a paragraph or passage?

☐ Is your reasoning in an explanatory paper clear and logical? Is your reasoning in an argumentative paper rigorous enough to withstand the scrutiny of readers? Have you avoided generalizing too broadly or illogically connecting generalizations and particulars?

■ **ACTIVITY 7.7:** Reasoning Inductively and Deductively

Look through a recent magazine for an article that explores a health, environmental, or economic issue. Read the article, looking for paragraphs organized inductively and deductively. Why do you think the writer chose one pattern or the other in the various sections of the article? How well do those patterns work from a reader's point of view?

ANALYZING A SUBJECT

Analyzing a subject means dividing it into its parts and then examining one part at a time. If you have taken a chemistry course, you probably analyzed water: you separated it into hydrogen and oxygen, its two elements. You've heard many a television commentator analyze the news, telling us what made up an event—who participated, where it occurred, what happened. Analyzing a news event may produce results less certain and clear-cut than analyzing a chemical compound, but the principle is similar: by taking something apart, by examining its components, you can understand it better.

Analysis helps readers grasp something complex: they can more readily take in the subject in a series of bites than in one gulp. For this reason, college textbooks do a lot of analyzing. An economics text divides a labor union into its component parts; an anatomy text divides the hand into its bones, muscles, and ligaments. In your college papers, you might analyze and explain to readers anything from a contemporary subculture (What social groups make up the homeless population of Los Angeles?) to an ecosystem (What animals, plants, and minerals coexist in a rain forest?). Analysis is so useful that you can apply it in many situations: separating the stages in a process to see how it works, breaking down the components of a subject to classify them, or identifying the possible results of an event to project consequences. (For more on process analysis, see pp. 128–30. For more on division and classification, see pp. 131–33. For more on cause and effect, see pp. 136–38.)

In *Cultural Anthropology: A Perspective on the Human Condition* (St. Paul: West, 1987), Emily A. Schultz and Robert H. Lavenda briefly but effectively demonstrate by analysis how a metaphor like "the Lord is my shepherd" makes a difficult concept ("the Lord") easy to understand.

> The first part of a metaphor, the metaphorical subject, indicates the domain of experience that needs to be clarified (e.g., "the Lord"). The second part of a metaphor, the metaphorical predicate, suggests a domain of experience which is familiar (e.g., sheep-herding) and which may help us understand what "the Lord" is all about.

In much the same way, Lillian Tsu, a government major at Cornell University, uses analysis in her essay "A Woman in the White House" to identify major difficulties faced by female politicians in the United States:

> Although traditionally paternalistic societies like the Philippines and Pakistan and socially conservative states like Great Britain have elected female leaders, particular characteristics of the United States' own electoral system make it difficult for this country to follow suit and elect a female president. Despite social modernization and the progress of the women's movement, the voters of the United States still lag far behind those of other nations in their willingness to trust in the leadership of a female executive. While the women's movement

succeeded in changing Americans' attitudes as to what roles are socially acceptable for women, female candidates still face a more difficult task in U.S. elections than their male counterparts face. Three factors are responsible for this situation—political socialization, lack of experience, and open discrimination.

Tsu treats the three factors in turn, beginning each section with a transition that emphasizes the difficulties female candidates in the United States face: "One obstacle," "A second obstacle," "A third obstacle." The opening list and the transitions give readers clear direction in a complicated essay, guiding them through the explanation of the three factors to the final section on the implications of the analysis.

When you plan an analysis, you might label slices in a pielike circle or arrange subdivisions in a list running from smallest to largest or from least to most important. Make sure that your analysis has a purpose, that it demonstrates something about your subject or tells your readers something they didn't know before. For example, to show the ethnic composition of New York City, you might divide the city geographically into neighborhoods—Harlem, Spanish Harlem, Yorkville, Chinatown, Little Italy. To explain New York's social classes, however, you might start with homeless people and work up to the wealthy elite. The way you slice your subject into pieces will depend in part on the point you want to make about it. And the point you end up making will depend in part on how you've sliced it up. As you develop your ideas, you may also find that you have a stronger point to make—that New York City's social hierarchy is oppressive and unstable, for example.

How can you help your readers follow your analysis? Some writers begin by identifying the subdivisions into which they will slice their subject ("The federal government has three branches"). If you name or label each part you mention, define the terms you use, and clarify with examples, you will also distinguish each part from the others. You can make your essay as readable as possible by using transitions, leading readers from one part to the next. (For more on transitions, see pp. 104–7.)

Use the Analysis Checklist for questions to consider when you want to analyze a subject.

ANALYSIS CHECKLIST

- ☐ Exactly what will you try to achieve in your analysis? What is its purpose?
- ☐ How does your analysis support your main idea or thesis?

□ How will you break your subject into parts?
□ How can you make each part clear to your readers?
□ What definitions, details, and examples would help clarify each part?

ACTIVITY 7.8: Analyzing a Subject

Analyze one of the following subjects by making a list of its basic parts or elements. Be sure to identify the purpose or point of your analysis. Compare your analysis with those of others in your class who chose the same subject.

a college	a choir, orchestra, or other musical group
a news source	a computer or other technological device
a reality TV show	a basketball, baseball, hockey, or other team
effective teaching	a family, tribe, clan, or neighborhood
a healthy lifestyle	leadership, heroism, or service

ANALYZING A PROCESS

Analyzing a process means telling step by step how something is, was, or could be done. You can analyze an action or a phenomenon—how a skyscraper is built, how a revolution begins, how sunspots form, how to make chili. This strategy can also explain large, long-ago happenings that a writer couldn't possibly have witnessed and complex technical processes that a writer couldn't personally duplicate. Here, for instance, is an excerpt from Tom Foster's article, "Can Artificial Meat Save the World?" (*Popular Science*, November 18, 2013), which explains the process of producing an innovative meat-free "meat." This *informative process analysis* sets forth how something happens:

On the other side of Columbia, at a biotech start-up incubator on the edge of the University of Missouri campus, the scientists at Modern Meadow are working on a very different solution to the meat-production crisis. When I visit, a 3-D printer about the size of an HP desktop unit streams a line of yellowish goo onto a petri dish. Back and forth, the machine creates a series of narrow rows a hair's breadth apart. After covering a few inches of the dish, the printer switches direction and lays new rows atop the first ones in a crosshatch pattern. There's no noise but an electric whir, no smell, nothing to suggest that the goo is an embryonic form of meat that will turn into a little sausage. Once the printer finishes its run, the result looks something like a large Band-Aid.

To reach this stage, about 700 million beef cells spent two weeks growing in a cell-growth medium in a wardrobe-size incubator. The cells were then spun free in a centrifuge, and the resulting slurry, which is the consistency of honey, was transferred to a large syringe that acts as the business end of the printer.

The printed cells will now go back into an incubator for a few more days, during which time they will start to develop an extracellular matrix, a naturally occurring scaffold of collagens that gives cells structural support. The result is actual muscle tissue.

The *directive* (how-to) *process analysis* tells readers how to do something (how to box, invest for retirement, clean a painting) or how to make something (how to draw a map, blaze a trail, set up a computer). Especially on websites, directions may consist of simple step-by-step lists designed for browsers who want quick advice. In essays and articles, however, the basics may be supplemented with advice, encouragement, or relevant experience. In the following example from "Hand Feeding Wild Birds" (*Backyard Bird Newsletter*, December 2004), Diane Porter begins with the bird watcher's purpose in following the steps she explains:

> Your backyard birds can be landing on your shoulder and taking food from your hand this winter. With a little encouragement, some birds will accept you as a natural part of their environment—perhaps even as a friend. It's not too difficult to win the trust of the guests at your feeders. Here's how to do it.

Then she continues with the steps in the process:

> Begin by filling your feeders at the same time every day, preferably in the early morning, when birds actively seek food. Include a few chopped walnuts or pecans, which many birds relish, where the birds can get at them immediately. Certain birds will catch on and show up soon after you visit the feeder.
>
> On a cold morning, stand or sit quietly for a few minutes about 10 to 15 feet away from the feeder after you put out the food. It's OK to talk, and in fact the birds will learn to associate your voice with food, but avoid sudden movements.

She explains how, over time, you can move closer to the feeder, hold out your hand to offer food, and expand the feeding area as you gain the birds' acceptance. Her conclusion returns to the personal reward for the person interacting with the birds:

> Start any time of the year. I've hand tamed birds in Southern California who've never seen snow. But I think it goes faster and easier in winter. Whenever it happens, it will be summer in your heart.

Although generally used to supply accurate directions, process analysis can also be turned to humorous ends, as illustrated in this paragraph from "How to Heal a Broken Heart (in One Day)" by student Lindsey Schendel.

> To begin your first day of mourning, you will wake up at 11 a.m., thus banishing any feelings of fatigue. Forget eating a healthy breakfast; toast two waffles, and plaster them with chocolate syrup instead of maple. Then make sure you have a room of serenity so you may cry in peace. It is important that you go through the necessary phases of denial and depression. Call up a friend or family member while you are still in your serious, somber mood. Explain to that person the hardships you are facing and how you don't know if you can go on. Immediately afterwards, turn on any empowering music, get up, and dance.

Like more serious process directions, this paragraph includes steps or stages (sleeping late, eating breakfast, crying and calling, and getting up and dancing). They are arranged in chronological order with transitions marking the movement from one to the other (*To begin, Then, while, Immediately afterwards*).

Process analyses are wonderful ways to show your readers the inside workings of events or systems, but they can be difficult to follow. Divide the process into logical steps or stages, and put the steps in a sensible chronological order. Add details or examples wherever your description seems ambiguous or abstract, and use transitions to mark the end of one step and the beginning of the next. (For more on transitions, see pp. 104–7.)

The Process Checklist includes questions to consider when you use process analysis.

PROCESS CHECKLIST

☐ Do you thoroughly understand the process you are analyzing?

☐ Do you have a good reason to analyze a process at this point in your writing? How does your analysis support your main idea or thesis?

☐ Have you divided the process into logical and useful steps? Have you adjusted your explanation of the steps for your audience?

☐ Is the order in which you present these steps the best possible?

☐ Do you use transitions to guide readers from one step to the next?

■ **ACTIVITY 7.9**: Analyzing a Process

Analyze one of the following processes or procedures in a paragraph . or short essay. Then share your process analysis with classmates. Can they follow your analysis easily? Do they spot anything you left out?

registering for college classes
studying for a test
having the flu (or another illness)

hunting for a job
buying a used car
moving

DIVIDING AND CLASSIFYING

To *divide* is to break something down, identifying or analyzing its components. (For more on analyzing a subject, see pp. 125–28.) It's far easier to take in a subject, especially a complex one, a piece at a time. The subject divided may be as concrete as a medical center (which a writer might divide into specialty units) or as abstract as a person's knowledge of art (which the writer might divide into knowledge of sculpture, painting, drawing, and other forms). To *classify* is to make sense of a complicated and potentially bewildering array of things—works of literature, this year's movies—by sorting them into categories (*types* or *classes*) that you can deal with one at a time. Literature is customarily arranged by genre—novels, stories, poems, plays; movies might be sorted by audience (movies for children, teenagers, or mature audiences).

Dividing and classifying are like two sides of the same coin. Both are common in textbooks and nonfiction articles and books that want to make it easy for readers to grasp complex categories or topic components—for instance, levels of wildlife management, types of newborn infants, or useful methods of development for writers. In theory, any broad subject can be *divided* into components, which can then be *classified* into categories. In practice, it's often difficult to tell where division stops and classification begins.

In the following paragraph from *David and Goliath: Underdogs, Misfits, and the Art of Battling Giants* (Boston: Little, Brown, 2013), Malcolm Gladwell uses division to simplify for modern readers what might be an unfamiliar subject—the types of warriors deployed in ancient battles:

Ancient armies had three kinds of warriors. The first was cavalry— armed men on horseback or in chariots. The second was infantry—foot soldiers wearing armor and carrying swords and shields. The third were projectile warriors, or what today would be called artillery: archers and, most important, slingers. Slingers had a leather pouch attached on two sides by a long strand of rope. They would put a rock or lead ball into the pouch, swing it around in increasingly wider and faster circles, and then release one end of the rope, hurling the rock forward.

Gladwell's intent, however, is less to enlighten readers about historical warfare than, as the book's subtitle suggests, to help them think differently about contemporary contests by considering the advantages of disadvantages. After he classifies Goliath as "heavy infantry" and David as "a slinger, and slingers beat infantry, hands down," readers are equipped to interpret their ancient biblical contest differently.

Classification also helps to identify patterns and relationships that might otherwise be missed. In "How Wonder Works" (*Aeon Magazine*, June 21, 2013), Jessie Prinz explores the nature of wonder, "humanity's most important emotion," fed and unified by science, religion, and art. To do so, he classifies various human reactions to novelty, spectacle, and all sorts of natural and creative works—in short, responses that identify and express wonder.

> These bodily symptoms point to three dimensions that might in fact be essential components of wonder. The first is *sensory*: wondrous things engage our senses—we stare and widen our eyes. The second is *cognitive*: such things are perplexing because we cannot rely on past experience to comprehend them. This leads to a suspension of breath, akin to the freezing response that kicks in when we are startled: we gasp and say "Wow!" Finally, wonder has a dimension that can be described as *spiritual*: we look upwards in veneration; hence Smith's invocation of the swelling heart.

When you divide and classify, your point is to use systematic grouping to make order out of a complex or overwhelming jumble.

- Identify sensible components and categories, given your purpose, and follow the same principle of classification or analysis for all categories. For example, to discuss campus relations, it makes sense to divide the school population into *instructors, students,* and *support staff;* it would make less sense to divide it into *people from the South, people from the other states,* and *people from overseas.*
- Try to group apples with apples so that all the components or categories are roughly equivalent. For example, if you're classifying television shows and you've come up with *sitcoms, dramas, talk shows, children's shows, news,* and *cartoons,* then you've got a problem: the last category is probably part of *children's shows.*

- Check that your final system is simple and easy for your readers to understand. Most people can handle only about seven things at once. If you've got more than six or seven components or categories, perhaps you may need to combine or eliminate some.

Use the Division and Classification Checklist when you plan to divide and classify.

DIVISION AND CLASSIFICATION CHECKLIST

☐ How does your division or classification support your main idea or thesis?

☐ Do you use the most logical principle to divide or classify for your purpose?

☐ Do you stick to one principle throughout?

☐ Have you identified components or categories that are comparable?

☐ Have you arranged your components or categories in the best order?

☐ Have you given specific examples for each component or category?

☐ Have you made a complex subject more accessible to your readers?

■ **ACTIVITY 7.10:** Dividing and Classifying

Choose two of the following subjects. Brainstorm for five minutes on each, trying to come up with as many components as you can. With classmates, create one large list by combining items for each subject. Working together, try to classify the items on the largest list into logical categories. Add or change components or categories as needed.

students	customers	sports	families
teachers	websites	vacations	drivers

COMPARING AND CONTRASTING

Often you can develop ideas by setting a pair of subjects side by side, comparing and contrasting them. When you *compare,* you point out similarities; when you *contrast,* you discuss differences. In daily life, we compare and contrast to decide which menu item to choose, which car (or other product) to buy, which college course to sign up for. A comparison and contrast can lead to a final evaluation and a decision about which thing is better, but it doesn't have to.

Working together, these twin strategies use one subject to clarify another. The dual method works well for a pair similar in nature—two cities, two films, two economic theories. Because this method shows that you have observed and understood both subjects, college instructors will often ask you to compare and contrast on exams ("Discuss the chief similarities and differences between nineteenth-century French and English colonial policies in West Africa").

You can use two basic methods of organization for comparison and contrast: the opposing pattern and the alternating pattern. Using the *opposing pattern,* you discuss all the characteristics or subdivisions of the first subject in the first half of the paragraph or essay and then discuss all the characteristics of the other subject. Using the *alternating pattern,* you move back and forth between the two subjects. This pattern places the specifics close together for immediate comparison and contrast. Whichever pattern you choose, be sure to cover the same subpoints for each subject and to follow the same order in each part.

OPPOSING PATTERN, SUBJECT BY SUBJECT	ALTERNATING PATTERN, POINT BY POINT
Subject A	Point 1
Point 1	Subject A
Point 2	Subject B
Point 3	Point 2
Subject B	Subject A
Point 1	Subject B
Point 2	Point 3
Point 3	Subject A
	Subject B

In the following selection, Monica Luhar uses a brief opposing pattern to contrast her experience with that of her mother and her friends in "Being the Daughter of an Arranged Marriage" (*Alternet,* May 13, 2013).

> At the age of 19, my mother fastened a red bindi in the middle of her forehead, wrapped herself in a silk sari, and walked seven times around a sacred fire in Karamsad, India, with a 26-year-old man she hardly knew.
>
> At 19, I was a single Indian American college sophomore who certainly did not have any plans to have an arranged marriage like my parents. And a relationship was not really an option, because my par-

ents did not allow me to date. For years, they had one strict rule: I was to focus on school until I graduated from college. Meanwhile, most of my friends were in committed relationships and some were even engaged to their high school sweethearts. I resented the rule, and felt that they were limiting me from dating because they did not have any experience themselves.

The next selection comes from "The Epidemic of Childhood Obesity: Learn the Facts" on the *Let's Move* website. To answer "How did we get here?" this passage begins with the alternating pattern, first contrasting lifestyles (in alternating paragraphs) of children three decades ago with those of children today. Next it shifts to snacks, portion sizes, and total caloric intake, each topic alternating within its own paragraph.

Thirty years ago, most people led lives that kept them at a healthy weight. Kids walked to and from school every day, ran around at recess, participated in gym class, and played for hours after school before dinner. Meals were home-cooked with reasonable portion sizes and there was always a vegetable on the plate. Eating fast food was rare and snacking between meals was an occasional treat.

Today, children experience a very different lifestyle. Walks to and from school have been replaced by car and bus rides. Gym class and after-school sports have been cut; afternoons are now spent with TV, video games, and the Internet. Parents are busier than ever and families eat fewer home-cooked meals. Snacking between meals is now commonplace.

Thirty years ago, kids ate just one snack a day, whereas now they are trending toward three snacks, resulting in an additional 200 calories a day. And one in five school-age children has up to six snacks a day.

Portion sizes have also exploded—they are now two to five times bigger than they were in years past. Beverage portions have grown as well—in the mid-1970s, the average sugar-sweetened beverage was 13.6 ounces; compared to today, kids think nothing of drinking 20 ounces of sugar-sweetened beverages at a time.

In total, we are now eating 31 percent more calories than we were forty years ago—including 56 percent more fats and oils and 14 percent more sugars and sweeteners. The average American now eats fifteen more pounds of sugar a year than in 1970.

The selection concludes with a final contrast to guide readers to solutions.

Now that's the bad news. The good news is that by making just a few lifestyle changes, we can help our children lead healthier lives—and we already have the tools we need to do it. We just need the will.

Consider the Comparison and Contrast Checklist when you use this strategy for development.

COMPARISON AND CONTRAST CHECKLIST

☐ Is your reason for comparing and contrasting unmistakably clear? Does it support or develop your main idea or thesis?

☐ Have you chosen to write about *major* similarities and differences?

☐ Have you compared or contrasted like things? Have you discussed the same categories or features for each item?

☐ Have you selected points of comparison and supporting details that will intrigue, enlighten, and persuade your audience?

☐ Have you used the best possible arrangement, given your subject and the point you're trying to make?

☐ If you are making a judgment, have you treated both subjects fairly?

☐ Have you avoided moving mechanically from "On the one hand" to "On the other hand"?

ACTIVITY 7.11: Comparing and Contrasting

Write a paragraph or two in which you compare and contrast the subjects in one of the following pairs:

baseball and football (or two other sports)
living in an apartment (or dorm) and living in a house
two communities or neighborhoods you are familiar with
two musicians or performers
communication by two methods
watching a sports event on television and in person

IDENTIFYING CAUSES AND EFFECTS

From the time we are children, we ask why. Why can't I go out and play? Why is the sky blue? Why did my goldfish die? Searching for causes and effects continues into adulthood, so it's natural that explaining causal relationships is a common method of development. To use this method successfully, you must think about the subject critically, gather evidence, draw judicious conclusions, and clarify relationships.

In the following passage from "On the Origin of Celebrity" (*Nautilus*, September 5, 2013), Professor Robert Sapolsky brings his background in biology and neurology to his topic:

> We all feel the magnetic pull of celebrities—we track them, know their net worth, their tastes in furniture, the absurd names of their pets and children. We go under the knives of cosmetic surgeons to look like them. We feel personal connections with them, are let down by their moral failings, care about their tragedies. As I write, my family of musical fanatics is mourning the death of Cory Monteith. We not only feel for the pointless loss of a talented young actor, and for his girlfriend, Lea Michele, but in some confused, inchoate way, also feel heartbroken for Finn and Rachel, the characters they play on *Glee*.
>
> Why the obsession? Because we're primates with vested interests in tracking social hierarchies and patterns of social affiliation. And celebrities provide our primate minds with stimulating gyrations of hierarchy and affiliation (who is sleeping with, feuding with, out-earning whom). Celebrities also reflect the peculiar distance we have traveled culturally since our hominid past, and reveal how distorted our minds can become in our virtual world. We obsess over celebrities because, for better or worse, we feel a deep personal sense of connection with people who aren't real.

Instead of focusing on causes *or* effects, often writers trace a *chain* of cause-and-effect relationships. That's what Charles C. Mann and Mark L. Plummer do in "The Butterfly Problem" (*Atlantic Monthly*, January 1992):

> More generally, the web of species around us helps generate soil, regulate freshwater supplies, dispose of waste, and maintain the quality of the atmosphere. Pillaging nature to the point where it cannot perform these functions is dangerously foolish. Simple self-protection is thus a second motive for preserving biodiversity. When DDT was sprayed in Borneo, the biologists Paul and Anne Ehrlich relate in their book *Extinction* (1981), it killed all the houseflies. The gecko lizards that preyed on the flies ate their pesticide-filled corpses and died. House cats consumed the dying lizards; they died too. Rats descended on the villages, bringing bubonic plague. Incredibly, the housefly in this case was part of an intricate system that controlled human disease. To make up for its absence, the government was forced to parachute cats into the area.

Use the following checklist when you investigate causes and effects.

CAUSE-AND-EFFECT CHECKLIST

☐ Is your use of cause and effect clearly tied to your main idea or thesis?

☐ Have you identified actual causes? Have you supplied evidence that will persuade readers to support them?

☐ Have you identified actual effects, or are they conjecture? If conjecture, are they logical possibilities? Can you find persuasive evidence to support them?

☐ Have you judiciously drawn conclusions concerning causes and effects? Have you avoided logical fallacies? (See pp. 208–9.)

☐ Have you presented your points clearly and logically so that your readers can easily follow them?

☐ Have you considered other causes or effects, immediate or long-term, that readers might find relevant?

ACTIVITY 7.12: Identifying Causes and Effects

1. Identify some of the *causes* of five of the following. Then discuss the possible causes with your classmates.

failing an exam	stage fright	losing a job
an automobile accident	losing or winning a game	losing weight
poor or good health	stress	arriving late going to college
	getting a job	getting a scholarship

2. Identify some of the *effects* of five of the following. Then discuss the possible effects with your classmates.

an insult	speeding	traveling to another country
a compliment	winning the lottery	
learning to read	divorce	drinking while driving
dieting	changing jobs	

3. Identify some of the *causes and effects* of one of the following. You may need to do a little research to identify the chain of causes and effects for the event. Discuss your findings with your classmates.

the online shopping boom	recycling
the attacks on September 11, 2001	a gay marriage court case
the discovery of atomic energy	the uses of solar energy
a major U.S. Supreme Court decision	global climate change racial tension

ADDING VISUAL EVIDENCE

At times you may feel that a project, report, or essay would benefit from visual as well as textual development. Visual evidence—graphs, maps, diagrams, photographs, or other materials—can clarify an explanation or argument. In fact, well-selected visual evidence can do even more—engage the attention of your audience, show directly something that might otherwise require a long explanation, or emphasize relationships or complexities so that readers truly "see" what you are saying.

Sometimes visual materials represent or reflect the same method of development that you are using in your text. For example, a visual might illustrate a procedure, an activity, a set of directions, or the stages in a process, as the "How to Study Model" in Figure 7.1 does. Visuals can also present complex information in an especially clear, attractive, or persuasive manner. A straightforward chart, graph, or table can help readers quickly grasp information. For example, the line graph and table in Figure 7.2 illustrate two ways of showing how driver distraction contributes

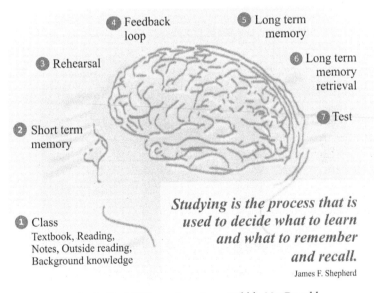

Fig. 1. "How to Study Model," figure from Lucy Tribble MacDonald, *Howtostudy.org.* (Teach Learn Online, 2013); Web; 30 Nov. 2013.

Figure 7.1   Using and Citing a Visual (MLA style)

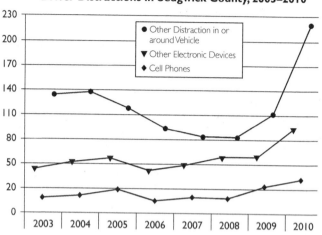

Number of Automobile Accidents Attributed to Driver Distractions in Sedgwick County, 2003–2010

- ● Other Distraction in or around Vehicle
- ▼ Other Electronic Devices
- ◆ Cell Phones

Number of Automobile Accidents Attributed to Driver Distractions in the State of Kansas and Sedgwick County

Year	Cell Phones		Other Electronic Devices		Other Distraction in or around Vehicle	
	KS	▼ SG	KS	◆ SG	KS	● SG
2003	198	45	81	12	956	133
2004	260	53	111	16	991	138
2005	292	58	104	19	909	119
2006	350	44	104	8	843	96
2007	350	49	111	14	802	84
2008	394	61	102	13	832	84
2009	499	61	201	23	1,020	113
2010	536	95	180	35	1,303	223

Source: Kansas, Sedgwick County, Sedgwick County Health Dept.; *Sedgwick County Health Department Data Book*; Mar. 2012; Web; 16 June 2014; sec. 4.5: Automobile Accidents Attributed to Driver Distractions.

Figure 7.2   Using and Citing a Graph and a Table (MLA style)

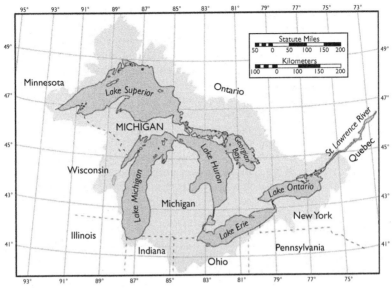

States/provinces of the Great Lakes basin.

Fig. 3. United States, Dept. of Homeland Security, Federal Emergency Management Agency; *Great Lakes Coastal Flood Study*. "States/Provinces of the Great Lakes Basin." Map. *greatlakescoast.org*, 5 Apr. 2012. Web. 16 June 2014.

Figure 7.3   Using and Citing a Map (MLA style)

to accidents. Similarly, the map in Figure 7.3 shows the geographical range of the Great Lakes basin, a large international coastal region whose risk during a 100-year flood or a storm surge is the subject of a collaborative FEMA study.

Carefully selected visuals reinforce or supplement your text; they function as evidence, not decoration. For example, color effectively highlights key information, perhaps distinguishing slices in a pie chart. However, too much color can overload readers as can hard-to-see colors on a white page or a tinted screen.

If you have never before created charts, graphs, or tables, try your software's tools for making them. Typically, tables clearly label both the columns (running up and down) and the rows (running across). Within this grid, they can display numerical findings, group items in categories, or align information for comparison or contrast. Besides creating your own visuals, you also can use an image editor to add digital photos or a scanner to integrate printed material from sources. If you are unfamiliar with these options, ask for advice at the computer lab.

Providing a context for a visual also helps your readers make sense of it. In an introductory sentence, identify the number or letter of the visual (for example, "Figure 6"), its content, and the point that it helps you make. Place the visual close to the related discussion, and size it so that it supports, not overshadows, the text.

Whenever you adapt or borrow visuals from another source, printed or electronic, credit that source in your paper. If you download an image from the web, check the site for its guidelines for using images; follow them, requesting permission when required and giving credit to the copyright owner. If you are uncertain about whether you can use an image from a source, check with your instructor.

Use the Visual Evidence Checklist to help you add visual evidence to your text.

VISUAL EVIDENCE CHECKLIST

☐ Have you mentioned all the visuals in your text so that readers can easily connect them to your discussion? Have you labeled all the visuals so that they are easy to identify?

☐ Have you selected diagrams, photographs, or other illustrations that clarify your content for readers?

☐ Do your graphs, charts, and tables help readers absorb complicated information?

☐ Have you provided whatever explanation or interpretation readers might need to understand your visuals?

☐ Have you integrated each visual effectively using appropriate placement, sizing, and alignment?

☐ Have you secured any permission needed to use copyrighted material? Have you credited the source of each visual?

■ ACTIVITY 7.13: Using Visual Evidence

Working individually or with a group, gather a variety of materials that use visuals—for example, a textbook, a pamphlet or brochure, a flyer, a catalog, and a magazine article. Evaluate the types of visuals used and their effectiveness in helping readers understand the information presented.

8

Strategies for Revising

Good writing is rewriting. In this chapter we provide strategies for revising—ways to rethink muddy ideas and emphasize important ones, ways to rephrase obscure passages and restructure garbled sentences. Whether you are rewriting a whole essay or specific sentences and paragraphs, revision is your opportunity to make adjustments based on changes in your thinking and responses from others, as illustrated below.

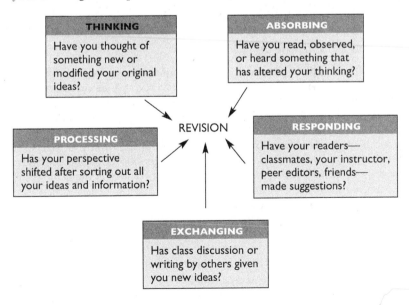

THINKING
Have you thought of something new or modified your original ideas?

ABSORBING
Have you read, observed, or heard something that has altered your thinking?

REVISION

PROCESSING
Has your perspective shifted after sorting out all your ideas and information?

RESPONDING
Have your readers—classmates, your instructor, peer editors, friends—made suggestions?

EXCHANGING
Has class discussion or writing by others given you new ideas?

RE-VIEWING AND MACROREVISING

Revision means "seeing again"—discovering again, conceiving again, shaping again. It can occur at any and all stages of the process, and most writers do a lot of it. *Macrorevising* is making large, global, or fundamental changes that affect the overall direction or impact of writing—its purpose, organization, or audience. Its companion is *microrevising*, paying attention to the language aspects of writing—sentences, words, grammar—including ways to create emphasis, eliminate wordiness, and increase clarity (see pp. 154–58).

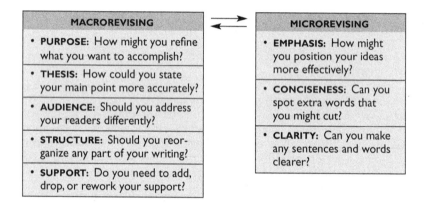

MACROREVISING	MICROREVISING
• **PURPOSE:** How might you refine what you want to accomplish?	• **EMPHASIS:** How might you position your ideas more effectively?
• **THESIS:** How could you state your main point more accurately?	• **CONCISENESS:** Can you spot extra words that you might cut?
• **AUDIENCE:** Should you address your readers differently?	• **CLARITY:** Can you make any sentences and words clearer?
• **STRUCTURE:** Should you reorganize any part of your writing?	
• **SUPPORT:** Do you need to add, drop, or rework your support?	

Revising for Purpose and Thesis

When you revise for purpose, you make sure that your writing accomplishes what you want it to do. If your goal is to create an interesting profile of a person, have you done so? If you want to persuade your readers to take a certain course of action, have you succeeded? Of course, if your complex project has evolved or your assignment is now clearer to you, the purpose of your final essay may be different from your purpose when you began. To revise for purpose, try to step back and see your writing as other readers will. Concentrate on what's actually in your paper, not what you assume is there.

At this point you'll probably want to create a thesis sentence (if you haven't) or revise your working thesis statement (if you've developed one) (see pp. 69–72). First, reconsider how it is worded:

- Is it stated exactly in concise yet detailed language?
- Is it focused on only one main idea?

- Is it stated positively rather than negatively?
- Is it limited to a demonstrable statement?

Then consider how accurately your thesis now represents your main idea and your draft as a whole:

- Does each part of your essay relate directly to your thesis?
- Does each part of your essay develop and support your thesis?
- Does your essay deliver everything your thesis promises?

If you find unrelated or contradictory passages, you have several options: revise the thesis, revise the essay, or revise both.

You may find that your ideas have deepened, your topic has become more complex, or your essay has developed along new lines during the process of writing. If so, you may want to refine or expand your thesis.

WORKING THESIS	The *Herald*'s coverage of the Senate elections was more thorough than the *Courier*'s.
REVISED THESIS	The *Herald*'s coverage of the Senate elections was less timely but more thorough and fairer than the *Courier*'s.
WORKING THESIS	As the roles of men and women have changed in our society, old-fashioned formal courtesy has declined.
REVISED THESIS	As the roles of men and women have changed in our society, old-fashioned formal courtesy has declined not only toward women but also toward men.

See the following checklist for helpful questions about revising for purpose and thesis.

REVISION CHECKLIST FOR PURPOSE AND THESIS

- ☐ Do you know exactly what you want your essay to accomplish? Can you put it in one sentence: "In this paper I want to . . ."?
- ☐ Is your thesis stated outright in the essay? If not, have you provided clues so that your readers will know precisely what it is?

- ☐ Does every part of the essay work to achieve the same goal?
- ☐ Have you tried to do too much? Does your coverage seem thin? If so, how might you reduce the scope of your thesis and essay?
- ☐ Does your essay say all that needs to be said? Is everything— ideas, connections, supporting evidence—on paper, not just in your head?
- ☐ While writing, have you changed your mind, rethought assumptions, made a discovery? Does anything now need to be recast?
- ☐ Do you have enough evidence? Is every point developed fully enough to be clear and convincing?

Revising for Audience

What works with one audience can fall flat with another. Your organization, selection of details, word choice, and tone all affect your particular readers. Visualize one of them poring over the essay, sentence by sentence, reacting to what you have written. What expressions do you see on that reader's face? Where does he or she have trouble understanding? Where have you hit the mark?

Use the checklist below to revise for your readers.

REVISION CHECKLIST FOR AUDIENCE

- ☐ Who will read this essay? What will they expect of it?
- ☐ Does the essay tell your readers what they want to know rather than what they probably know already? Does it tell them something worth knowing?
- ☐ Are there any places where readers might fall asleep? If so, can you shorten, delete, or enliven those passages?
- ☐ Does the opening of the essay mislead your readers by promising something that the essay never delivers?
- ☐ Do you unfold each idea in enough detail to make it both clear and interesting? Would readers appreciate more detailed evidence?

□ Have you anticipated questions readers might ask?

□ Where might readers raise objections? How might you anticipate and answer them?

□ Have you used any specialized or technical language that your
readers might not understand? If so, have you worked in brief
definitions?

□ What is your attitude toward your readers? Are you chummy,
angry, superior, apologetic, condescending, preachy? Should
you revise to improve your attitude? Ask your peers for an
opinion.

Revising for Structure and Support

When you revise for structure and support, you make sure that the order
of your ideas and your selection and arrangement of supporting material
are as effective as possible. You may have all the ingredients of a successful essay, but they may be a jumbled, confusing mess.

In a well-structured essay, each paragraph, sentence, and phrase
serves a clear function. Are your opening and closing paragraphs relevant, concise, and interesting? Is everything in each paragraph on the
same topic? Are all of your ideas adequately developed? Are the paragraphs arranged in the best possible order? Finally, do you lead readers
from one idea to the next with clear and painless transitions?

A revision outline can help you diagnose a draft that you suspect
doesn't quite make sense. Instead of outlining to plan, try outlining to
show what you've gotten on paper. Start by finding the topic sentence of
each paragraph in your draft (or creating one, if necessary) and listing
them in order. Label the sentences *I, II, A, B,* and so on to indicate the
logical relationships of ideas in your essay. Do the same with the supporting details under each topic sentence, labeling them also with letters
and numbers and indenting appropriately. (For more on outline format,
see pp. 84–86.)

Now look at the outline. Does it make sense on its own, without the
essay to explain it? Would a different order or arrangement be more
effective? Do any sections look thin, in need of more evidence? Are the
connections between parts on paper, not just in your head? Maybe too
many ideas are jammed into too few paragraphs. Maybe you need
more—or stronger—details and examples. Work on the outline until
you get it into good shape, and then rewrite the essay to follow it.

You'll find helpful questions on this topic in the Revision Checklist
for Structure and Support.

REVISION CHECKLIST FOR STRUCTURE AND SUPPORT

☐ Does your introduction set up the whole essay? Does it both grab readers' attention and hint at what is to follow?

☐ Does the essay deliver all that you promise in your opening?

☐ Would any later passage make a better beginning?

☐ Is your thesis clear early in the essay? If explicit, is it positioned prominently?

☐ Do the paragraph breaks seem logical?

☐ Is the main idea of each paragraph clear? Is it stated in a topic sentence?

☐ Is the main idea of each paragraph fully developed? Where might you need more or better evidence to be convincing?

☐ Is each detail or piece of evidence relevant to the topic sentence of the paragraph and to the main point of the essay? Should you move or omit any stray bits?

☐ Would any paragraphs make more sense in a different order?

☐ Does everything follow clearly? Does one point smoothly lead to the next? Would transitions help make the connections clearer?

☐ Does the conclusion follow logically or seem tacked on?

■ **ACTIVITY 8.1:** Tackling Macrorevision

Select a draft that would benefit from revision. Then, based on your sense of its greatest need, choose one of the revision checklists to guide a first revision. Let the draft sit for a while. Then work with one of the remaining checklists.

WORKING WITH A PEER EDITOR

There's no substitute for having someone else read your draft. Whether you write for an audience of classmates, the town council, or readers of *Newsweek*, having a classmate read over your essay is a worthwhile revision strategy.

To gain all you can as a writer from a peer review, you need to play an active part in the discussion of your work.

- Ask your reader questions. (Or bring a "Dear Editor" letter or memo, written ahead, to your meeting.)
- Be open to new ideas for focus, organization, or details.
- Use what's helpful, but trust yourself as the writer.

To be a helpful, supportive peer editor, try to respond and advise, not correct. Offer honest, intelligent feedback, not judgment.

- Look at the big picture: purpose, focus, clarity, coherence, organization, support.
- When you spot strengths or weaknesses, be specific. Note examples.
- Answer the writer's questions, and also use the questions supplied throughout this book. Concentrate on essentials, not details.

As a writer, you can ask your peer editor to begin with your specific questions or to select applicable questions from the following list.

QUESTIONS FOR A PEER EDITOR

General Questions

What is your first reaction to this paper?

What is this writer trying to tell you?

What are this paper's greatest strengths?

Does the paper have any major weaknesses?

What one change would most improve the draft?

Questions on Meaning

Do you understand everything? Is any information missing?

Does this paper tell you anything you didn't know before?

Is the writer trying to cover too much territory? Too little?

Does any point need to be explained or illustrated more fully?

When the paper ends, has it delivered what it promised?

Could this paper use a down-to-the-ground revision?

Questions on Organization

Has the writer grabbed your interest and quickly drawn you in?
Would you suggest beginning at some later point?

Does the paper have one main idea, or juggle more than one?

Would the main idea stand out better if anything were removed
or added?

Might the ideas in the paper be more effectively arranged? Do
any ideas belong together that now seem too far apart?

Can you follow the ideas easily? Are transitions needed? If so,
where?

Does the writer keep to one point of view, one angle of seeing?

Does the ending seem as if the writer meant to conclude or ran
out of gas? How might the writer strengthen the conclusion?

Questions on Writing Strategies

Do you feel that this paper addresses you personally?

Do you dislike or object to any of the writer's statements or
wording? Is the problem word choice, tone, or inadequate support? Should the writer keep or change this part?

Does the draft contain anything distracting or unneeded?

Do you get bored at any point? What would keep you reading?

Is the language too lofty and abstract? If so, where does the
writer need to get specific?

Do you understand all the words used? Do any specialized words
need clearer definition?

Campus e-mail or your LMS (Learning Management System) can
help writers and readers efficiently exchange drafts. Always keep your
numbered or dated original file, and copy it for exchanges. Change the
file name or add a plus sign (+) and your peer's initials to help you keep
track of different versions.

You and your classmates might agree to use an editing tool, such as
Track Changes. It distinguishes comments by readers so several peers
can respond individually in their own copies of a file (without the influence of others) or in turn to a shared file (with the option of discussing
suggestions or adding immediate second opinions). This tool also highlights advice with color, underlining, and strikeouts. (If you or your class-

mates prefer, you can also simply use all capitals for comments within each other's drafts.)

Although electronic exchanges are convenient for sending drafts back and forth, a face-to-face meeting can be inspiring. When the peer editing is finished, try to meet with your peer editor or editing group to talk through your drafts. During the meeting, writers can ask about readers' suggestions, respond to questions, get advice about possible changes, and add their own notes to the draft.

▌ ACTIVITY 8.2: Exchanging Drafts

Working with a partner or a small editing group, have everyone exchange drafts. Let each writer select one of the sets of peer editing questions (see pp. 149–50) for his or her reader, based on the type of revision that the draft probably needs most. Read each other's drafts, add suggestions, and meet to discuss everyone's revision suggestions.

A Sample Student Peer Exchange

Erin Schmitt's first major college assignment was to write an essay reflecting on the significance of a personal experience. She decided to focus on her last day at her job assisting Mr. Hertli, a highly intelligent elderly man growing increasingly blind. She opened her essay by leading her readers toward his house and into his office, loaded with books and research materials. There, he wanted to locate the country of Georgia, currently in the news. Following is the concluding section of Erin's paper with peer and instructor responses:

I placed the wide atlas across his wobbly knees, in his lap, facing him. 6
Taking his hand, I slowly directed Mr. Hertli's finger around the perimeter of each country, saying. "This is Turkey. To the east, here is Georgia." He pointed and repeated the countries back to me, and I asserted that, yes, that was Azerbaijan or Russia.

Peer: Spelled right?

It was as though I were teaching a small child, who could not read, 7
and who did not know the least about geography. And how strange it was to be feeling such a way. After all, I was helping a well-educated, cultured man, in this most elementary, basic way. In this aged man, nearing the end of his life, I saw the character of a young boy, beginning to learn a concept new to him.

Peer: When I read your draft online, my software said this was a fragment. Is it? Are fragments OK in here?

<table>
<tr><td>Peer: I get
what you're
saying,
but maybe
explain it
more? This
flat state-
ment seems
too abrupt.</td><td>This would be the last time I helped Mr. Hertli, as I would be
beginning college just a few days later. Mr. Hertli was now completely blind.
Like a mother afraid to send her child to school for the first time, I was
afraid to cease my assistance of this somewhat helpless man. For when I
had seen this connection—the young, new child in the old, I came to
realize just how valuable life itself is.</td><td>8</td></tr>
</table>

Erin also received some overall comments with suggestions for revision.

> Peer: *I really think you did a good job creating the experience. You're*
> *a very descriptive writer, and I liked being able to imagine the*
> *experience—the road, the animals, the flowers by the house.*
> *I also liked how you used contrasting paragraphs—long para-*
> *graph 5 to explain the situation and then short paragraph 6*
> *for the outcome. (But I still think 5 might be too wordy.)*
> *You got the reflection part started at the beginning, too, so*
> *I knew you were thinking about it. I just wasn't that sure*
> *about how you ended with it. My own son traces things with*
> *his hands, so I could see what you meant about Mr. Hertli,*
> *but I expected you to explain it more. Maybe you could add*
> *here to make the conclusion stronger when you revise.*

Erin met with her peers and her instructor, collecting all the comments about her draft. To help her focus on the purpose of the essay, she reread the assignment. She decided that reflecting more would strengthen her main idea, or thesis—and her instructor had already pointed out the importance of a strong thesis in college writing. Erin concentrated first on revising her conclusion because all her readers had suggested strengthening it. Her revision based on the peer review follows:

<table>
<tr><td>¶ 5 set up
situation—
this ¶ tells
what hap-
pened</td><td>I placed the wide atlas across his wobbly knees, in his lap, facing him.
fragile
Taking his hand, I slowly directed Mr. Hertli's finger around the perimeter
        ^
of each country, saying. "This is Turkey. To the east, here is Georgia." He</td><td>6</td></tr>
<tr><td>Luckily my
reader asked
about the
spelling.</td><td>pointed and repeated the countries <s>back</s> to me, and I asserted that, yes,
        indeed   , Armenia,
that was Azerbaijan or Russia.</td><td></td></tr>
<tr><td>Combine
with ¶ 6—
event with
meaning?</td><td>   ^   ^ felt
<s>It</s> This moment <s>was</s> as though I were teaching a small child/ who could
               ^
not read/ and who did not know the least about geography. And how strange
it was to be feeling such a way. After all, I was helping a well-educated,</td><td>7</td></tr>
</table>

cultured man/ in a this most elementary, basic way/ In this aged man,
nearing the end of his life, I saw the character of a ~~young~~ ^{small} boy, beginning
to learn a concept new to him.

My big goal here is to add more reflection.

This would be the last time I helped Mr. Hertli, as I would ~~be begin-~~
~~ning~~ ^{begin} college just a few days later. Mr. Hertli was now completely blind. Like^{, one hundred percent}
a mother afraid to send her child to ~~school for the first time~~ ^{kindergarten}, I was afraid to ^{now}
cease my ~~assistance of this somewhat~~ helpless man. For when I had seen ^{care for this seemingly}
this connection, the young~~, new~~ child ~~in the~~ old, I came to realize just how ^{new, still learning within an man}
valuable life itself is. *Mr. Hertli showed me how our younger selves provide deep* ^{and how unified}

roots for us as we get older and how our older selves still preserve our youth.

Young and old, we are all somehow connected, one and the same, no one being of

greater worth than the other. No matter our age, we will always have this link,

through generations, and I have grown to appreciate this of life.

8

ACTIVITY 8.3: Exchanging Drafts Again

Meet again with a peer editor or editing group to exchange drafts. Let each writer select a focus for his or her reader, such as one of the following:

- Another set of peer editing questions (see pp. 149–50), based on the type of revision that the draft probably needs most
- The writer's short summary of the draft's audience and purpose, compared with the draft itself
- An issue—such as the draft's organization or evidence—already revised
- The writer's biggest concern about the paper
- The draft's success meeting a key requirement of the assignment
- A specific passage or paragraph—introduction, conclusion, first or last supporting paragraph, some other section—that might be more compelling
- A specific passage that seems weak to the writer
- A peer editing or checklist topic that continues to challenge the writer

Read each other's drafts, add suggestions, and meet to discuss everyone's revision suggestions. If the group favors second opinions, have two classmates respond to each writer's focus.

MICROREVISING FOR EMPHASIS, CONCISENESS, AND CLARITY

After you've revised for the large issues in your draft—purpose, thesis, audience, structure, and support—you're ready to turn your attention to microrevising. Now is the time to emphasize what matters most and communicate it concisely and clearly.

Stressing What Counts

An ineffective writer treats all ideas as equals. An effective writer decides what matters most and shines a bright light on it using the most emphatic positions in an essay, a paragraph, or a sentence—the beginning and the end.

Stating It First.   In an essay, you might start with what matters most. For an economics paper on import quotas, student Donna Waite first summed up her conclusion.

> Although an import quota has many effects, both for the nation imposing the quota and for the nation whose industries must suffer from it, I believe that the most important effect is generally felt at home. A native industry gains a chance to thrive in a marketplace of lessened competition.

A paper that takes a stand or makes a proposal might open with the writer's position:

> Our state's antiquated system of justices of the peace is inefficient.

> The United States should orbit a human observer around Mars.

In a single sentence, you can also stress a point at the start. Consider the following unemphatic (and confusing) sentence:

> When Congress debates the Hall-Hayes Act removing existing protections for endangered species, as now seems likely to occur on May 12, it will be a considerable misfortune if this bill should pass because the extinction of many rare birds and animals would certainly result.

The debate and its likely timing consume the start of the sentence. Here's a better use of this emphatic position:

> The extinction of many rare birds and animals would certainly follow passage of the Hall-Hayes Act.

Now the writer is stressing what he most fears—the consequences of the act. In a later sentence, he can add the date and his opinion about the likelihood of passage.

Stating It Last.   Placing an idea last also can give it weight. Emphatic order, proceeding from least important to most, is dramatic: it builds up and up. In a paper on import quotas, a dramatic buildup might look contrived. However, in an essay on how city parks can lure visitors to a city, the thesis sentence—summing up the point of the essay—might stand at the very end:

> For the urban core, improved parks could bring about a new era of prosperity.

Giving evidence first and leading up to the thesis at the end is particularly effective in editorials and informal persuasive essays.

A sentence that uses climactic order, suspending its point until the end, is called a *periodic sentence*. Notice how novelist Julian Green builds to his point of emphasis:

> Amid chaos of illusions into which we are cast headlong, there is one thing that stands out as true, and that is—love.

Cutting and Whittling

Like pea pickers who throw out dirt and pebbles, good writers remove unnecessary words that clog their prose. One of the chief joys of revising is to watch 200 paunchy words shrink to a svelte 150. Most writers know that the more succinctly they can state an idea, the clearer and more forceful it will be.

Cutting the Fanfare.   Why bother to announce that you're going to say something? Cut the fanfare. We aren't, by the way, attacking the usefulness of transitions that lead readers along. (For more on transitions, see pp. 104–6.)

WORDY	As far as getting ready for winter is concerned, I put antifreeze in my car.
REVISED	To get ready for winter, I put antifreeze in my car.
WORDY	The point should be made that . . . Let me make it perfectly clear that . . . In this paper I intend to . . . In conclusion I would like to say that . . .

Beginning Directly.   Words also tend to abound after *There is* or *There are.*

WORDY   There are many people who dislike flying.

REVISED   Many people dislike flying.

Using Strong Verbs.   Forms of the verb *be* (*am, is, are, was, were*) followed by a noun or an adjective can make a statement wordy. These weak verbs can almost always be replaced by active verbs.

WORDY   The Akron game was a disappointment to the fans.

REVISED   The Akron game disappointed the fans.

Using Relative Pronouns with Caution.   When a clause begins with a relative pronoun (*who, which, that*), you often can whittle it to a phrase.

WORDY   Venus, which is the second planet of the solar system, is
           called the evening star.

REVISED   Venus, the second planet of the solar system, is called the
           evening star.

Cutting Out Deadwood.   The more you revise, the more shortcuts you'll discover. Try reading the sentences below without the words in italics.

Howell spoke for the sophomores, and Janet *also spoke* for the seniors.

He is *something of* a clown but *sort of the* lovable *type.*

As a major in *the field of* economics, I plan to concentrate on *the area of* international banking.

The decision as to whether *or not* to go is up to you.

Cutting Descriptors.   Adjectives and adverbs are often dispensable. Contrast these two versions.

WORDY   Johnson's extremely significant research led to highly
           important major discoveries.

REVISED   Johnson's research led to major discoveries.

Selecting Short Words.   Although a long word may convey a shade of meaning that a shorter synonym doesn't, in general shun a long word when you can pick a short one. Instead of *the remainder,* write *the rest;* instead of *activate, start* or *begin;* instead of *adequate* or *sufficient, enough.* Look for the right word, one that wraps an idea in a smaller package.

WORDY   Andy has a left fist that has a lot of power in it.

REVISED   Andy has a potent left.

By the way, it pays to read. From reading, you absorb words like *potent* and set them to work for you.

Keeping It Clear

Finally, recall what you want to achieve—clear communication with your readers using specific, unambiguous words arranged in logical order. Aim for direct, forceful expression.

WORDY   He is more or less a pretty outstanding person in regard to good looks.

REVISED   He is strikingly handsome.

Try to read your draft as a first-time reader would. Be sure to return, after a break, to passages that you have struggled to write; heal any battle scars by focusing on clarity.

UNCLEAR   Thus, after a lot of thought, it should be approved by the board even though the federal funding for all the cow tagging may not be approved yet because it has wide support from local cattle ranchers.

CLEAR   In anticipation of federal funding, the Livestock Board should approve the cow-tagging proposal widely supported by local cattle ranchers.

The Microrevision Checklist includes questions to use in emphasizing, slimming, and clarifying your writing.

MICROREVISION CHECKLIST

☐ Have you positioned what counts at the beginning or the end?

☐ Do you announce an idea before you explain it? If so, consider chopping out the announcement.

☐ Are you direct, straightforward, and clear?

☐ Can you recast any sentence that begins *There is* or *There are*?

☐ Can you substitute an active verb wherever you use a form of the verb *be* (*is*, *was*, *were*)?

☐ Can you reduce to a phrase any clause beginning with *which*, *who*, or *that*?

- ☐ Can you cut out the deadwood and unnecessary adjectives and adverbs?
- ☐ Do you see any long words where short words would do?
- ☐ Have you kept your writing clear, direct, and forceful?

■ ACTIVITY 8.4: Tackling Microrevision

Think back over the revisions you've already made and the advice you've received from peers or other readers. Is your paper more likely to seem bland (because it lacks emphasis), wordy (because it needs a good trimming), or foggy (because it needs to be more clear, direct, and logical)? Focus on one issue for the moment, and concentrate on adding emphasis, cutting extra words, or expressing ideas clearly.

A SAMPLE STUDENT REVISION

For his composition class, Daniel Matthews was assigned a paper using a few sources. He was to write about an "urban legend," a widely accepted and emotionally appealing—but untrue—tale about events. The following selection from his paper, "The Truth about 'Taps,'" introduces his topic, briefly explaining the legend and the true story about it. You can see the thoughtful cuts and condensations that Matthews made with the help of his English instructor and his peer editor. His first draft illustrates macrorevisions (highlighted in the margin) and microrevisions (marked in the text). The clear and concise final version follows.

ROUGH DRAFT

Anyone who has ever
~~As you know, whenever you have~~ attended the funeral services for a
   ^

has
fallen veteran of the United States of America, ~~you have~~ stood fast as
   ^

a lone bugler filled the air with the mournful ~~and sullenly appropriate~~

nation
last tribute to a defender of the ~~United States of America~~. ~~As most of~~
   ^

T
~~us know,~~ ℓhe name of the bugle call is "Taps," and the ~~story~~ behind
  ^ *has*   *ed*   ^   *legend*

has
its origin ~~is one that is~~ gain~~ing a~~ popularity ~~of its own~~ as it ~~is more~~
   ^   ^   ^

~~and more frequently being~~ circulated in this time of war and terror.

Avoid "you" in case readers have not shared this experience.

Rework paragraph to summarize legend when first mentioned.

Although ~~it is clear that~~ this tale ~~of the origin~~ of a beautiful ode

to a fallen warrior is heartfelt ~~and full of purposeful intent~~, it is

As such, i
an "urban legend." ~~I~~t fails to provide due justice to the memories

of the men responsible for the true origin of "Taps."

true
    General Daniel Butterfield is the originator of the bugle call

"Taps⊙~~,~~" ~~formerly known as "Lights Out."~~ Butterfield served ~~as a~~

~~general~~ in the Union army during the Civil War and was awarded

the Medal of Honor for actions during that time. One of his most

endearing claims to fame is the bugle call "Taps," which he com-

posed at Harrison's Landing in 1862 (Warner 167). ~~The bugle call~~

                                       ,
"Taps" originates from another call named "Lights Out"~~; this call~~

~~was~~ used by the Army to signal the end of the day/ Butterfield,

wanting a new and original call unique to his command, summoned

                                  R
bugler Oliver Willcox Norton to his tent one night. ~~and~~ /ather than

compose an altogether new tune, he instead modified the notes to

Shortly thereafter
the call "Lights Out" (US Military District of Washington). ~~Then~~ this

call could be heard ~~being used~~ up and down the Union lines as the

other commanders ~~who had~~ heard the call ~~liked it~~ and adapted it for

their own use. ~~This call, the modified version of "Lights Out"~~ is also

and itself   "Tattoo," a
~~in a way~~ a derivative of ~~the~~ British bugle call ~~"Tattoo" which is very~~

similar in both sound and purpose ~~to "Lights Out,"~~ (Villanueva).

~~notes this as well in his paper "24 Notes That Tap Deep Emotion."~~

INSERT:
According to
this story,
Union Captain
Robert Ellicombe
discovered that
a Confederate
casualty was, in
fact, his son, a
music student
in the South.
The father
found "Taps" in
his son's pocket,
and the tune
was first played
at a military
burial as his son
was laid to rest
(Coulter).

Group all the
discussion of
the versions
in one place.

Divide long
sentence to
keep it clear.

Strengthen
paragraph
conclusion
by sticking
to its focus.

REVISED DRAFT

Anyone who has ever attended the funeral services for a fallen veteran of the United States of America has stood fast as a lone bugler filled the air with a mournful last tribute to a defender of the nation. The name of the bugle call is "Taps," and the legend behind its origin has gained popularity as it has circulated in this time of war and terror. According to this story, Union Captain Robert Ellicombe discovered that a Confederate casualty was, in fact, his son, a music student in the South. The father found "Taps" in his son's pocket, and the tune was first played at a military burial as his son was laid to rest (Coulter). Although this tale of a beautiful ode to a fallen warrior is heartfelt, it is an "urban legend." As such, it fails to provide due justice to the memories of the men responsible for the true origin of "Taps."

General Daniel Butterfield is the true originator of the bugle call "Taps." Butterfield served in the Union army during the Civil War and was awarded the Medal of Honor for actions during that time. One of his most endearing claims to fame is the bugle call "Taps," which he composed at Harrison's Landing in 1862 (Warner 167). "Taps" originates from another call named "Lights Out," used by the army to signal the end of the day and itself a derivative of "Tattoo," a British bugle call similar in both sound and purpose (Villanueva). Butterfield, wanting a new and original call unique to his command, summoned bugler Oliver Willcox Norton to his tent one night. Rather than compose an altogether new tune, he instead modified the notes to the call "Lights Out" (US Military District of Washington). Shortly thereafter this

call could be heard up and down the Union lines as other commanders heard

the call and adapted it for their own use.

After Daniel Matthews trimmed, clarified, and rearranged, his revision was both clearer and more forceful than his original draft. Next he edited and proofread his paper (see Ch. 9), making his final refinements. He also added citations to identify his sources (see Ch. 12) as he prepared the final version to submit.

9

Strategies for Editing and Proofreading

Editing and proofreading are needed at the end of the writing process because writers—all writers—find it difficult to write error-free and effective sentences the first time they try. Sometimes as a writer you pay more attention to what you want to say than to how you say it. Sometimes you forget spelling or grammar or punctuation conventions. At other times you are distracted by events around you, or you simply make keyboarding errors. Once you are satisfied that you have expressed your ideas, you should make sure that each sentence and word is concise, clear, and correct.

Editing means correcting wording, grammar, punctuation, and mechanics, as well as refining your voice and polishing your style. Proofreading means taking a final look at your paper to check correctness and to catch spelling and word-processing errors. Both activities allow you to refine your paper based on your own efforts and the advice of others, as illustrated in the graphic on the next page.

Don't edit and proofread too soon. In your early drafting, don't fret over the spelling of an unfamiliar word; it may be revised in a later version. If the word stays in, you'll have time to check it later. After you have revised, however, you are ready to refine and correct. In college, good editing and proofreading can make the difference between a C and an A. On the job, those skills may help you get a promotion. Readers, teachers, and bosses like careful writers who take time to edit and proofread.

EDITING

Editing provides a final opportunity to make your draft shine by polishing words and sentences so that you express yourself stylishly as well as correctly.

Making Corrections

As you edit, you need to set priorities—should you start as an error-hunter, stalking wild commas, or a wordsmith, polishing phrases? Many writers can tinker indefinitely with words and sentences, striving for the most satisfying expression. However, college writers face heavy workloads, frequent deadlines, and sharp-eyed readers who are likely to spot errors that can discredit a writer. Alternate between editing to correct and editing to refine as your deadlines allow, but edit first for errors if time is running short.

How do you find errors—especially those you don't know you're making? Pay attention to instructors' comments, especially those repeated. Note problems that your peer editors mention. Keep your own list of likely mistakes so that you can hunt for them in every paper until you master them.

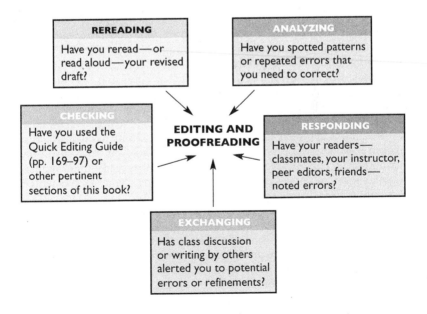

REREADING
Have you reread—or read aloud—your revised draft?

ANALYZING
Have you spotted patterns or repeated errors that you need to correct?

CHECKING
Have you used the Quick Editing Guide (pp. 169–97) or other pertinent sections of this book?

EDITING AND PROOFREADING

RESPONDING
Have your readers—classmates, your instructor, peer editors, friends—noted errors?

EXCHANGING
Has class discussion or writing by others alerted you to potential errors or refinements?

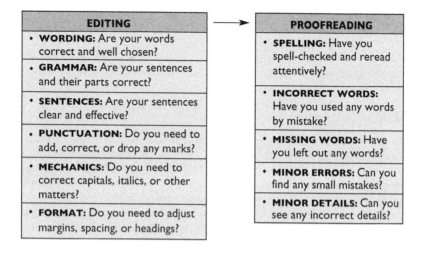

EDITING		PROOFREADING
• **WORDING:** Are your words correct and well chosen?	→	• **SPELLING:** Have you spell-checked and reread attentively?
• **GRAMMAR:** Are your sentences and their parts correct?		• **INCORRECT WORDS:** Have you used any words by mistake?
• **SENTENCES:** Are your sentences clear and effective?		• **MISSING WORDS:** Have you left out any words?
• **PUNCTUATION:** Do you need to add, correct, or drop any marks?		• **MINOR ERRORS:** Can you find any small mistakes?
• **MECHANICS:** Do you need to correct capitals, italics, or other matters?		• **MINOR DETAILS:** Can you see any incorrect details?
• **FORMAT:** Do you need to adjust margins, spacing, or headings?		

Whenever you question whether a word or construction is correct, consult a good handbook. Learn the grammar conventions you don't understand so you can spot and eliminate problems in your own writing. Practice until you easily recognize major errors such as fragments and comma splices. Ask for help from a peer editor or a tutor in the writing center if your campus has one.

If you use a grammar-checker to help you edit, you'll discover that it is a handy tool but not foolproof. A grammar-checker can alert you to many types of sentence problems. For example, it probably will spot problems with adjectives and adverbs, such as confusing *good* and *well*. However, it also may question long sentences and unusual constructions that are perfectly correct. Because it will not always correctly identify subjects or verbs, it may question whether a correct sentence is complete or the subject and verb agree. It is likely to miss faulty parallelism, misplaced modifiers, possessives without apostrophes, and commas in the wrong places. For these reasons, you always need to consider the grammar-checker's suggestions carefully before accepting them. As the writer, you, not your software, should have the final word.

Use the "Quick Editing Guide" on pages 169 to 197 of this chapter to get started making corrections. It briefly reviews problems with grammar, punctuation, and mechanics typically found in college writing. For each problem, it supplies definitions, examples, and a checklist to help you tackle the problem. Refer to the Quick Editing Guide Directory on page 169 for a checklist for the problems covered, along with the relevant section letters and numbers.

Refining Your College Voice

When you write a college paper, you face the challenge of finding your own voice—the choice and arrangement of language that expresses your vision. You probably want to present yourself as a thoughtful writer, someone with credible insights that a reader will want to share. You probably want to sound serious but not pompous, thoughtful but not too dry or distant. You may also adjust your voice to the field and type of writing project, perhaps speaking more formally in a lab report, more passionately in a position paper. When you revise, you may strengthen your voice, but you also must focus on broad issues such as structure and support. Now, as you edit, you can continue to refine your approach, your attitude, your wording, your tone.

Finding your own voice may be especially difficult in a source-based paper. After all, first you read carefully, and then you capture information by quoting, paraphrasing, summarizing, and synthesizing. You need to introduce what you learn, feed it into your draft, and credit it. After you've done all this, you may worry that your sources have taken over your paper. You may feel there's no room left for your own voice and, even if there were, it's too quiet to jostle past the powerful words of your sources. Now is the time to bolster your confidence by thinking about how you want to present yourself—and then to edit accordingly. Use these questions to help you strengthen your voice.

COLLEGE VOICE CHECKLIST

☐ Can you write a list or passage explaining what you'd like readers to hear from your voice? Where could you add more of this in your draft?

☐ Have you carefully created your voice as a college writer, balancing passion and personality with rock-solid reasoning?

☐ Have you concentrated on using your own voice to state your thesis, to open and conclude paragraphs, and to identify, introduce, and explain any source material you include?

☐ Have you chosen words and structured sentences to reassure readers that you are reliable, credible, thoughtful—demonstrating qualities they expect from a college writer?

☐ Do casual expressions—from conversation, text messaging, or social networking—ever creep into your writing? If so, can you drop them or translate them into concise conventional wording?

Polishing Your College Style

Like fashion designers and artists, writers may vary their style depending on the effect they want to create. They can choose words and design sentences for different purposes and audiences. In a novel or a script, slang and short phrases can create realistic dialogue that brings characters to life. In a college essay, however, readers expect a more formal style. As you read, write, and read some more for your classes, you will get a sense of the style preferred in different kinds of academic writing. By the time you select your major, you will be ready to write in the same style as others in the field.

COLLEGE STYLE CHECKLIST

☐ Have you chosen words that you understand? Are they direct and precise? Will they read smoothly and be clear to your readers as well?

☐ Have you mastered and integrated any specialized vocabulary about the topic?

☐ Do your sentences have clear subjects and active verbs to show their actions? Do you limit passive verbs to conventional or necessary uses?

☐ Have you varied your sentence structures? Do you favor shorter and simpler patterns for plain, direct statements? Do you add qualifications and more complicated structures for greater formality or complexity?

☐ Do you stick to a serious, earnest tone unless you are positive that readers will appreciate small injections of humor, passion, or personal anecdotes?

☐ Do you focus ideas and information for academic readers by emphasizing what matters most and by minimizing unnecessary words?

☐ Do you tell readers where you are going and then lead them along the way with plenty of previews, transitions, and summaries?

☐ Do you treat readers respectfully by acknowledging their views?

☐ Do you meet readers' expectations for critical thinking, especially the analysis, evaluation, and synthesis of specific supporting evidence?

☐ Do you treat all sources respectfully, using the expected citation style to acknowledge their contributions to your paper?

☐ Do the formatting, structural, and stylistic features of your paper match those assigned, expected by your readers, or typical of writing in the field?

PROOFREADING

Careful proofreading is especially important because many errors in writing occur unconsciously and easily become habits. If you have never looked closely at the spelling of *environment,* you may never have noticed the second *n.* A moment's break in concentration can also lead to errors. Because the mind works faster than the pencil (or the word processor), when you are distracted by someone talking or a phone beeping, you may leave out a word or add the wrong punctuation.

The very way our eyes work also leads to errors. When you read normally, you usually see only the shells of words—the first and last letters. You fix your eyes on the print only about three or four times per line. To proofread effectively, you must look at the letters in each word and the punctuation marks between words without sliding over them. Proofreading requires time and patience, but it is a skill you can develop. Here are some proofreading tips:

- All writers make mistakes when they put ideas on paper. You simply need to take the time to find and correct them.
- Let a paper sit several days, overnight, or at least a few hours before proofreading it.
- Budget enough time to proofread thoroughly.
- Read what you have written very slowly, looking at every word and letter. See what you have actually written, not what you think is there.
- Read your paper aloud. Speaking forces you to slow down and see more, and sometimes you will hear a mistake you haven't seen.
- Read the essay backward. This will force you to look at each word because you won't get caught up in the flow of ideas.
- Use a dictionary or a spell-checker (see pp. 190–91). Watch for common errors: misspellings, incorrect words, and missing words.
- Double-check for your habitual errors (such as leaving off *-s* or *-ed* or putting in unnecessary commas).

- Read your essay several times, focusing each time on a specific area of difficulty (once for spelling, once for punctuation, once for a problem that recurs in your writing).
- Ask someone else to read your paper and tell you if it is free of errors. But take pride in your own work. Don't let someone else do it for you.

◼ ACTIVITY 9.1: Editing and Proofreading

Read the following passage carefully. Assume that its organization is fine, but look for more than ten errors in the paragraph. Find these mistakes in sentence structure, grammar, spelling, punctuation, and capitalization, and correct them. After you have corrected the passage, discuss with your classmates the changes you have made and your reasons for making them.

Robert Frost, one of the most popular American poets. He was born in San Francisco in 1874, and died in Boston in 1963. His family moved to new England when his father died in 1885. There he completed highschool and attended colledge but never graduate. Poverty and problems filled his life. He worked in a woolen mill, on a newspaper, and at varous odd jobs. Because of ill health, he settled on a farm and began to teach school to support his wife and children. Throughout his life he dedicated himself to writing poetry, by 1915 he was in demand for public readings and speaking engagements. He was awarded the Pulitzer Prize for poetry four times-in 1924, 1931, 1937, and 1943. The popularity of his poetry rests in his use of common themes and images, expressed in everyday language. Everyone can relate to his universal poems, such as "Birches" and "Stopping by Woods on a Snowy Evening." Students read his poetry from seventh grade through graduate school, so almost everyone recognize lines from his best-loved poems. America is proud of it's son, the homespun poet Robert Frost.

◼ ACTIVITY 9.2: Proofreading in Pairs

Select a passage from this textbook or elsewhere that is about a hundred words long. Type up the passage, intentionally adding ten errors in grammar, spelling, punctuation, or capitalization. Swap passages with a classmate; proofread, and then check each other's work against the original. Share your proofreading strategies.

Quick Editing Guide

QUICK EDITING GUIDE DIRECTORY: CHECKLIST FOR COMMON AND SERIOUS PROBLEMS

Grammar Problems	Section
☐ Are any of your sentences actually fragments?	A1
☐ Are any of your sentences actually comma splices or fused sentences?	A2
☐ Have you used the correct form for all verbs in the past tense?	A3
☐ Do all verbs agree with their subjects?	A4
☐ Have you used the correct case for all pronouns?	A5
☐ Do all pronouns agree with their antecedents?	A6
☐ Have you used adjectives and adverbs correctly?	A7

Sentence Problems	
☐ Does each modifier clearly modify the appropriate sentence element?	B1
☐ Have you used parallel structure where needed?	B2

Punctuation Problems	
☐ Have you used commas correctly?	C1
☐ Have you used apostrophes correctly?	C2
☐ Have you punctuated quotations correctly?	C3

Mechanics and Format Problems	
☐ Have you used capital letters correctly?	D1
☐ Have you spelled all words correctly?	D2
☐ Have you used correct manuscript form?	D3

This Quick Editing Guide provides an overview of grammar, style, punctuation, and mechanics problems typical of college writing. Certain common errors in Standard Written English are like red flags to careful readers: they signal that the writer is either ignorant or careless. Use the Editing Checklist to check your paper for these problems; then use the editing checklists in each section to help you focus on and correct specific errors. Concentrate on your most frequent problems, the ones most likely to reappear in your writing.

A   EDITING FOR COMMON GRAMMAR PROBLEMS

A1   Check for sentence fragments.

A complete sentence has a subject,° has a predicate,° and can stand on its own. A *sentence fragment* lacks a subject, a predicate, or both, or for some other reason fails to convey a complete thought. It cannot stand on its own as a sentence. Although common in advertising and fiction, fragments are usually ineffective in college writing because they do not communicate coherent thoughts.

To edit for fragments, examine each sentence carefully to make sure that it has a subject and a verb and that it expresses a complete thought. To correct a fragment, make it into a complete sentence by adding a missing part, dropping an unnecessary subordinating conjunction,° or joining it to a complete sentence nearby, if that would make more sense.

FRAGMENT	Roberto has two sisters. Maya and Leeza.
CORRECT	Roberto has two sisters, Maya and Leeza.
FRAGMENT	The children going to the zoo.
CORRECT	The children were going to the zoo.
CORRECT	The children going to the zoo were caught in a traffic jam.
FRAGMENT	Last night when we saw Viola Davis's most recent movie.
CORRECT	Last night we saw Viola Davis's most recent movie.

---

subject: The part of a sentence that names something—a person, an object, an idea, a situation—about which the predicate makes an assertion: The *king* lives.   predicate: The part of a sentence that makes an assertion about the subject involving an action (Birds *fly*), a relationship (Birds *have feathers*), or a state of being (Birds *are warm-blooded*)   subordinating conjunction: A word (such as *because, although, if, when*) used to make one clause dependent on, or subordinate to, another: *Unless* you have a key, we are locked out.

EDITING CHECKLIST FOR FRAGMENTS

☐ Does your sentence have a subject?

☐ Does your sentence have a complete verb?

☐ If your sentence contains a subordinate clause, does it contain a clause that is a complete sentence too?

☐ If your sentence contains a subject and a complement that renames or describes the subject, does a verb connect them?

☐ If you find a fragment, can you link it to an adjoining sentence, eliminate its subordinating conjunction, or add a missing element?

A2   Check for comma splices or fused sentences.

A complete sentence has a subject and a predicate and can stand on its own. When two sentences are joined together to form one sentence, each sentence within the larger one is called a main clause.° However, writers need to follow the rules for joining main clauses to avoid creating serious sentence errors — comma splices or fused sentences. A *comma splice* is two main clauses joined with only a comma. A *fused sentence* (or *run-on*) is two main clauses joined with no punctuation at all.

COMMA SPLICE	I went to the store, I bought a new jacket.
FUSED SENTENCE	I went to the store I bought a new jacket.

To find comma splices and fused sentences, examine each sentence to be sure it is complete. If it has two main clauses, make sure they are joined correctly. If you find a comma splice or fused sentence, correct it in one of these four ways, depending on which makes the best sense:

ADD A PERIOD	I went to the store. I bought a new jacket.
ADD A COMMA AND A COORDINATING CONJUNCTION°	I went to the store, and I bought a new jacket.
ADD A SEMICOLON	I went to the store; I bought a new jacket.

main clause: A group of words that has both a subject and a verb and can stand alone as a complete sentence: *My sister has a car.*   coordinating conjunction: A one-syllable linking word (*and, but, for, or, nor, so, yet*) that joins elements with equal or near-equal importance: Jack *and* Jill, sink *or* swim.

ADD A SUBORDINATING   I went to the store before I bought a new
CONJUNCTION°   jacket.

**EDITING CHECKLIST FOR COMMA SPLICES
AND FUSED SENTENCES**

☐ Can you make each main clause a separate sentence?
☐ Can you link the two main clauses with a comma and a coordinating conjunction?
☐ Can you link the two main clauses with a semicolon or, if appropriate, a colon?
☐ Can you subordinate one clause to the other?

A3 Check for correct past-tense verb forms.

The *form* of a verb,° the way it is spelled and pronounced, can change to show its *tense*—the time when its action did, does, or will occur (in the past, present, or future). A verb about something in the present often is spelled and pronounced differently than a verb about something in the past.

PRESENT   Right now, I *watch* only a few minutes of television each day.

PAST   Last month, I *watched* television every evening.

Many writers fail to use the correct form of a verb in the past tense because they leave off the past tense ending on a regular verb or forget the past tense form of an irregular verb.

Regular verbs are verbs that form the past tense following the standard rule, by adding *-ed* or *-d* to the end of the present tense form: *watch/ watched, look/looked, hope/hoped.* Check all regular verbs in the past tense to be sure you have used one of these endings.

FAULTY   I *ask* my brother for a loan yesterday.

CORRECT   I *asked* my brother for a loan yesterday.

FAULTY   Nicole *race* in the track meet last week.

CORRECT   Nicole *raced* in the track meet last week.

subordinating conjunction: A word (such as *because, although, if, when*) used to make one clause dependent on, or subordinate to, another: *Unless* you have a key, we are locked out.   verb: A word that shows action (The cow *jumped* over the moon) or a state of being (The cow *is* brown).

TIP: If you say the final *-d* sound when you talk, you may find it easier to remember to add the final *-d* or *-ed* when you write past tense regular verbs.

Irregular verbs do not follow the standard rules to form the past tense, as Table 9.1 shows. Instead, their unpredictable past tense forms are different from their base forms and thus have to be memorized: *eat/ate, see/saw, get/got.* In addition, the past tense form may differ from the past participle:° "She *ate* the whole pie; she *has eaten* two pies this week." The most troublesome irregular verbs are actually very common, so if you make the effort to learn the correct forms, you will quickly improve your writing.

FAULTY	My cat *laid* on the tile floor to take her nap.
CORRECT	My cat *lay* on the tile floor to take her nap.

FAULTY	I *have swam* twenty laps every day this month.
CORRECT	I *have swum* twenty laps every day this month.

TIP: In college papers, follow convention by using the present tense, not the past, to describe the work of an author or the events in a literary work.

FAULTY	In "The Lottery," Shirley Jackson *revealed* the power of tradition. As the story *opened*, the villagers *gathered* in the square.
CORRECT	In "The Lottery," Shirley Jackson *reveals* the power of tradition. As the story *opens*, the villagers *gather* in the square.

EDITING CHECKLIST FOR PAST TENSE VERB FORMS

☐ Have you identified the main verb in the sentence?
☐ Is the sentence about the past, the present, or the future? Does the verb reflect this sense of time?
☐ Is the verb regular or irregular?
☐ Have you used the correct form to express your meaning?

---

participle: A form of a verb that cannot function alone as a main verb, including present participles, which end in *-ing (dancing)*, and past participles, which often end in *-ed* or *-d (danced)*.

TABLE 9.1   Principal Parts of Common Irregular Verbs

Base Form	Past Tense	Past Participle
be	was	been
become	became	become
begin	began	begun
blow	blew	blown
break	broke	broken
bring	brought	brought
burst	burst	burst
catch	caught	caught
choose	chose	chosen
come	came	come
do	did	done
draw	drew	drawn
drink	drank	drunk
drive	drove	driven
eat	ate	eaten
fall	fell	fallen
fight	fought	fought
freeze	froze	frozen
get	got	got, gotten
give	gave	given
go	went	gone
grow	grew	grown
have	had	had
hear	heard	heard
hide	hid	hidden
know	knew	known
lay	laid	laid
lead	led	led
let	let	let
lie	lay	lain
make	made	made
raise	raised	raised
ride	rode	ridden
ring	rang	rung
rise	rose	risen
run	ran	run

say	said	said
see	saw	seen
set	set	set
sing	sang	sung
sit	sat	sat
slay	slew	slain
slide	slid	slid
speak	spoke	spoken
spin	spun	spun
stand	stood	stood
steal	stole	stolen
swim	swam	swum
swing	swung	swung
teach	taught	taught
tear	tore	torn
think	thought	thought
throw	threw	thrown
wake	woke, waked	woken, waked
write	wrote	written

For the forms of irregular verbs not in this table, consult your dictionary. (Some dictionaries list principal parts for all verbs, some just for irregular verbs.)

A4   Check for subject-verb agreement.

The *form* of a verb,° the way it is spelled and pronounced, can change to show *number*—whether the subject° is singular (one) or plural (more than one). It can also show *person*—whether the subject is *you* or *she*, for example.

SINGULAR	Our instructor *grades* every paper carefully.
PLURAL	Most instructors *grade* tests using a standard scale.
SECOND PERSON	You *write* well-documented research papers.
THIRD PERSON	She *writes* good research papers, too.

verb: A word that shows action (The cow *jumped* over the moon) or a state of being (The cow *is* brown).   subject: The part of a sentence that names something—a person, an object, an idea, a situation—about which the predicate makes an assertion: The *king* lives.

TABLE 9.2   Forms of be and have

Verb	Present Tense	Past Tense
be	I am you are he/she/it is we are you are they are	I was you were he/she/it was we were you were they were
have	I have you have he/she/it has we have you have they have	I had you had he/she/it had we had you had they had

A verb must match, or *agree with,* its subject in terms of number and person. Regular verbs (those that follow a standard rule to make the different forms) are problems only in the present tense. There they have two forms: one that ends in *-s* or *-es* and one that does not. Only the subjects *he, she, it,* and singular nouns use the verb form that ends in *-s* or *-es.*

I like	we like	Dan likes
you like	you like	the child likes
he/she/it likes	they like	the children like

The verbs *be* and *have* do not follow the *-s*/no *-s* pattern to form the present tense; they are irregular verbs, so their forms must be memorized. The verb *be* is also irregular in the past tense (Table 9.2).

Problems in agreement often occur when the subject is difficult to find, is an indefinite pronoun,° or is confusing for some other reason. In particular, make sure that you have not left off any *-s* or *-es* endings and that you have used the correct form for irregular verbs (see Table 9.1).

FAULTY   Jim *write* his research papers in the library.

CORRECT   Jim *writes* his research papers in the library.

indefinite pronoun: A pronoun that stands for an unspecified person or thing, including singular forms (*each, everyone, no one*) and plural forms (*both, few*): *Everyone* is soaking wet.

FAULTY   The students *has* difficulty with the assignment.

CORRECT   The students *have* difficulty with the assignment.

FAULTY   Every one of the cakes *were* sold at the fund raiser.

CORRECT   Every one of the cakes *was* sold at the fund raiser.

EDITING CHECKLIST FOR SUBJECT-VERB AGREEMENT

☐ Have you correctly identified the subject and the verb in the sentence?

☐ Is the subject singular or plural? Does the verb match?

☐ Have you used the correct form of the verb?

A5   Check for correct pronoun case.

Depending on the role a pronoun° plays in a sentence, it is said to be in the *subjective case, objective case*, or *possessive case*. Use the subjective case if the pronoun is the subject° of a sentence, the subject of a subordinate clause, or a subject complement° (after a linking verb). Use the objective case if the pronoun is a direct or indirect object° of a verb or the object of a preposition. Use the possessive case to show possession.

SUBJECTIVE   *I* will argue that our campus needs more parking.

OBJECTIVE   This issue is important to *me*.

POSSESSIVE   *My* argument will be quite persuasive.

Only some of the many types of pronouns change form to show case. The personal pronouns *I, you, he, she, it, we,* and *they* and the relative pronoun *who* each have at least two forms (Table 9.3).

---

pronoun: A word that stands in place of a noun (*he, him,* or *his* for *Nate*)   **subject:** The part of a sentence that names something—a person, an object, an idea, a situation—about which the predicate makes an assertion: The *king* lives.   **subject complement:** A noun, an adjective, or a group of words that follows a linking verb (*is, become, feel, seem,* or another verb that shows a state of being) and that renames or describes the subject: This plum tastes *ripe*.   **object:** The target or recipient of the action of a verb: Some geese bite *people*.

TABLE 9.3   Pronoun Cases

Subjective	Objective	Possessive
I	me	my, mine
you	you	your, yours
he	him	his
she	her	hers
it	it	its
we	us	our, ours
they	them	their, theirs
who	whom	whose

Two errors in pronoun case are common. First, writers often use the subjective case when they should use the objective case—sometimes because they are trying to sound formal and correct. Instead, choose the correct form for a personal pronoun based on its function in the sentence. If the sentence pairs a noun and a pronoun, try the sentence with the pronoun alone.

FAULTY	My company gave my husband and *I* a trip to Hawaii.
TRIAL	My company gave I a trip?
CORRECT	My company gave my husband and *me* a trip to Hawaii.

FAULTY	My uncle and *me* had different expectations.
TRIAL	Me had different expectations?
CORRECT	My uncle and *I* had different expectations.

If the sentence leaves out implied words, try filling them in.

FAULTY	Jack ran faster than *me*.
TRIAL	Jack ran faster than me ran.
CORRECT	Jack ran faster than *I*.

The second common error with pronoun case involves gerunds.° Whenever you need a pronoun to modify a gerund, use the possessive case.

FAULTY	Our supervisor disapproves of *us* talking in the hallway.
CORRECT	Our supervisor disapproves of *our* talking in the hallway.

gerund: A form of a verb, ending in *-ing,* that functions as a noun: Lacey likes *playing* in the steel band.

EDITING CHECKLIST FOR PRONOUN CASE

☐ Have you identified all the pronouns in the sentence?

☐ Does each one function as a subject, an object, or a possessive?

☐ Given the function of each pronoun, have you used the correct form?

A6   Check for pronoun-antecedent agreement.

The *form* of a pronoun,° the way it is spelled and pronounced, changes depending on its use in a particular sentence. The form can change to show *number*—whether the subject is singular (one) or plural (more than one). It can change to show *gender*—masculine, feminine, or neuter. It can also change to show *person*—first (*I, we*), second (*you*), or third (*he, she, it, they*).

SINGULAR	My brother took *his* coat and left.
PLURAL	My brothers took *their* coats and left.
MASCULINE	I talked to Steven before *he* had a chance to leave.
FEMININE	I talked to Stephanie before *she* had a chance to leave.
FIRST PERSON	*I* ordered a sandwich.
THIRD PERSON	*She* ordered a sandwich.

In most cases, a pronoun refers to a specific noun or pronoun mentioned nearby; that word is called the pronoun's *antecedent.* The connection between the pronoun and the antecedent must be clear so that readers know what the pronoun means in the sentence. One way to make this connection clear is to be sure that the pronoun and the antecedent match (or *agree*) in number and gender.

A common error in pronoun agreement is using a plural pronoun to refer to a singular antecedent. This error often crops up when the antecedent is difficult to find, when the antecedent is an indefinite pronoun, or when the antecedent is confusing for some other reason. First, find the correct antecedent, and decide whether it is singular or plural. Then make the pronoun match its antecedent.

pronoun: A word that stands in place of a noun (*he, him,* or *his* for *Nate*).

FAULTY	Each of the boys in the Soccer Club has *their* own bag.
CORRECT	Each of the boys in the Soccer Club has *his* own bag.
	[The word *each*, not *boys*, is the antecedent. *Each* is an indefinite pronoun and is always singular, so any pronoun referring to it must be singular as well.]
FAULTY	Everyone in the meeting had *their* own coffee.
CORRECT	Everyone in the meeting had *his or her* own coffee.
	[*Everyone* is an indefinite pronoun that is always singular, so any pronoun referring to it must be singular as well.]
FAULTY	Neither Juanita nor Paula has received approval of *their* financial aid yet.
CORRECT	Neither Juanita nor Paula has received approval of *her* financial aid yet.
	[*Neither Juanita nor Paula* is a compound subject joined by *nor*. Any pronoun referring to it must agree with only the nearer part of the compound. In other words, *her* needs to agree with *Paula*, which is singular.]

Indefinite pronouns as antecedents are troublesome when they are grammatically singular but create a plural image in the writer's mind. Fortunately, most indefinite pronouns are either always singular or always plural (Table 9.4). A few (such as *some* or *all*) can vary in number to fit the noun represented.

SINGULAR	*Some* of the stew lost *its* flavor.
PLURAL	*Some* of the players lost *their* equipment.

TABLE 9.4 Indefinite Pronouns

Always Singular			Always Plural
anybody	everyone	nothing	both
anyone	everything	one (of)	few
anything	much	somebody	many
each (of)	neither (of)	someone	several
either (of)	nobody	something	
everybody	no one		

EDITING CHECKLIST FOR PRONOUN-ANTECEDENT AGREEMENT

- ☐ Have you identified the antecedent for each pronoun?
- ☐ Is the antecedent singular or plural? Does the pronoun match?
- ☐ Is the antecedent masculine, feminine, or neuter? Does the pronoun match?
- ☐ Is the antecedent in the first, second, or third person? Does the pronoun match?

A7   Check for correct adjectives and adverbs.

Adjectives and *adverbs* are modifiers° that describe or give more information about (*modify*) other words in a sentence. Many adverbs are formed by adding -*ly* to adjectives: *simple/simply; quiet/quietly.* Because adjectives and adverbs resemble each other, writers sometimes mistakenly use one instead of the other. To edit, find the word that the adjective or adverb modifies. If that word is a noun or pronoun, use an adjective. (An adjective typically describes which or what kind.) If that word is a verb, adjective, or another adverb, use an adverb. (An adverb typically describes how, when, where, or why.)

FAULTY	Kelly ran into the house *quick.*
CORRECT	Kelly ran into the house *quickly.*
FAULTY	Gabriela looked *terribly* after her bout with the flu.
CORRECT	Gabriela looked *terrible* after her bout with the flu.
FAULTY	His scar healed so *good* that it was barely visible.
CORRECT	His scar healed so *well* that it was barely visible.

Adjectives and adverbs with similar comparative and superlative forms can cause trouble (Table 9.5). Always ask whether you need an adjective or an adverb in the sentence, and then use the correct word.

---

modifier: A word (such as an adjective or adverb), phrase, or clause that provides more information about another part of a sentence: Plays *staged by the drama class* are *always successful.*

TABLE 9.5   Comparison of Irregular Adjectives and Adverbs

Modifier	Positive	Comparative	Superlative
ADJECTIVES	good	better	best
	bad	worse	worst
	little	less, littler	least, littlest
	many, some, much	more	most
ADVERBS	well	better	best
	badly	worse	worst
	little	less	least

EDITING CHECKLIST FOR ADJECTIVES AND ADVERBS

☐ Have you identified which word the adjective or adverb modifies?

☐ If the word modified is a noun or pronoun, have you used an adjective?

☐ If the word modified is a verb, adjective, or adverb, have you used an adverb?

☐ Have you used the correct comparative or superlative form?

B   EDITING TO ENSURE EFFECTIVE SENTENCES

B1   Check for misplaced and dangling modifiers.

For a sentence to be clear, the connection between a modifier° and the thing it modifies must be obvious. Usually a modifier should be placed right before or right after the sentence element it modifies. If the modifier is placed too close to some other sentence element, it is a ***misplaced modifier.*** If there is nothing in the sentence that the modifier can logically modify, it is a ***dangling modifier.*** Both of these errors can confuse readers—and they sometimes create unintentionally humorous images. As

---

modifier: A word (such as an adjective or adverb), phrase, or clause that provides more information about another part of a sentence: Plays *staged by the drama class* are *always successful.*

you edit, place a modifier directly before or after the word being modified to connect the two clearly.

MISPLACED	George found the leftovers when he visited in the refrigerator.
CORRECT	George found the leftovers in the refrigerator when he visited.
	[In the faulty sentence, *in the refrigerator* seems to modify George's visit. Obviously the leftovers are in the refrigerator, not George.]
DANGLING	Looking out the window, the clouds were beautiful.
CORRECT	Looking out the window, I saw that the clouds were beautiful.
CORRECT	When I looked out the window, the clouds were beautiful. [In the faulty sentence, *looking out the window* should modify *I,* not *the clouds,* but *I* is not in the sentence. The modifier is left without anything logical to modify—a dangling modifier. To correct this, the writer has to edit so that *I* is in the sentence.]

EDITING CHECKLIST FOR MISPLACED AND DANGLING MODIFIERS

☐ What is each modifier meant to modify? Is the modifier as close as possible to that sentence element? Is any misreading possible?

☐ If a modifier is misplaced, can you move it to clarify the meaning?

☐ What noun or pronoun is a dangling modifier meant to modify? Can you make that word or phrase the subject of the main clause? Or can you turn the dangling modifier into a clause that includes the missing noun or pronoun?

B2   Check for parallel structure.

A series of words, phrases, clauses, or sentences with the same grammatical form is said to be ***parallel.*** Using parallel form for elements that are parallel in meaning or function helps readers grasp the meaning of a sentence more easily. A lack of parallelism can distract, annoy, or even confuse readers.

To use parallelism, put nouns with nouns, verbs with verbs, and phrases with phrases. Parallelism is particularly important in a series, with correlative conjunctions,° and in comparisons using *than* or *as*.

FAULTY	I like to go to Estes Park for skiing, ice skating, and to meet interesting people.
CORRECT	I like to go to Estes Park to ski, to ice skate, and to meet interesting people.
FAULTY	The proposal is neither practical, nor is it innovative.
CORRECT	The proposal is neither practical nor innovative.
FAULTY	A parent should have a few firm rules rather than having many flimsy ones.
CORRECT	A parent should have a few firm rules rather than many flimsy ones.

Edit to reinforce parallel structures by repeating articles, conjunctions, prepositions, or lead-in words as needed.

AWKWARD	His dream was that he would never have to give up his routine but he would still find time to explore new frontiers.
PARALLEL	His dream was that he would never have to give up his routine but *that* he would still find time to explore new frontiers.

EDITING CHECKLIST FOR PARALLEL STRUCTURE

☐ Are all the elements in a series in the same grammatical form?
☐ Are the elements in a comparison parallel in form?
☐ Are the articles, conjunctions, or prepositions between elements repeated rather than mixed or omitted?
☐ Are lead-in words repeated as needed?

---

correlative conjunction: A pair of linking words (such as *either/or, not only/but also*) that appear separately but work together to join elements of a sentence: *Neither* his friends *nor* hers like pizza.

C   EDITING FOR COMMON PUNCTUATION PROBLEMS

C1   Check for correct use of commas.

The *comma* is a punctuation mark that indicates a pause. By setting some words apart from others, commas help clarify relationships. They prevent the words on a page and the ideas they represent from becoming a jumble. Here are some important conventional uses of commas.

- Use a comma before a coordinating conjunction *(and, but, for, or, so, yet, nor)* that joins two main clauses° in a compound sentence.

  The discussion was brief, *so* the meeting was adjourned early.

- Use a comma after an introductory word or word group unless it is short and cannot be misread.

  After the war, the North's economy developed rapidly.

- Use commas to separate the items in a series of three or more items.

  The chief advantages will be *speed, durability,* and *longevity.*

- Use commas to set off a modifying clause or phrase if it is nonrestrictive° (nonessential) rather than restrictive.°

  Good childcare, *which is difficult to find,* should be provided by the employer.

  Good childcare *that is reliable and inexpensive* is every employee's hope.

- Use commas to set off an appositive,° an expression that comes directly after a noun or pronoun and renames it, if it is nonrestrictive (nonessential) rather than restrictive.

  Sheri, my sister, has a new job as an events coordinator.

  My dog, Rover, is better trained than my cat, Sheba.

  My dog Rover is better trained than my dog Homer.

main clause: A group of words that has both a subject and a verb and can stand alone as a complete sentence: *My sister has a car.*   nonrestrictive modifier: an expression (set off by commas) that adds nonessential, though perhaps interesting or valuable, information that could be left out.   restrictive modifier: an expression (not set off by commas) that adds limiting information, essential to specify what it modifies.   appositive: A word or group of words that adds information about a subject or object by identifying it in a different way: my dog *Rover,* Hal's brother *Fred.*

- Use commas to set off parenthetical expressions,° conjunctive adverbs,° and other interrupters.

The proposal from the mayor's commission, however, is not feasible.

EDITING CHECKLIST FOR COMMAS

☐ Have you added a comma between two main clauses joined by a coordinating conjunction?

☐ Have you added the commas needed after introductory words or word groups?

☐ Have you separated items in a series with commas?

☐ Have you avoided putting commas before the first item in a series or after the last?

☐ Have you used commas before and after each nonrestrictive (nonessential) phrase or clause?

☐ Have you avoided using commas around a restrictive word, phrase, or clause?

☐ Have you used commas to set off parenthetical expressions, conjunctive adverbs, and other interrupters?

C2   Check for correct use of apostrophes.

An **apostrophe** is a punctuation mark that either shows possession (*Sylvia's*) or indicates that one or more letters have intentionally been left out to form a contraction (*didn't*). Because apostrophes are easy to overlook, writers often omit a necessary apostrophe. They also may use an apostrophe where it is not needed or put one in the wrong place. An apostrophe is never used to create the possessive form of a personal pronoun; use the possessive pronoun form (Table 9.6) instead.

FAULTY	*Mikes* car was totaled in the accident.
CORRECT	*Mike's* car was totaled in the accident.
FAULTY	*Womens'* pay is often less than *mens'*.
CORRECT	*Women's* pay is often less than *men's*.

---

parenthetical expression: An aside to readers or a transitional expression such as *for example* or *in contrast*.   conjunctive adverb: A linking word that can connect independent clauses and show a relationship between two ideas: Armando is a serious student; *therefore,* he studies every day.

TABLE 9.6 Possessive Personal Pronouns

Personal Pronoun	Possessive Case
I	my, mine
you	your, yours (not your's)
he	his
she	her, hers (not her's)
it	its (not it's)
we	our, ours (not our's)
they	their, theirs (not their's)
who	whose (not who's)

FAULTY Che *did'nt* want to stay home and study.
CORRECT Che *didn't* want to stay home and study.

FAULTY The dog wagged *it's* tail happily. [it's = it is? No.]
CORRECT The dog wagged *its* tail happily.

FAULTY *Its* raining.
CORRECT *It's* raining. [it's = it is]

EDITING CHECKLIST FOR APOSTROPHES

☐ Have you used an apostrophe to create the possessive form of a noun?
☐ Have you used an apostrophe to show that letters have been left out in a contraction?
☐ Have you used the possessive case—rather than an apostrophe—to show that a pronoun is possessive?
☐ Have you used *it's* correctly (to mean *it is*)?

C3   Check for correct punctuation of quotations.

When you quote the exact words of a person you have interviewed or a source you have read, be sure to enclose those words in *quotation marks*. Notice how student Betsy Buffo presents the words of her subject in this excerpt from "Interview with an Artist."

Derek is straightforward when asked about how his work is received in the local community: "My work is outside the mainstream. Because it's controversial, it's not easy for me to get exposure."

If your source is quoting someone else (a quotation within a quotation), put your subject's words in quotation marks and the words he or she is quoting in single quotation marks. Always put commas and periods inside the quotation marks; put semicolons and colons outside.

Substitute an *ellipsis mark* (. . .)—three spaced dots—for any words you have omitted from the middle of a direct quotation. If you are following MLA style, you may place ellipsis marks inside brackets ([. . .]) when necessary to avoid confusing your ellipsis marks with those of the original writer. If an ellipsis mark comes at the end of a sentence, add another period to conclude the sentence. You don't need an ellipsis mark to show the beginning or ending of a quotation that is clearly incomplete.

In this selection from "Playing Games with Women's Sports," student Kelly Grecian indicates two omissions from her quotation.

Rounds observed decades ago that "The importance of what women athletes wear can't be underestimated" (44). She notes how "Beach volleyball, which is played . . . by bikini-clad women, rates network coverage. . . ." (44) while other women's leagues fail.

She adds her source—"Why Men Fear Women's Teams," an article by Kate Rounds from *Ms.* magazine—to her list of references at the end of her paper.

Common errors in punctuating quotations include leaving out necessary punctuation marks or putting them in the incorrect place or sequence. Each source-citation guide, such as MLA and APA, also recommends its own preferences for presenting quotations. (See pp. 230–33 and pp. 244–47.)

EDITING CHECKLIST FOR PUNCTUATION WITH QUOTATIONS

☐ Are the exact words quoted from your source enclosed in quotation marks?

☐ Are commas and periods placed inside closing quotation marks?

☐ Are colons and semicolons placed outside closing quotation marks?

☐ Have you used an ellipsis mark to show where any words have been omitted from the middle of a quotation?

D EDITING FOR COMMON MECHANICS AND FORMAT PROBLEMS

D1 Check for correct use of capital letters.

Capital letters are used in three general situations: to begin a new sentence; to begin names of specific people, places, dates, and things (proper nouns); and to begin main words in titles. Writers sometimes use capital letters where they are not needed—for emphasis, for example—or fail to use them where they are needed.

FAULTY	During my Sophomore year in College, I took World Literature, Biology, History, Psychology, and French—courses required for a Humanities Major.
CORRECT	During my sophomore year in college, I took world literature, biology, history, psychology, and French—courses required for a humanities major.

EDITING CHECKLIST FOR CAPITALIZATION

☐ Have you used a capital letter at the beginning of each complete sentence, including sentences that are quoted?

☐ Have you used capital letters for proper nouns and pronouns?

☐ Have you used a capital letter for each main word in a title, including the first word and the last word?

☐ Have you avoided using capital letters for emphasis?

CAPITALIZATION AT A GLANCE

Capitalize the following cases.

THE FIRST LETTER OF A SENTENCE, INCLUDING A QUOTED SENTENCE

She called out, "Come in! The water's warm."

PROPER NAMES AND ADJECTIVES MADE FROM THEM

Marie Curie	Smithsonian Institution	a Freudian reading

A RANK OR TITLE BEFORE A PROPER NAME

Ms. Olson   Professor   the president
                       Santocolon

A FAMILY RELATIONSHIP ONLY WHEN IT SUBSTITUTES
FOR OR IS PART OF A PROPER NAME

Grandma Jones   Father Time   my father

RELIGIONS, THEIR FOLLOWERS, AND DEITIES

Islam   Orthodox Jew   Buddha

PLACES, REGIONS, GEOGRAPHIC FEATURES, AND NATIONALITIES

Palo Alto   the Berkshire   Egyptians
the Midwest   Mountains   Chinese

DAYS OF THE WEEK, MONTHS, AND HOLIDAYS

Wednesday   July   Labor Day

HISTORICAL EVENTS, PERIODS, AND DOCUMENTS

the Boston Tea Party   the Middle Ages   the Constitution

SCHOOLS, COLLEGES, UNIVERSITIES, AND SPECIFIC COURSES

Temple University   Introduction to   a psychology
                       Psychology   course

FIRST, LAST, AND MAIN WORDS IN TITLES OF PAPERS, BOOKS,
ARTICLES, WORKS OF ART, TELEVISION SHOWS, POEMS, AND
PERFORMANCES

The Decline and Fall   "The Road Not Taken"   *King Lear*
of the Roman Empire   "The Lottery"   *Hamlet*

D2   Check spelling.

Misspelled words are difficult to spot in your own writing. You usually see
what you think you wrote. However, readers usually see what you actually did write. Based on what's on the page, they may conclude—fairly or
not—that you are careless, sloppy, or lazy. Pronunciation or faulty memory (*calvary, cavalry; nuclear, nucular*) can interfere with correct spelling.
On the other hand, if you quote from sources, you need to quote exactly,
even if their spellings occasionally differ from the ones familiar to you.

Spell-checkers offer a handy alternative to the dictionary, but you need to know their limitations. A spell-checker compares the words in your text with the words listed in its dictionary, and it highlights words that do not appear there. A spell-checker cannot help you to distinguish words you intend from words you don't (if all are spelled correctly). It also cannot help you spell words that its dictionary does not contain. Watch for one word spelled as another (*heel, heal*), the same word with alternate spellings (*hegira, hejira*), words that vary in different Englishes (*color, colour*), proper nouns (*moose lake* vs. *Moose Lake, Minnesota*), and other potentially confusing variations.

Spell-checkers may also skip over acronyms, sets of initials used as if they were words, such as FBI (the familiar Federal Bureau of Investigation) or ACD (the less familiar Australian Cattle Dog). Spell-checkers also ignore one-letter words. For example, they will not flag a typographical error such as *s truck* for *a truck*. Nor will they highlight *homonyms*, words that sound alike but are spelled differently (Table 9.7), or words that are misspelled as different words—*their* for *there, to* for *too*, or *own* for *won*. Always check the spelling in your text by eye after you've used your spell-checker.

TABLE 9.7 Commonly Confused Homonyms

accept (v., receive willingly); **except** (prep., other than)

　　Mimi could *accept* all of Lefty's gifts *except* his ring.

affect (v., influence); **effect** (n., result)

　　If the new rules *affect* us, what will be their *effect*?

allusion (n., reference); **illusion** (n., fantasy)

　　Any *allusion* to Norman's mother may revive his *illusion* that she is upstairs, alive, in her rocking chair.

capital (adj., uppercase; n., seat of government); **capitol** (n., government building)

　　The *Capitol* building in our nation's *capital* is spelled with a *capital C*.

cite (v., refer to); **sight** (n., vision or tourist attraction); **site** (n., place)

　　Did you *cite* Aunt Peggy as your authority on which *sites* feature the most interesting *sights*?

complement (v., complete; n., counterpart); **compliment** (v. or n., praise)

　　For Lee to say that Sheila's beauty *complements* her intelligence may or may not be a *compliment*.

(Continued)

TABLE 9.7   (Continued)

desert (v., abandon; n., hot, dry region); **dessert** (n., end-of-meal sweet)

Don't *desert* us by leaving for the *desert* before *dessert*.

elicit (v., bring out); **illicit** (adj., illegal)

By going undercover, Sonny should *elicit* some offers of *illicit* drugs.

formally (adv., officially); **formerly** (adv., in the past)

Jane and John Doe-Smith, *formerly* Jane Doe and John Smith, sent cards *formally* announcing their marriage.

led (v., past tense of *lead*); **lead** (n., a metal)

Gil's heart was heavy as *lead* when he *led* the mourners to the grave.

principal (n. or adj., chief); **principle** (n., rule or standard)

The *principal* problem is convincing the media that our school *principal* is a person of high *principles*.

stationary (adj., motionless); **stationery** (n., writing paper)

Hubert's *stationery* shop stood *stationary* until a flood swept it away.

their (pron., belonging to them); **there** (adv., in that place); **they're** (contraction of *they are)*

Sue said *they're* going over *there* to visit *their* aunt.

to (prep., toward); **too** (adv., also or excessively); **two** (n. or adj., numeral: one more than one)

Let's not take *two* cars *to* town—that's *too* many unless Lucille and Harry are coming *too.*

who's (contraction of *who is*); **whose** (pron., belonging to whom)

Who's going to tell me *whose* dog this is?

your (pron., belonging to you); **you're** (contraction of *you are)*

You're not getting *your* own way this time!

Many commonly misspelled words have similar tricky features such as letters that double in some words but not in others (*academic, accessible*), letters that may not be pronounced (*arctic, exhaust*), and letter pairs that may fall in one sequence or another (*chief, foreign*). See Table 9.8 for a few examples of words that are commonly misspelled. Your spell-checker can catch these unless it confuses the word you intend with a similar or related word (*analysis, analyze*).

If you habitually misspell certain words, use your software's Search or Find function to locate all instances. Consider keeping track of misspelled

TABLE 9.8   Examples of Commonly Misspelled Words

a lot	dissatisfied	neither
achievement	doesn't	niece
acknowledgment	don't	ninety
advice	drunkenness	ninth
advise	efficiency	omission
all right	eighth	omitted
all together (in one group)	embarrass	perceive
allege	entirety	persistence
already	environment	precede (go before)
altogether (entirely)	excel	predominant
answer	excellence	prejudice
athletics	familiar	privilege
beneficial	foresee	proceed (continue)
benefited	forth	quiet
breath (noun)	forty	quite
breathe (verb)	fourth (number four)	recede
bureaucracy	friend	receipt
casualties	genuine	receive
certain	government	reminisce
changeable	height	reminiscence
choose (present tense)	heroes	repetition
chose (past tense)	humorous	rhythm
column	illiterate	seize
commitment	illogical	separate
committed	incredible	succeed
conscience	irrelevant	supersede
conscientious	irresistible	technical
conscious	irritable	technique
criticism	it's (it is, it has)	thorough
criticize	its (possessive)	though
deceive	judgment	thought
dependent	knowledge	throughout
descendant	loose (adjective)	unanimous
development	lose (verb)	unnecessary
device (noun)	lying	warrant
devise (verb)	mischievous	weather
disappoint	misspell	weird
disastrous	necessary	whether

words in your papers for a few weeks so you can take advantage of this feature to simplify your editing. If you search for the correct spelling of a word, you will simply leave it as it is when you find it. However, if you search for each of the spellings of similar words, you can then check and correct each instance as needed. Likewise, if you search for your favorite spelling variations, you can correct all of your typical mistakes—and maybe learn the correct spelling during the process.

EDITING CHECKLIST FOR SPELLING

☐ Have you checked for words you habitually misspell?

☐ Have you checked for commonly confused or misspelled words?

☐ Have you checked a dictionary for any words you are unsure about?

☐ Have you run your spell-checker? Have you read your paper carefully for errors that it would miss?

D3   Check for correct manuscript form.

In case you have received no particular instructions for the form of your paper, here are some general, all-purpose guidelines.

General Manuscript Style for College Essays, Articles, and Reports

1. Pick a conventional, easy-to-read typeface such as Times New Roman, which academic style guides recommend. Make sure you have a fresh cartridge in your printer. If you handwrite your paper, make sure your writing is legible even if you feel the pressure of a time limit.

2. Print in black ink. Use dark blue or black ink if you write by hand.

3. Write or print on just one side of standard letter-size bond paper ($8\frac{1}{2}$ by 11 inches). If you handwrite your paper, use $8\frac{1}{2}$-by-11-inch paper with smooth edges (not torn from a spiral-bound notebook). If you are writing on a quiz page or in an exam booklet, follow any specific directions from your instructor. You need to write legibly but also explain your answer in limited space. Be clear if any answers continue on the back of a page.

4. For a paper without a separate title page, place your name, your instructor's name, the number and section of the course, and the date in the upper left or right corner of the first page, each item on a new line. (Ask whether your instructor has a preference for which side.) Double-space and center your title. Don't underline the title, don't put it in quotation marks or use all capital letters, and don't put a period after it. Capitalize the first and last words, the first word after a colon or semicolon, and all other words except prepositions,° coordinating conjunctions,° and articles.° Double-space between the title and the first line of your text. (Most instructors do not require a title page for short college papers. If your instructor asks for one but doesn't give you any guidelines, see the first item under Additional Suggestions for Research Papers, below.)

5. Number your pages consecutively, including the first page. For a paper of two or more pages, use a running header to put your last name in the upper right corner of each sheet along with the page number. (Use the Header option under View or Edit.) Do not type the word *page* or the letter *p* before the page number, and do not follow the number with a period or parenthesis.

6. Leave ample margins—at least an inch—left, right, top, and bottom.

7. Double-space your manuscript; if you handwrite, use wide-ruled paper or skip every other line.

8. Indent each new paragraph five spaces or one-half inch.

9. Long quotations should be double-spaced like the rest of your paper but indented from the left margin—ten spaces (one inch) if you're following MLA (Modern Language Association) guidelines, five spaces (one-half inch) if you're using APA (American Psychological Association) guidelines. Put the source citation in parentheses immediately after the final punctuation mark of the block quotation. (See the examples on p. 233 and pp. 246–47.)

10. Label all illustrations. Make sure any insertions are bound securely to the paper.

11. Staple the paper in the top left corner, or use a paper clip as MLA advises. Don't use any other method to secure the pages unless one is recommended by your instructor.

12. For safety's sake and peace of mind, always make a copy of your paper, and back up your file.

---

preposition: A word (such as *in, on, at, of, from*) that shows a connection and leads into a phrase.   **coordinating conjunction:** A one-syllable linking word (*and, but, for, or, nor, so, yet*) that joins elements with equal or near-equal importance.   **article:** The word *a, an,* or *the.*

Additional Suggestions for Research Papers

For research papers, the format is the same as recommended in the previous section, with the following additional specifications.

1. The MLA guidelines do not recommend a title page. If your instructor wants one, type the title of your paper, centered and double-spaced, about a third of the way down the page. Go down two to four more lines and type your name, the instructor's name, the number and section of the course, and the date, each on a separate line and double-spaced.
2. Do not number your title page; number your outline, if you submit one with your paper, with small roman numerals (i, ii, iii, and so on). Number consecutively all subsequent pages in the essay, including your works cited or references pages, using arabic numerals (1, 2, 3, and so on) in the upper right corner of the page.
3. Double-space your works cited or references list.

How to Make a Correction

Before you produce your final copy, make any large changes in your draft, edit and proofread carefully, and run your spell-checker. When you give your paper a last once-over, however, don't be afraid to make small corrections in pen. In making last-minute corrections, you may find it handy to use these symbols and marks used by proofreaders. (See the last page of this book for a list of correction symbols.)

- A transposition mark (⁀) reverses the positions of two words or two letters:

  The nearby star Tau Ceti closely resmebles our sun.

- Close-up marks (⌒) bring together the parts of a word accidentally split. A separation mark (|) inserts a space where one is needed:

  The nearby star Tau Ceti closely re sembles our sun.

- To delete a letter or punctuation mark, draw a line with a curlicue through it:

  The nearby star Tau Ceti closely ressembles our sun.

- Use a caret (∧) to indicate where to insert a word or letter:

  The nearby star Tau Ceti closely resemble our sun.

- The symbol ¶ before a word or a line means "start a new paragraph":

  Recently, astronomers have reduced their efforts to study dark nebulae. ¶That
  other solar systems may also support life makes for another fascinating
  speculation.

- To make a letter lowercase, draw a slanted line through it. To make a letter uppercase, put three short lines under it:

  i read it for my History class.

- You can always cross out a word neatly, with a single horizontal line, and write a better one above it:

  closely
  The nearby star Tau Ceti somewhat resembles our sun.

- Finally, if a page has many handwritten corrections on it, print or write it over again.

■ ACTIVITY 9.3: Editing with a Computer

Try using computer software to help you edit your draft more closely. Always make and save a backup copy of your file before you work on changes.

1. Automatically isolate each sentence so that you are less likely to skip over errors. Select the Find and Replace function in your Home or Edit menu. Then ask the software to find every period in the file and replace it with a period and two returns. This change will create a version with every sentence separated by several spaces—ready for focused editing. (Restore the usual paragraph format after you edit.)

   a. Concentrate on each sentence, looking for fragments, comma splices, and other problems. Edit or rewrite to correct or improve.

   b. Check other characteristics, such as length. If most sentences are the same length, add variety by combining, expanding, or trimming some of them.

   c. Skim a series of sentences for similar opening patterns or expressions. If many sentences begin in the same way, edit to relieve the monotony.

2. Search for your personal editing problems. Keep track of your mistakes or review comments on past papers to develop an "error hit list." Use the Find and Replace function to check quickly for some of these problems. For instance, search for *each* (always singular) or *few* (always plural) to see if all the verbs agree, for *its* and *it's* to turn up apostrophe errors, or for *There* to discover whether you overuse sentences beginning with *There is* or *There are*.

PART THREE

Resources

10

Resources for Arguing

Both in and out of class, you'll hear controversial issues discussed—immigration policy, standardized testing, disaster preparedness, income disparities, health insurance, global outsourcing of jobs. In many fields of study, experts don't always agree, and some academic issues—the merits of a literary work, the effectiveness of a social policy, the benefits of a risky procedure—remain controversies for years. On the surface, these issues often are simplified, presented as either/or debates between two battling opponents. In reality, most civic discussions encompass multiple points of view, and most responses to problems need to incorporate multiple ideas and compromises. Whatever the issue or type of argument you tackle, you'll want to argue effectively as you acknowledge the exchanges around you.

DEVELOPING AN ARGUMENT

The strategies you have used for developing other papers may also be useful for an argument. (See Chs. 7 and 11.) However, readers typically expect an argument to be both logical and persuasive, and those expectations set the standard for your thesis, your reasons, and your supporting evidence. The following advice should help you write powerful arguments that successfully appeal to readers.

Beginning with an Issue and a Thesis

A solid argument begins with a specific issue about which people hold different opinions. The issue might be a widely debated civic controversy (such as immigration policy) or a local matter (such as a zoning dispute). It might be a disagreement among researchers about the likely effects of a food additive or among readers about interpretations of a short story. Your working thesis states your initial position on an issue, usually a perspective you will refine as you gain understanding of the issue. (For more on thesis statements, see pp. 68–76 and 144–46.)

WORKING THESIS   We should expect advertisers to fight rather than reinforce stereotypes of people with disabilities.

REVISED THESIS   Consumers should spend their shopping dollars thoughtfully, holding advertisers accountable for feeding rather than fighting stereotypes of people with disabilities.

When you draft your argument paper, you will probably want to open with enough background about the issue to justify your concern about it and to help your readers appreciate the controversy. You'll need to define key terms, especially the words and expressions on which your points hinge. As you investigate the issue, you'll also identify or develop substantial reasons for agreeing with your thesis (and perhaps recognize a valid point or two that you'll need to counter). Your reasons will help you focus and build persuasive supporting paragraphs where you present the evidence to support your thesis.

Because a thesis identifies and states your position, it generally forms the basis of a strong argument. Use these questions to improve yours.

THESIS CHECKLIST

☐ Have you stated your thesis clearly? Could you sharpen any vague or imprecise wording?

☐ Does your thesis stick to one main idea? Is it focused?

☐ Is your thesis stated positively, not negatively?

☐ Is your thesis limited? Can you support it with enough evidence in a short essay?

☐ Does your thesis need any other revision to attract your readers' attention?

Making a Claim

As you plan an argument, consider three general types of claims: those that require substantiation, endorse policy, and provide evaluation. Although these three categories overlap somewhat and often can be made about the same topic, you should develop the claim that is most likely to speak to your audience. Suppose, for example, that the local school board is examining a proposal for an early childhood center at South High for students' babies. High school students, their parents, school administrators, counselors, and early childhood specialists might all agree that an on-site facility would benefit the babies and their teen parents. They might disagree, however, about whether district policies allow the use of funds to support this kind of project or whether the facility's presence would be a good or bad influence on South High students who do not have children. Different claims and different evidence might appeal to each group in the effort to reach consensus.

Claims of Substantiation.   Claims of substantiation require examining and interpreting information to resolve disputes over facts, circumstances, causes or effects, definitions, or even the extent of a problem.

> Certain types of cigarette advertisements, such as e-cigarette ads, significantly encourage smoking among teenagers.

> Despite a few well-publicized exceptions to the rule, police brutality is not a major problem in this country.

> On the whole, bilingual education programs help students learn English more quickly than total immersion programs do.

Claims of Policy.   Claims of policy challenge or defend methods of achieving generally accepted goals.

> The federal government should support the distribution of clean needles to reduce the rate of HIV infection among intravenous drug users.

> Denying children of undocumented workers enrollment in U.S. public schools will reduce the problem of illegal immigration.

> Any teenager accused of murder should be tried as an adult.

Claims of Evaluation.   Claims of evaluation consider the rightness, appropriateness, or worth of an issue.

> Research using fetal tissue is unethical in a civilized society.

> English-only legislation promotes cultural intolerance in our society.

Keeping children in foster care for years, instead of releasing them for adoption, is wrong.

■ ACTIVITY 10.1: Making a Claim with a Group

Have each member of your group write out a one-sentence claim or position. Ask the group to suggest possible supporting evidence, opposing evidence, and arguments to counter the opposing evidence. When you are finished, have each writer reconsider his or her position based on the group's discussion.

Selecting Persuasive Evidence

Gather facts, statistics, expert testimony, firsthand observations, and other kinds of evidence to support your position and the type of claim you are making. Credible evidence is accurate, reliable, up-to-date, relevant, and representative. It also needs to be complex, not oversimplified, so that it is sufficient and strong enough to support your thesis and persuade your readers. Cluster and organize the evidence to back up your reasons for thinking as you do.

Besides hunting for evidence to support your stand, look carefully at the stands others take. Your evidence may easily persuade those who already agree with you; the challenge is to engage or persuade those who are undecided or who see things differently. Be sure to consider your own assumptions about both the nature of the issue and the authority of your view. What you assume, readers may question. Your best answer to such questions is compelling evidence. (For a checklist for testing evidence, see pp. 39–40. For criteria for research sources, see pp. 215–16.)

Use the following questions as a guide to building strong and persuasive evidence.

PERSUASIVE EVIDENCE CHECKLIST

- ☐ What do you assume about the issue and your stand? What seems unquestionably logical or true to you?
- ☐ What evidence supports your assumptions? How logical and relevant is that evidence?
- ☐ How can you integrate your evidence so that readers understand and perhaps come to share your assumptions?
- ☐ What are your readers likely to think about the issue? Which of their opinions or claims differ from yours?

□ What evidence supports those other views? How logical and relevant is that evidence?

□ What evidence can you use to show why those views are weak, only partially true, misguided, or just plain wrong?

□ Which alternative views might you want to recognize, concede, or even integrate into your position?

□ Which other views or evidence might you want to question or challenge?

Using Evidence to Support an Appeal

One way to select evidence and to judge whether it is appropriate and sufficient is to consider the types of appeal—logical, emotional, and ethical. Most effective arguments work on all three levels, using evidence that supports each type of appeal.

Logical Appeals (Logos). When writers use a logical appeal (*logos* or "word" in Greek), they appeal to the reader's mind or intellect. This appeal relies on evidence that is factual, objective, clear, and relevant. Critical readers expect to find logical evidence supporting major claims and statements. For example, if a writer were arguing for term limits for legislators, she wouldn't want to base her argument on evidence that some long-term legislators weren't reelected last term (irrelevant) or that the current system is unfair to young people who want to get into politics (not logical). Instead she might argue that the absence of term limits encourages corruption, using evidence of legislators who repaid lobbyists for campaign contributions with key votes.

Emotional Appeals (Pathos). When writers use an emotional appeal (*pathos* or "suffering" in Greek), they appeal to the reader's heart. They choose language, facts, quotations, examples, and images that evoke an emotional response. Of course, convincing writing does touch readers' hearts as well as their minds. Without this heartfelt tug, a strict logical appeal may seem cold and dehumanized. If a writer opposed hunting seals for their fur, he might combine statistics about the number of seals killed each year and the overall population decrease with a vivid description of baby seals being slaughtered. Some writers use emotional words and sentimental examples to manipulate readers—to arouse their sympathy, pity, or anger in order to convert them without much logical evidence—but dishonest emotional appeals may alienate readers. Instead of basing an argument against a political candidate on pitiful images of scrawny children living in roach-infested squalor, a good writer would report the candidate's voting record on issues that affect children.

Ethical Appeals (Ethos).   When writers use an ethical appeal (*ethos* or "character" in Greek), they call on the reader's sense of fairness and trust. They select and present evidence in a way that will make the audience trust them, respect their judgment, and believe what they have to say. The best logical argument in the world falls flat when readers don't take the writer seriously. How can you use an ethical appeal to establish your credibility as a writer? First, you need to establish your credentials in the field through experience, reading, or interviews that help you learn about the subject. If you are writing about environmental pollution, tell your readers that your allergies have been irritated by chemicals in the air. Identify medical or environmental experts you have contacted or whose publications you have read. Demonstrate your knowledge through the information you present, the experts and sources you cite, and the depth of understanding you convey. Establish a rapport with readers by pointing to values and attitudes you share with them and by responding seriously to opposing arguments. Finally, use language that is precise, clear, and appropriate in tone.

The logical appeal engages readers' intellect; the emotional appeal touches their hearts; the ethical appeal draws on their sense of fairness and reasonableness. A persuasive argument usually operates on all three levels. For example, you might develop a thesis about the need to curb accidental gunshot deaths in your county, as Table 10.1 illustrates.

TABLE 10.1   Appeals and Evidence: Curbing Accidental Gunshot Deaths

Type of Appeal	Ways of Making the Appeal	Possible Supporting Evidence
Logical (logos)	• Rely on clear reasoning and sound evidence to influence your readers' thinking. • Demonstrate what you claim, and don't claim what you can't demonstrate. • Test and select your evidence.	• Supply current and reliable statistics about gun ownership and accidental shootings. • Prepare a bar graph that shows the number of incidents during the past ten years, using data from the county records. • Describe the immediate and long-term consequences of a typical shooting accident.

(Continued)

TABLE 10.1   (Continued)

Type of Appeal	Ways of Making the Appeal	Possible Supporting Evidence
Emotional (pathos)	• Choose examples and language that will influence your readers' feelings. • Include effective images, but don't overdo them. • Complement logical appeals, but don't replace them.	• Describe the wrenching scenario of a father whose college-age son unexpectedly returns home at 3:00 A.M. The father mistakes his son for an intruder and shoots him, throwing the family into turmoil. • Use quotations and descriptions from newspaper accounts to show the reactions of family, friends, and neighbors.
Ethical (ethos)	• Use a tone and approach that appeal to your readers' sense of fairness and reasonableness. • Spell out your values and beliefs, and acknowledge the values and beliefs of others with different opinions. • Establish your credentials, if any, and the credentials of experts you cite. • Instill confidence in your readers so that they see you as a caring, trustworthy person with reliable views.	• Establish your reasonable approach by acknowledging the views of hunters and others who store guns at home and follow recommended safety procedures. • Supply the credentials or affiliation of experts ("Ray Fontaine, public safety director for the county"). • Note ways in which experts have established their authority ("During my interview with Ms. Dutton, she related several recent incidents involving gun accidents in the home, testifying to her extensive knowledge of this issue in our community.").

■ **ACTIVITY 10.2:** Identifying Types of Appeals

Bring to class the editorial or opinion page from a newspaper or newsmagazine. Read some of the letters or articles. Identify the types of appeals each author uses to support his or her point.

Reasoning Logically

Why do you have to be logical? Isn't it enough just to tell everybody else what you think? That tactic probably works fine when you and your friends are solving the problems of the world at two in the morning. After all, your friends already know you, your opinions, and the way you typically think. They may even find your occasional rant entertaining.

Whether they agree or disagree with you, they probably tolerate your ideas because they are your friends.

When you write an argument paper in college, however, you face a different type of audience, one that needs to learn what you assume, what you advocate, and why you hold to that position. Your readers also want to learn the specifics of your argument—the reasons you find compelling, the evidence that supports your views, and the connections that relate each point to your position. Finally, they expect reasoning, not pleading or bullying. How you reason—and how you present your reasoning—is an important part of gaining readers' confidence, acknowledgment, and eventual agreement.

As you plan a particular college paper, read the assignment carefully. It may suggest the kind of reasoning or evidence that your instructor will find logical. The readings that accompany the assignment may do the same, acting as strong or weak examples of the kind of argument assigned or as reliable sources for supporting evidence. In addition, a college writing assignment often assumes that you are contributing to an exchange of knowledge. It expects you to draw on the opinions and supporting evidence of others. Your argument, however, needs to integrate the work of others with your own views and to supply logical transitions that connect each idea or bit of evidence with the next. Use the following questions as you plan your draft or revise it, refining your reasoning and demonstrating it to others.

LOGICAL REASONING CHECKLIST

- ☐ Have you built your argument on a solid foundation? Are your premises, your initial assumptions, sound?

- ☐ Is your thesis or claim clearly stated? Are its terms explained or defined?

- ☐ What are your reasons or supporting arguments for thinking your thesis is sound? Have you identified and arranged them in a sequence to persuade your audience? Have you used transitions to introduce them so readers can't miss them?

- ☐ Have you located and identified credible evidence to support each reason you present? Have you favored objective, research-based evidence (facts, statistics, and expert testimony) rather than personal experiences or beliefs?

- ☐ Have you explained and connected your evidence so your audience can see how it applies or relates to your argument? Have you added transitions to clarify relationships for readers?

☐ Have you enhanced your own credibility by acknowledging other points of view? Have you effectively integrated or countered those views?

☐ Have you adjusted your tone and style so that you come across as reasonable and fair-minded? Have you avoided arrogant claims about proving (rather than showing) points? Have you avoided wishy-washy evasions?

☐ Have you credited all your sources?

Avoiding Logical Fallacies

Logical fallacies are common mistakes in thinking that may lead to faulty conclusions or distort evidence. Table 10.2 describes a few of the most familiar logical fallacies.

TABLE 10.2   Recognizing Logical Fallacies

Term and Explanation	Example
Non sequitur: Stating a claim that doesn't follow from your first premise or statement; Latin for "It does not follow"	Liza should marry Mateo. In college he got all A's.
Oversimplification: Offering easy solutions for complicated problems	If we want to end substance abuse, let's send every drug user to prison for life. [Even aspirin users?]
Post hoc, ergo propter hoc: Assuming a cause-and-effect relationship where none exists even though one event preceded another; Latin for "after this, therefore because of this"	After Jenny's black cat crossed my path, everything went wrong, and I failed my midterm.
Allness: Stating or implying that something is true of an entire class of things, often using *all, everyone, no one, always,* or *never*	Students enjoy studying. [All students? All subjects? All the time?]
Proof by example or too few examples: Presenting an example as proof rather than as illustration or clarification; overgeneralizing (the basis of much prejudice)	Armenians are great chefs. My neighbor is Armenian, and can he cook!

Term and Explanation	Example
Begging the question: Proving a statement already taken for granted, often by repeating it in different words or by defining a word in terms of itself	Rapists are dangerous because they are menaces. Happiness is the state of being happy.
Circular reasoning: Supporting a statement with itself; a form of begging the question	He is a liar because he simply isn't telling the truth.
Either/or reasoning: Oversimplifying by assuming that an issue has only two sides, a statement must be true or false, a question demands a yes or no answer, or a problem has only two possible solutions (and one that's acceptable)	What are we going to do about climate change? Either we stop using all energy-consuming vehicles and products that contribute to it, or we just learn to live with it.
Argument from dubious authority: Using an unidentified authority to shore up a weak argument or an authority whose expertise lies outside the issue, such as a TV personality selling insurance	According to some of the most knowledgeable scientists in America, smoking two packs a day is as harmless as eating oatmeal cookies.
Argument ad hominem: Attacking an individual's opinion by attacking his or her character, thus deflecting attention from the merit of a proposal; Latin for "against the man"	Diaz may argue that we need to save the polar bears, but he's the type who gets emotional over nothing.
Argument from ignorance: Maintaining that a claim has to be accepted because it hasn't been disproved or that it has to be rejected because it hasn't been proved	Despite years of effort, no one has proved that ghosts don't exist; therefore, we should expect to see them at any time. No one has ever shown that life exists on any other planet; clearly the notion of other living things in the universe is absurd.
Argument by analogy: Showing the similarities between familiar and unfamiliar items (while ignoring differences) as evidence rather than as a useful way of explaining	People are born free as the birds; it's cruel to expect them to work.
Bandwagon argument: Suggesting that everyone is joining the group and that readers who don't may miss out on happiness, success, or a reward	Purchasing the new Global Glimmer admits you to the nation's most elite group of smartphone users.

■ ACTIVITY 10.3: Checking for Logical Reasoning

Gather some print or online editorials and letters to the editor. (Consider your campus or community newspaper as well as big-city or national publications.) Working with a classmate, sort these examples, looking for both reasonable and flawed arguments. Analyze several of these by identifying the claims and appeals, outlining the sequence of points, and evaluating the supporting evidence. Present to classmates your conclusions about what strengthens or weakens an argument.

PRESENTING YOUR ARGUMENT

After you have worked out your argument and found evidence to substantiate it, you need to shape it into final form for readers. To influence your audience as you hope, you will need a carefully crafted argument. Many arguments follow this long-established pattern:

1. Introduce your topic in a way that will interest your readers.
2. State your thesis.
3. Provide an overview of the situation along with any necessary or useful background.
4. Present the reasons that support your thesis or the points that justify it, along with persuasive supporting evidence.
5. Acknowledge opposing points of view, conceding or challenging them as appropriate.
6. Reaffirm your main point.

Argument assignments, like civic and academic exchanges, take many forms. Common types include taking a stand on an issue, proposing a solution to a problem, and evaluating something using specific criteria. The purposes and challenges of these typical arguments are reviewed here.

Taking a Stand

A common argument assignment is to take a stand on a controversy that engages your interest. Taking a stand on an issue will help you understand the controversy and clarify what you believe. Writing of this kind serves a twofold purpose: (1) to state an opinion and (2) to win readers' respect for it. To do so, you must first know exactly where you stand and why. You will need to state what you believe, give reasons with evidence to support your position, enlist readers' trust, respect what your readers are likely to think and feel, and choose strategies to garner their support.

Your major challenge will be gathering enough relevant evidence to support your position. Without that evidence, you'll convince only those who agreed with you in the first place. You also won't persuade readers by ranting, insulting those who disagree with you, or being wishy-washy. Instead, build respect—yours for the views of your readers and theirs for you—by anticipating their objections, showing awareness of alternate views, and presenting evidence that both addresses the concerns of others and strengthens your argument.

TAKING A STAND CHECKLIST

☐ Have you selected an issue or controversy that you know and care about?

☐ Have you settled on your position and identified alternative or opposing views?

☐ Have you identified the main reasons for your view or the main persuasive points that justify it?

☐ Have you gathered enough relevant evidence to support your position?

☐ Have you defined all the critical or potentially ambiguous key terms that you plan to use in your argument?

☐ Have you respectfully anticipated the objections and arguments that your skeptical readers are likely to make?

☐ Have you sustained a suitable tone—that is, a tone neither hostile nor weakly apologetic?

Proposing a Solution

Sometimes when you learn about a problem—climate change, homelessness, or famine, for example—you say to yourself, "Something should be done about that." You can do something constructive yourself by writing powerfully and persuasively. Your purpose in this type of writing, as politicians and advertisers well know, is to rouse your audience to action. That's what Thomas Jefferson and the others who wrote the Declaration of Independence did, and it's what you can do even in your daily life at college. Does some school policy irk you? Do you think students should rally for a cause or an organization? Do you want to encourage members of your college community to volunteer for a worthy effort? You can write a letter to your college newspaper or to someone in authority in order to stir your readers to action.

Your major challenge in a proposal is developing a detailed and convincing solution. Finding problems is much easier than finding solutions. To generate a viable solution, begin with a close analysis of the problem. Try to understand how it might affect different groups of people—conservatives and liberals, parents and children, men and women, for example. Your task is to propose a realistic way to solve or alleviate the problem while addressing readers' concerns about all its aspects.

PROPOSING A SOLUTION CHECKLIST

☐ Have you identified a problem or a condition in need of improvement?

☐ Have you analyzed the problem to determine its impact?

☐ Have you included background information and evidence to substantiate the nature and severity of the problem?

☐ Have you noted any experiences or beliefs that qualify you to recommend a solution to the problem?

☐ Have you proposed a realistic solution to solve the problem in ways that make sense to your audience? Have you supplied logical and persuasive reasons to support your solution?

☐ Have you conveyed the practicality of your solution by estimating the resources and time needed for implementation, outlining step-by-step actions for implementation, and anticipating possible difficulties?

Writing an Evaluation

Evaluating means judging. You evaluate when you decide which candidate gets your vote, pick which digital camera to buy, watch a game and size up a team's prowess, or recommend a new restaurant to your friends. In everyday situations, people often make snap judgments, but writing an evaluation calls for critical thinking. (See Ch. 3.) A written evaluation begins with a specific subject. Then you must decide on criteria, or standards for judging, and apply them to your subject. You inspect the subject carefully and come to a considered opinion based on evidence that backs up your judgment.

In writing an evaluation, your purpose is twofold: (1) to set forth your assessment of the quality of your subject and (2) to convince your readers that your judgment is reasonable. Your major challenge is to make clear to readers your criteria for arriving at your opinion. Identify the features or standards you'll use for evaluating your topic, briefly explain each of them, and then consider what judgment or evaluation the criteria support. Doing so will help you move from an unsubstantiated opinion or a neutral summary to a judgment that you can justify to your readers.

MAKING A JUDGMENT CHECKLIST

☐ Have you selected something to evaluate that deserves thoughtful consideration?

☐ What criteria do you plan to use in making your evaluation? Are they clear and reasonably easy to apply?

☐ Have you reached a clear judgment? Have you supplied evidence to support each of the reasons for your evaluation?

☐ Have you been fair and reasonable? Have you acknowledged the disadvantages or faults of something you champion? Have you acknowledged any virtues of something you condemn?

☐ Have you anticipated and answered any possible objections of your audience?

■ ACTIVITY 10.4: Responding to an Argument with a Group

Working with a small group, exchange the drafts of your argument papers. Ask each reader to identify the writer's thesis and most persuasive evidence and then to present them to the group. Let the group suggest additional logical reasons or points and evidence that might make the argument more compelling.

11

Resources for Integrating Sources

College assignments often require you to find and use sources in your writing. This requirement is generally intended to guide, lead, or tug you into the intellectual exchange that underlies college writing, reading, and thinking. Whether you plan to use only a few sources or to conduct substantial research, you'll need to read, evaluate, and integrate your evidence ethically and effectively. You're probably wondering exactly how to do that. How can you tell if you've found a source of reliable support for your ideas? How can you record useful information so it's easy to integrate in your writing? How can you smoothly add such information as you write? How should you identify where you found the information? This chapter will help you get started answering those questions.

SELECTING SUPPORTING EVIDENCE

The value of every source remains potential until you capture its facts, statistics, expert testimony, examples, or other information in a form that you can incorporate into your paper. In addition, you must accurately credit, both in the text of your paper and in a final list, each source whose words or ideas you use. (Follow the advice of the Modern Language Association or the American Psychological Association, both illustrated here, or whatever other system your instructor requires.) If you add source information skillfully and credit each source conscientiously, your research will probably accomplish its purpose: supporting your thesis so that your paper satisfies you and meets your readers' standards.

Evaluating Sources for Reliable and Appropriate Evidence

When you use evidence from sources to support your points in a college paper, you and your readers are likely to hold two simple expectations:

1. That your sources are reliable so you can trust their information
2. That information you select from them is appropriate for your paper

After all, how could an unreliable source successfully support your ideas? And what could unsuitable or mismatched information contribute to your paper? The difficult task, of course, is learning how to judge what is reliable and appropriate. The following checklist suggests how you can use the time-tested reporter's questions—who, what, where, when, why, and how—to evaluate each print or online source you consider using.

SOURCE EVALUATION CHECKLIST

Who?

☐ Who is the author of the source? What are the author's credentials? What seems to be the author's point of view?

☐ Who is the intended audience of the source? Experts in the field? Professionals? People with a special interest? General readers? How does the tone or evidence appeal to them?

☐ Who publishes the source or sponsors the site? A business? Scholarly organization? Professional association? Government agency? Issue-oriented group? Have you heard of this publisher or sponsor before? Is it well regarded? Does it seem reputable? Does it take an academic or popular approach?

☐ Who reviewed the source before publication? Only the author? Peer reviewers expert in the area? Editorial staff?

What?

☐ What is the purpose of the publication or website? To sell a product or service? To entertain? To supply information? To publish new research? To shape opinion about an issue?

☐ What bias or point of view might affect its reliability?

□ What kind of information does the source supply? Is it a primary source (a firsthand account) or a secondary source (an analysis of primary material)? If it is a secondary source, does it rely on evidence from sound primary sources?

□ What evidence does the source present? Does it seem trust-worthy, sufficient, and relevant given what you know about the subject? Does its argument or analysis seem logical and complete, or does it leave key questions unanswered? Does it identify its sources? If it is online, are any links active and appropriate?

Where?

□ Where did you find the source? Is it a prescreened source available through your campus library? Is it a website that popped up during a general search?

□ Where has the source been recommended? On an instructor's syllabus or web page? On a library list? In another reliable source? During a conference with an instructor or librarian?

When?

□ When was the source published or created?

□ When was the source last revised or updated? Is it current?

Why?

□ Why should you use this source rather than others?

□ Why is information in this source relevant to your topic or research question?

How?

□ How does the selection of evidence in the source reflect the interests and expertise of its author, publisher, sponsor, or audience? How might you need to qualify its use in your paper?

□ How would the source's information add to your paper? How would it support your thesis and provide compelling evidence to persuade your readers?

Reading Your Sources Critically

Size up each source to decide what it covers and what it offers to you. If you can't understand a source because you lack the necessary background, don't use it in your paper. If its ideas, facts, claims, or viewpoints seem unusual, incorporate only what you can substantiate in other unrelated sources. On the other hand, if the source seems enlightening and pertinent, examine it carefully to determine what evidence it might offer in support of your thesis.

Targeting Your Reading.   If you can predict what you'll need from a certain source, focus your reading on finding that information:

- Facts and statistics that substantiate a situation
- Examples that illustrate comparable or possible situations
- Analytical systems that may help you classify or organize
- Similar or contrasting viewpoints or research findings
- Historical events that provide background or suggest trends
- Expert opinions, including reasons, for predicting certain outcomes
- Unexpected views that may make you reconsider assumptions
- Novel solutions that may stimulate your creativity

Reading Actively.   Instead of simply hoping for brilliant insights as you read, try reading actively. This approach can help you search more deeply for reasons and evidence to support your thesis or answer your questions. It can challenge you to think more deeply and creatively about just which answers are possible. Record your own thoughts in a special reading file or notebook so they aren't overwhelmed by your source notes. Try active reading strategies like these:

- Jot down your own notes relating one reading to others or combining ideas from several sources.
- Look for strengths and weaknesses, especially if they challenge your preconceptions.
- Try to figure out what a persuasive writer takes for granted or what a dull writer expresses ineffectively; then reassess the merits of each view.
- Write out your own views, passionately or calmly.
- Sum up the changes in your thinking as you have conducted your research. Where did you begin? Where are you now? How and why have your views changed?

Avoiding Plagiarism in Academic Writing

Discussions of research ethics sometimes reduce that issue to one topic: plagiarism. Plagiarists intentionally present someone else's work as their own—whether they dishonestly submit a paper purchased online, pretend that passages copied from an article are their own writing, appropriate ideas or theories of others without naming their sources, or use someone else's graphics without acknowledgment or permission. Plagiarism, an especially serious offense in college, shows a deep disrespect for the intellectual work of the academic world—analyzing, comparing, interpreting, creating, investigating, and assessing ideas.

Even if you do not intend to plagiarize—to use another writer's words or ideas without appropriately crediting them—a paper full of sloppy or careless shortcuts can look just like a paper deliberately copied from unacknowledged sources. Instead, borrow carefully and honestly, fully crediting the writers from whom you borrow anything. Allow enough time to add information from sources skillfully and correctly. Find out exactly how your instructor expects you to credit sources.

Identify the source of any information, idea, summary, paraphrase, or quotation right away, as soon as you write it in your notes. Carry that acknowledgment into your first draft and all that follow. You generally do not need to identify a source if you use what is called *common knowledge*—quotations, expressions, or information widely known and widely accepted. If you are uncertain about whether you need to cite a source, ask your instructor, or simply provide the citation.

Table 11.1 reviews accepted methods of adding source material and identifies good research practices. These practices will help prevent common errors that may call into question your integrity or your attentiveness as a research writer.

TABLE 11.1   Accepted Methods of Adding and Crediting Source Material

Method and Its Objectives	Good Practices to Avoid Errors
Quotation: Select and identify the exact words of a source in order to capture its vitality, authority, or incisiveness for your paper.	• Fully identify the source. • Provide the page number or other location of the quotation in the source. • Use both opening and closing quotation marks. • Repeat the exact words of the source or properly indicate changes.
Paraphrase: Reword the detailed ideas of a source in your own words and your own sentences, giving credit to the original, in order to capture the content of a passage.	• Read carefully so that you can paraphrase accurately without distorting the source. • Fully identify the source. • Provide the page number or other location of the original passage in the source.

Method and Its Objectives	Good Practices to Avoid Errors
	• Rephrase or add quotation marks to identify words or phrases from the source that creep into your paraphrase. • Apart from brief quotations, use your own words and sentences to avoid following the pattern, sequence, or wording of the original. • Clearly distinguish the paraphrase from your own ideas to avoid confusing switches.
Summary: Very briefly express the main point or key ideas of a source or passage in your own words, giving credit to the original source, in order to capture its essential ideas or conclusion in your paper.	• Read carefully so that you can summarize accurately without distorting the source. • Fully identify the source. • Rephrase or add quotation marks to identify words or phrases from the source that creep into your summary. • Give specific credit to the source for ideas that you add to your discussion. • Clearly distinguish the summary from your own ideas to avoid confusing switches.
In-text citation: Credit each quotation, paraphrase, summary, or reference to a source in short form by giving the author's last name in the text of your paper or in parentheses—adding the page number, date, or other details required by your citation style.	• Supply consistent citations without forgetting or carelessly omitting sources. • Spell names of authors and titles correctly. • Provide accurate page or location references, especially for quotations, paraphrases, or other specific information. • Add any other information such as dates required by your citation style.
Concluding list of works cited or references: Credit each source cited in the text with a corresponding full entry in a list of sources at the end of the paper.	• Provide consistent entries without forgetting or carelessly omitting sources. • Match each source citation in the text with an entry in the final list. • Supply every detail expected in an entry, even if you must go online or to the library to complete your source notes. • Follow the exact sequence, capitalization, punctuation, indentation pattern, and other details required by your citation style. • Check that each entry in your final list appears in the expected alphabetical or numerical order.

Ask yourself the following questions as you consider how to meet college research standards.

RESEARCH ETHICS CHECKLIST

☐ Have you reviewed your school's standards for ethical academic conduct? Do your syllabus and course handouts explain how those standards apply in your class?

☐ Do you have any paper-writing habits, such as procrastination, that might create ethical problems for you? How might you change those habits to avoid problems?

☐ Have you found the section in this book that explains the documentation style you'll use in your paper?

☐ Are you keeping track of the author, title, and publication information for every source you use? (For more advice about identifying sources, see Ch. 12.)

☐ Are you carefully distinguishing your own ideas from those of sources when you record notes or gather material?

☐ Do you need to master or polish research skills—such as quoting, paraphrasing, or summarizing?

☐ Have you recorded contact information so that you can request permission to include any visual materials from sources in your paper?

☐ Have you asked your instructor's advice about any other ethical issues that have come up in the course of your research?

CAPTURING, LAUNCHING, AND CITING SOURCE MATERIAL

Before you pop any source material into your paper, think about the reliability and suitability of the source. If its evidence seems accurate, logical, and relevant, consider exactly how you might want to capture it for your paper—by quoting, paraphrasing, or summarizing.

Quoting Accurately

When an author expresses an idea so memorably that you want to reproduce those words exactly, quote them word for word. Direct quotations can add life, color, and authority to a paper. Quote accurately, including punctuation and capitalization (though APA allows adjusting capitalization of the first word to fit its placement in a sentence). Use an ellipsis mark—three dots (. . .) midsentence or four dots (. . . .) counting the period ending a sentence—to show where you leave out any original wording. (For more on punctuating quotations and using ellipsis marks, see pp. 187–88. For examples of specific formats for quotations, see p. 203 on MLA and pp. 246–47 on APA.)

Select what you quote carefully; leave out wording that doesn't relate to your point, but don't distort the original meaning. For example, if a reviewer calls a movie "a perfect example of poor directing and inept acting," you can't quote this comment as "perfect . . . directing and . . . acting." Limit your direct quotations to compelling selections. A quotation in itself is not necessarily effective evidence, and too many quotations suggest that your writing is padded or lacks original thoughts.

QUOTATION CHECKLIST

☐ Have you limited your quotations to impressive, persuasive passages that might strengthen your paper?

☐ Have you checked the quotation against the original to be sure that it repeats the source word for word?

☐ Have you marked the beginning and the ending of the quotation with quotation marks?

☐ Have you used ellipsis (. . .) marks to indicate where you have left out words in the original?

☐ Have you identified the source of the quotation in a launch statement (see pp. 226–27) or in parentheses?

☐ Have you specified the page number or numbers where the quotation appears in the source?

Paraphrasing Carefully

Paraphrasing involves restating an author's ideas in your own language. A paraphrase is generally about the same length as the original; it expresses the ideas and emphasis of the original using your words and sentences. A sloppy paraphrase—one that sounds too much like the language of the source—will stick out in your paper, resulting in awkward jumps between your style and that of your source. On the other hand, a fresh and creative paraphrase not only avoids plagiarism but also expresses your own style and helps your paper read smoothly.

Be careful to avoid slipping in the author's words or shadowing the original sentence structures too closely. If a source says, "President Wilson called an emergency meeting of his cabinet to discuss the new crisis," and you say, "The president called his cabinet to hold an emergency meeting to discuss the new crisis," your words are too close to those of the source. One option is to quote the original, though it doesn't seem worth quoting word for word in this case. Or, better, you could write: "Summoning the full cabinet to an urgent session, Wilson laid out the challenge before them."

PARAPHRASE CHECKLIST

☐ Have you read the passage critically to be sure that you fully understand it?

☐ Have you paraphrased accurately, reflecting both the main points and the supporting details in the original?

☐ Does your paraphrase use your own words without repeating or echoing the words or sentence structure of the original?

☐ Does your paraphrase stick to the ideas of the original without tucking in your own thoughts?

☐ Have you reread and revised your paraphrase so that it reads smoothly and clearly?

☐ Have you identified the source of the paraphrase in a launch statement (see pp. 226–27) or in parentheses?

☐ Have you specified the page number or numbers where the passage appears in the source?

Summarizing Fairly

Summarizing is a useful way of incorporating the general point of a whole paragraph or section of a work. You briefly state the main sense of the original in your own words and tell where you got the idea. A summary is generally much shorter than the original; it expresses only the most important ideas—the essence—of the original. In your text, a summary can efficiently present a key idea from a source; a pair of summaries can simplify comparing, contrasting, merging, or synthesizing central ideas from two different sources.

SUMMARY CHECKLIST

☐ Have you fairly stated the author's thesis or main point in your own words in a sentence or two?

☐ Have you briefly stated any supporting ideas that you want to summarize?

☐ Have you stuck to the overall point without getting bogged down in details or examples?

☐ Has your summary remained respectful of the ideas and opinions of others, even if you disagree with them?

☐ Have you revised so your summary is smooth and clear?

☐ Have you identified the source of the summary in a launch statement (see pp. 226–27) or in parentheses?

☐ Have you specified the page number or numbers where any specific passage appears in the source?

SAMPLE QUOTATIONS, PARAPHRASE, AND SUMMARY

Passage from Original Source

Obesity is a major issue because (1) vast numbers of people are affected; (2) the prevalence is growing; (3) rates are increasing in children; (4) the medical, psychological, and social effects are severe; (5) the behaviors that cause it (poor diet and inactivity) are themselves major contributors to ill health; and (6) treatment is expensive, rarely effective, and impractical to use on a large scale.

Biology and environment conspire to promote obesity. Biology is an enabling factor, but the obesity epidemic, and the consequent human tragedy, is a function of the worsening food and physical activity environment. Governments and societies have come to this conclusion very late. There is much catching up to do.

Sample Quotations from Second Paragraph

Although human biology has contributed to the pudgy American society, everyone now faces the powerful challenge of a "worsening food and physical activity environment" (Brownell and Horgen 51).

As Brownell and Horgen conclude, "There is much catching up to do" (51).

Sample Paraphrase of First Paragraph

The current concern with increasing American weight has developed for half a dozen reasons, according to Brownell and Horgen. They attribute the shift in awareness to the number of obese people and the increase in this number, especially among youngsters. In addition, excess weight carries harsh consequences for individual physical and mental health and for society's welfare. Lack of exercise and unhealthy food choices worsen the health consequences, especially because there's no cheap and easy cure for the effects of eating too much and exercising too little (51).

Sample Summary

After outlining six reasons why obesity is a critical issue, Brownell and Horgen urge Americans to eat less and become more active (51).

Works Cited Entry (MLA Style)

Brownell, Kelly D., and Katherine Battle Horgen. *Food Fight: The Inside Story of the Food Industry, America's Obesity Crisis, and What We Can Do about It.* Chicago: Contemporary-McGraw, 2004. Print.

Developing an Annotated Bibliography

An annotated bibliography is a list of your sources—read to date or credited in your final paper—that includes a short summary or annotation for each entry. This common assignment quickly informs a reader about the direction of your research. It also shows your mastery of two major research skills: identifying a source and writing a summary.

To develop an annotated bibliography, find out which format you are expected to use to identify sources and what your annotations should do—summarize only, add evaluation, or meet a special requirement (such as interpretation). A summary is a brief, neutral explanation in your own words of the source's thesis or main points. In contrast, an evaluation is a judgment of the source's accuracy, reliability, or relevance.

Using Summary with Source Identification and Proposed Use.   Several drafts of Schyler Martin's annotated bibliography were due as he identified possible sources for his MLA-style essay, "Does Education Improve Social Ills in Native American Communities?" He identified each source as primary (a firsthand or eyewitness account) or secondary (a secondhand analysis based on primary material), summarized it, and described how he expected it to support his position.

> Loew, Patty. *Indian Nations of Wisconsin: Histories of Endurance and Renewal.* Madison: Wisconsin Historical Society Press, 2001. Print.
>
> > Secondary source. Professor Loew, a member of the Ojibwe tribe, presents Wisconsin history from a Native point of view. I will be using Loew's interviews to support my claims of education changing lives.
>
> Wildcat, Daniel R. "Practical Professional Indigenous Education." *Power and Place: Indian Education in America.* Comp. Vine Deloria, Jr., and Daniel R. Wildcat. Golden: Fulcrum, 2001. 113–21. Print.
>
> > Secondary source. This book compares and contrasts the "Western" idea of education with Native American beliefs, showing where the "holes" are in today's educational policies. I will use Wildcat's chapter to demonstrate the argument of education only being useful when it is applied.

For her history paper, Shari O'Malley summed up relevance:

> Goodman, Phil. "Patriotic Femininity: Women's Morals and Men's Morale During the Second World War." *Gender & History* 10.2 (1998): 278–93. Print. Goodman examines British attitudes about women replacing men in the workplace and related wartime issues.

Using Summary with Evaluation. When Stephanie Hawkins prepared her APA-style paper "Japanese: Linguistic Diversity" for an independent study, she added an annotated bibliography summarizing her sources and evaluating their contributions, relationships, or usefulness to her study.

> Abe, H. (1995). From stereotype to context: The study of Japanese women's language. *Feminist Studies* 21(3), 647–671.
>
> > Abe discusses the roots of Japanese women's language, beginning in ancient Japan and continuing into modern times. I was able to use this peer-reviewed source to expand on the format of women's language and the consequences of its use.

Kristof, N. (1995, September 24). On language: Too polite for words. *New York Times Magazine*, pp. SM22–SM23.

> Kristof, a regular columnist for the *New York Times Magazine*, briefly describes the use of honorifics as an outlet for sarcasm and insults. Although the article discusses cultures other than Japanese, it provides insight into the polite vulgarity of the Japanese language.

■ ACTIVITY 11.1: Annotating a Source

Select one of your sources (or a reading for another class), and write a few sentences to describe what the source covers and why it is relevant to your project. If your instructor has specified a particular approach, tailor your annotation to follow those directions. Exchange annotation drafts with a classmate or small group, and discuss ways to clarify contents or relevance.

Launching Each Quotation, Paraphrase, and Summary

Instead of dropping ideas from sources into your paper as if they had just arrived by flying saucer, weave them in so that they effectively support the point you want to make. Launch each quotation, paraphrase, summary, or other reference to a source with an introduction that tells readers who wrote it or why it's in your paper. College instructors tend to favor launch statements that comment on the source, establish its authority, connect it to the paper's thesis, or relate it to other sources. Use strategies such as these, illustrated in MLA style, to vary your statements and add emphasis.

- Name the author in the sentence that introduces the source:

  As Wood explains, the goal of American education continues to fluctuate between gaining knowledge and applying it (58).

- Add the author's name in the middle of the source material:

  In *Romeo and Juliet*, "That which we call a rose," Shakespeare claims, "By any other word would smell as sweet" (2.2.43–44).

- Name the author only in the parenthetical source citation if you want to keep your focus on the topic:

  A second march on Washington followed the first (Whitlock 83).

- Mention the professional title, affiliation, or experience of an author or person you've interviewed to add authority or credibility.

- Tell readers why you have selected and included the material.
- Interpret what you see as the point or relevance of the material.
- Relate the source clearly to the paper's thesis or to the specific point it supports.
- Compare or contrast the point of view or evidence of one source with that of another source.
- Supply transitions to connect several sources mentioned in a sentence or paragraph.
- Vary your introductory language (*says, claims, observes, emphasizes, documents, implies, reports, studies, analyzes, interprets*) to portray the contribution of the source accurately.
- Lead smoothly from your launch statement into the source material instead of tossing a stand-alone quotation into your paragraph without any introduction.

Citing Each Source Accurately

Identify the source of your material following whatever style you are using. Although MLA and APA styles have their own conventions (see pp. 228–42 on MLA style and pp. 242–54 on APA style), both expect you to accomplish the following things:

- Acknowledge all material from a source—words directly quoted, information or opinions recast in your own words, summaries of ideas or theories, references to research studies and findings, specific reasons or examples, and anything else drawn from that source.
- Identify the source material at the exact point where you add it to your text, generally by identifying the author (in MLA style) or the author and year of publication (in APA style) in parentheses (unless already identified in your launch statement).
- Begin the citation with the first words of the title if a source does not identify an individual or group author.
- Add the page number (or another specific location) for each quotation or paraphrase so that a reader could easily locate the original passage.
- Link the short identification of each source in your paper—supplied in your text wording or in parentheses—to the full description of your sources in a list of works cited or reference list at the end of your paper.
- Follow the conventional patterns for identifying sources, supplying the same details in the same order with the same capitalization and punctuation.

12

Resources for
Crediting Sources

The following sections explain how to cite a source in the text and how to list it at the end of a paper in MLA style or APA style. The core of each source entry is the author's name, recorded first in both styles. Next, the type of source determines the pattern you should follow in the rest of the full entry identifying the source. To help you focus on the information needed to credit your sources, both the MLA and APA sections are organized around two questions: Who wrote it? What type of source is it?

CITING AND LISTING SOURCES IN MLA STYLE

In MLA style (the format recommended by the Modern Language Association and often required in English classes), your sources need to be identified twice in your paper: first, briefly, in the text where you draw upon the source material and later, in full, at the end of your paper. The short citation includes the name of the author of the source (or a short form of the title if the source does not name an author) so that a reader can easily connect the short entry in your text with the related full entry in the final alphabetical list. Because instructors expect source references to be formatted carefully, follow the style guidelines and any special directions supplied by your instructor. For more extensive advice, turn to the *MLA Handbook for Writers of Research Papers* (7th ed.; New York: MLA, 2009), usually available in your campus bookstore and library.

MLA DIRECTORY

Citing Sources in Your Text

Right in the text, at the precise point where you insert a quotation, a paraphrase, or a summary, you need to identify the source. Your citation often follows a simple pattern: name the author, and note the page or pages in the original where the material is located.

(Last Name of Author ##)   (Talia 35)   (Smitt and Gilbert 152–53)

This basic form applies whatever the type of source—article, book, or web page—though your purposes as a writer, the nature of the material, and the type of source will influence exactly how you integrate a citation into your discussion. (See the checklist on p. 233.) Keep in mind the two key questions: Who wrote it? What type of source is it?

Who Wrote It?

The core of an MLA citation is the author of the source. Crediting that author is part of your ethical obligation as a researcher and a writer. Whether you decide to integrate the author's name into your discussion or cite it in parentheses will vary with your purpose as a writer and the type of material or source you have used.

INDIVIDUAL AUTHOR NOT NAMED IN SENTENCE

Place this citation immediately after a direct quotation or paraphrase.

When "The Lottery" begins, the reader thinks of the "great pile of stones" (Jackson 191) as children's entertainment.

INDIVIDUAL AUTHOR NAMED IN SENTENCE

When the author is named in your launch statement, the citation can be even simpler.

According to Hunt, the city faced "deficits and drought" (54) for ten more years.

TWO OR THREE AUTHORS

Include each author's last name either in your text or in the citation.

> Taylor and Wheeler present yet another view (25).

FOUR OR MORE AUTHORS

Give the names of all the authors, or use only the last name of the first author listed, followed by the abbreviation *et al.* (Latin for "and others"). Present the source the same way in your list of works cited (see p. 234).

> In the years between 1870 and 1900, the nation's cities grew at an astonishing rate (Roark et al. 671).

UNIDENTIFIED AUTHOR

For a source with an unknown author, use the complete title in your sentence or the first main word or two of the title in parentheses. If a source is sponsored by a corporation or other group, name the sponsor as the author.

> Due to download codes and vinyl's beauty, album sales are up ("Back to Black" 1).

What Type of Source Is It?

Because naming the author is the core of your citation, the basic form applies to any type of source though a few types present complications.

MULTIVOLUME WORK

For a work with multiple volumes, provide the author's name and the volume number, followed by a colon and the page number.

> In ancient times, astrological predictions were sometimes used as a kind of black magic (Sarton 2: 319).

INDIRECT SOURCE

If possible, cite the original source. If that source is not available (as often happens with published accounts of spoken remarks), use the abbreviation *qtd. in* (for "quoted in") before citing the secondary source.

> Zill says that, psychologically, children in stepfamilies most resemble children in single-parent families, even if they live in a two-parent household (qtd. in Derber 119).

NOVEL OR SHORT STORY

Give the page number from your own copy first. If possible, add the section or chapter where the passage could be found in any edition.

> In *A Tale of Two Cities,* Dickens describes the aptly named Stryver as "shouldering himself (morally and physically) into companies and conversations" (110; bk. 2, ch. 4).

PLAY

For a verse play, list the act, scene, and line numbers, separated by periods.

> "Love," Iago says, "is merely a lust of the blood and a permission of the will" (*Oth.* 1.3.326).

POETRY

When quoting poetry, add a slash mark to show where each new line begins. Use the word *line* or *lines* in the first reference but only numbers in subsequent references, as in these examples from William Wordsworth's "The World Is Too Much with Us." Here is the first reference:

> "The world is too much with us; late and soon / Getting and spending, we lay waste our powers" (lines 1–2).

Here is the subsequent reference:

> "Or hear old Triton blow his wreathed horn" (14).

If a poem has multiple parts, cite the part and line numbers, separated by a period. Do not include the word *line*.

> In "Ode: Intimations of Immortality," Wordsworth ponders the truths of human existence, "Which we are toiling all our lives to find, / In darkness lost, the darkness of the grave" (8.116–17).

WORK IN AN ANTHOLOGY

For works in an anthology, cite the author of the selection—not the editor of the collection. (See p. 238 for entries for Tan's essay in Martin's anthology.)

> Amy Tan explains the "Englishes" of her childhood and family (32).

LONG QUOTATION

When a quotation is longer than four typed lines, indent the entire quotation one inch, or ten spaces. Double-space it, but don't place quotation marks around it. If the quotation is one paragraph or less, begin the first line without any extra paragraph indentation. Use ellipsis marks (. . .) to show where you omit anything from the middle of the quotation. Place your citation in parentheses after the punctuation that ends the quotation.

> Cynthia Griffin Wolff comments on Emily Dickinson's incisive use of language:
>
> Language, of course, was a far subtler weapon than a hammer. Dickinson's verbal maneuvers would increasingly reveal immense skill in avoiding a frontal attack; she preferred the silent knife of irony to the strident battering of loud complaint. . . . Scarcely submissive, she had acquired the cool calculation of an assassin. (170–71)

MLA CITATION CHECKLIST

☐ Have you double-checked to be sure that you have acknowledged all material from a source?

☐ Have you placed your citation right after your quotation, paraphrase, summary, or other reference to the source?

☐ Have you identified the author of each source in your text or in parentheses?

☐ Have you used the first few words of the title to cite a work without an identified author?

☐ Have you noted a page number or other specific location whenever needed?

☐ Have you added any necessary extras, whether volume numbers or poetry lines?

☐ Have you checked your final draft to be sure that every source cited in your text also appears in your list of works cited?

Listing Sources at the End

On a new page at the end of your paper, add a double-spaced list of your sources called Works Cited. For each source mentioned in the text, supply a corresponding full entry here. Arrange the entries alphabetically by author's last name or, for works with no author, by title. Indent lines after the first one-half inch. (Use your software to set this "hanging" indentation.)

The secret to figuring out what to include in a Works Cited entry generally comes down to two questions about your source: Who wrote it? What is it? Once you identify the number and type of authors plus the type of source you have used, look for a general pattern for the entry in this book or in the MLA style guide. Then examine the title page or other parts of your source to find the details needed to complete the pattern. Also add the medium of publication: Print, Web, Television, CD, PDF file, and so forth. Using the following examples as guides, supply the same details in the same order with the same punctuation and other features. (See the checklist on p. 242.)

Who Wrote It?

INDIVIDUAL AUTHOR

Finkel, David. *Thank You for Your Service.* New York: Farrar, 2013. Print.

TWO OR THREE AUTHORS

Name the authors in the order in which they are listed on the title page.

Steil, Benn, and Manuel Hinds. *Money, Markets, and Sovereignty.* New Haven: Yale UP, 2009. Print.

FOUR OR MORE AUTHORS

Name all the authors, or follow the name of the first author with the abbreviation *et al.* (Latin for "and others"). Identify the source in the same way you cite it in the text.

Roark, James L., et al. *The American Promise.* 5th ed. Boston: Bedford, 2012. Print.

SAME AUTHOR WITH MULTIPLE WORKS

Arrange the author's works alphabetically by title. Use the author's name for the first entry only, then replace the name with three hyphens.

Gould, Stephen Jay. *Dinosaur in a Haystack: Reflections in Natural History.* Cambridge: Belknap-Harvard UP, 2011. PDF file.

---. *Punctuated Equilibrium.* Cambridge: Belknap-Harvard UP, 2007. Print.

ORGANIZATION AUTHOR

Name the organization as author, omitting any initial article ("a," "an," or "the"). (The name may reappear as the publisher.)

> Canadian Standards Association. *Manufactured Homes.* Mississauga: Canadian
>> Standards Assn., 2009. Print.

UNIDENTIFIED AUTHOR

> "2014 Cars: Safety." *Consumer Reports* Apr. 2014: 79–83. Print.

What Type of Source Is It?

Once you have found the format that fits the author, look for the type of source and the specific entry that best matches yours. Mix and match the patterns shown here as needed.

Article in a Printed or Electronic Periodical

ARTICLE FROM A PRINTED JOURNAL

Provide the volume number, issue number, year, page numbers, and medium for all journals.

> McHaney, Pearl Amelia. "Eudora Welty (1909–2001)." *South Atlantic Review*
>> 66.4 (2001): 134–36. Print.

ARTICLE FROM AN ONLINE JOURNAL

Supply the information you would for a printed article, using "n. pag." if the source does not provide page numbers. End with the medium and your access date.

> Purdy, James P., and Joyce R. Walker. "Digital Breadcrumbs: Case Studies of
>> Online Research." *Kairos* 11.2 (2007): n. pag. Web. 29 May 2014.

**ARTICLE ACCESSED ONLINE THROUGH A LIBRARY
OR SUBSCRIPTION DATABASE**

If you find a source through a library subscription service, include the name of the service, the medium, and your access date.

> Vanacore, Andrew. "Free TV Could Get Its Curtain Call." *Boston Globe* 30 Dec.
>> 2009: B1. *Newsbank: America's Newspapers.* Web. 1 Mar. 2013.

ARTICLE FROM A PRINTED MAGAZINE

Give the month and year of the issue, or its specific date, after the title of the magazine. If the article's pages are not consecutive, add a + (plus sign) after the initial page.

> Jenkins, Lee. "He's Gotta Play Hurt." *Sports Illustrated* 26 Oct. 2009: 42–43.
>   Print.
>
> "Reinventing College." *Time* 29 Oct. 2012: 31+. Print.

ARTICLE FROM AN ONLINE MAGAZINE

> Epps, Garrett. "Is There a Right to Lie in Politics?" *TheAtlantic.com*. Atlantic
>   Monthly Group, 16 June 2014. Web. 18 June 2014.

ARTICLE FROM A PRINTED NEWSPAPER

If the newspaper has different editions, indicate the one where the article can be found. If the pages for the article are not consecutive, add a + after its initial page.

> Ostrow, Joanne. "Horrors!" *Denver Post* 11 May 2014: E2+. Print.

ARTICLE FROM AN ONLINE NEWSPAPER

> Cave, Damien. "Long Border, Endless Struggle." *New York Times*. New York
>   Times, 3 Mar. 2013, late ed. Web. 10 Mar. 2013.

EDITORIAL FROM A PRINTED PERIODICAL

> McGrath, Neal. "Concussion Care for Student-Athletes." Editorial. *Boston
>   Globe* 30 Dec. 2009, Opinion sec.: 17. Print.
> "Taking the Initiatives." Editorial. *Nation* 13 Nov. 2000: 3–4. Print.

EDITORIAL FROM AN ONLINE PERIODICAL

> Duncan, Arne. "Investing in Students, Not the Banks." Editorial. *Washington
>   Post*. Washington Post, 26 Feb. 2010. Web. 1 Mar. 2014.

LETTER TO THE EDITOR

> Ryan, Beth. Letter. *Smithsonian* Sept. 2012: 12. Print.

REVIEW

Include "Rev. of " before the title of the work reviewed.

> Coukell, Allan. "The Cell That Wouldn't Die." Rev. of *Culturing Life: How Cells Became Technologies*, by Hannah Landecker. *Discover* Feb. 2007: 68. Print.

Printed or Electronic Book

PRINTED BOOK

> Wrangham, Richard W. *Catching Fire: How Cooking Made Us Human*. New York: Basic, 2009. Print.

ONLINE BOOK

For an online book, supply what you would for a printed book. Then add the name of the site (italicized), the medium of publication, and your access date.

> Wharton, Edith. *The Age of Innocence*. New York: Appleton, 1920. *Bartleby.com: Great Books Online*. Web. 16 June 2014.

E-BOOK

> Quammen, David. *Spillover: Animal Infections and the Next Pandemic*. New York: Norton, 2012. Nook file.

MULTIVOLUME WORK

To cite the full work, include the number of volumes ("vols.") after the title.

> *Who Built America? Working People and the Nation's Economy, Politics, Culture, and Society*. 2 vols. New York: Worth, 2000. Print.

To cite only one volume, give its number after the title. If you wish, you then can add the total number of volumes after the medium.

> *Who Built America? Working People and the Nation's Economy, Politics, Culture, and Society*. Vol. 1. New York: Worth, 2000. Print. 2 vols.

ESSAY, SHORT STORY, OR POEM FROM AN EDITED COLLECTION

> Cash, Johnny. "Folsom Prison Blues." *Good Poems, American Places.* Ed.
> Garrison Keillor. New York: Viking-Penguin, 2011. 24. Print.

TWO OR MORE WORKS FROM THE SAME EDITED COLLECTION

If you list more than one selection from an anthology, prepare an entry for the collection (instead of repeating it for each selection). Then simply refer to it from the entries for the separate readings.

> Cisneros, Sandra. "Only Daughter." Martin 10–13.
>
> Martin, Wendy, ed. *The Beacon Book of Essays by Contemporary American Women.* Boston: Beacon, 1996. Print.
>
> Tan, Amy. "Mother Tongue." Martin 32–37.

SELECTION FROM AN ONLINE BOOK

> Webster, Augusta. "Not Love." *A Book of Rhyme.* London, 1881. *Victorian Women Writers Project.* Web. 16 June 2014.

ARTICLE FROM A PRINTED REFERENCE WORK

It is not necessary to supply the editor, publisher, or place of publication for well-known references. No volume and page numbers are needed when a reference book is organized alphabetically. If an article's author is identified by initials, check the book's list of contributors, which should supply the full name.

> Raymer, John D., and Margarita Nieto. "Octavio Paz." *Notable Latino Writers.* Pasadena: Salem, 2006. Print.

ARTICLE FROM AN ONLINE REFERENCE WORK

> "'Hansel and Gretel' by the Brothers Grimm." *Encyclopedia Mythica.* 2004. Web. 1 Mar. 2014.

Other Printed or Electronic Document

PRINTED GOVERNMENT DOCUMENT

If the document names an author or editor, that name may be provided either before the title or after it, if you identify the agency as author.

United States. Census Bureau. *Statistical Abstract of the United States: 2012.*
131st ed. Washington: GPO, 2011. Print.

ONLINE GOVERNMENT DOCUMENT

United States. National Institutes of Health. "Protect Your Tendons." *NIH
News in Health.* NIH, June 2014. Web. 18 June 2014.

ONLINE DOCUMENT

Carter, Jimmy. "Inaugural Address of Jimmy Carter." 20 Jan. 1977. *The
Avalon Project.* Yale Law School. Web. 20 Mar. 2014.

Internet or Electronic Source

See the directory on pp. 235–38 for entries for other electronic sources,
including books and articles.

PERSONAL WEB PAGE

If no title is available, include an identification such as "Home page."

Tannen, Deborah. Home page. Georgetown U and Deborah Tannen, 2009.
Web. 10 Mar. 2014.

ORGANIZATION WEB PAGE

"Library Statistics." *American Library Association.* Amer. Lib. Assn., 2012.
Web. 17 June 2014.

HOME PAGE FOR A CAMPUS DEPARTMENT OR COURSE

CSUN Department of Communication Studies. CSUN, n.d. Web. 16 June 2014.

BLOG OR BLOG ENTRY

To cite a blog entry, give the title of the entry in quotation marks. If a
blog comment does not have a title, use a label such as "Blog comment."
If there is no apparent sponsor of the blog you are citing, use "N.p." for
no publisher.

Knight, Christopher. "The Watts Towers' Perpetual State of Crisis." *Culture
Monster.* Los Angeles Times, 28 May 2010. Web. 29 May 2010.
Wray, William. Blog comment. *Culture Monster.* Los Angeles Times, 28 May
2010. Web. 29 May 2010.

Visual or Audio Source

ADVERTISEMENT

Invest in Better Futures. Advertisement. *Time* 3 Mar. 2014: 25. Print.

COMIC OR CARTOON

Supply the cartoonist's name, and identify the work as a comic strip or cartoon.

Adams, Scott. "Dilbert." Comic strip. *Denver Post* 17 June 2014: 11B. Print.

PHOTOGRAPH OR WORK OF ART

Supply the place (museum or gallery and city) where the item is housed. If you are citing it from a publication, identify that source. For a family or personal photograph, identify who took the photograph and when.

Stieglitz, Alfred. *Self-Portrait*. J. Paul Getty Museum, Los Angeles. *Stieglitz:*
    A Beginning Light. By Katherine Hoffman. New Haven: Yale UP, 2004,
    251. Print.
Black Forest. Personal photograph by author. 6 Aug. 2013. JPEG file.

AUDIOTAPE OR RECORDING

Begin with the name of the artist, composer, speaker, writer, or other contributor, based on your interest in the recording. Include the medium using a designation such as "Audiocassette," "CD," or "LP."

Byrne, Gabriel. *The James Joyce Collection*. Dove Audio, 1996. Audiocassette.

PROGRAM ON TELEVISION OR RADIO

"TB Silent Killer." *Frontline*. PBS. WGBH, Boston, 25 Mar. 2014. Television.
"Can Detroit Be Saved?" *Weekend Edition*. Natl. Public Radio. KCFR, Denver,
    2 Mar. 2013. Radio.

FILM

Start with the title unless you want to emphasize the work of a person connected with the film.

True Grit. Dir. Ethan Coen and Joel Coen. Perf. Jeff Bridges and Hailee
    Steinfeld. Paramount, 2010. Film.
Coen, Ethan, and Joel Coen, dir. *True Grit*. Paramount, 2010. Film.

PERFORMANCE

> *Sense and Sensibility: The Musical.* Lyrics by Jeffrey Haddow. Dir. Marcia
> Milgram Dodge. Denver Center Theatre Company, Denver. 5 Apr. 2013.
> Performance.

Conversation or Field Artifact

PERSONAL, TELEPHONE, OR E-MAIL INTERVIEW

Indicate whether you conducted the interview in person, by telephone,
or by e-mail.

> Santos, Cece. Personal interview. 5 Feb. 2014.

BROADCAST INTERVIEW

Identify the source by the person interviewed; if you want, you may
also identify the interviewer ("Interview by X") or the URL to locate a
podcast.

> Schatz, Amy. "Net Neutrality: Who's in Charge of the Internet?" Interview by
> Terry Gross. *Fresh Air.* Natl. Public Radio. KCFR, Denver. 25 May 2010.
> Radio.

PUBLISHED INTERVIEW

> Kerry, John. Interview. *Newsweek* 8 Mar. 2004: 26. Print.

E-MAIL

Use the subject line as a title to identify the message, or describe it as
shown below.

> Moore, Jack. Message to the author. 11 May 2014. E-mail.

ONLINE POSTING

Use the subject line as the title. Use the label "Online posting" if the posting has no title.

> Robinson, Meena. "Mansfield Park." *PBS Discussions.* PBS, 28 Jan. 2008. Web.
> 18 May 2008.

MLA WORKS CITED CHECKLIST

☐ Have you begun each entry with the correct pattern for the author's name?

☐ Have you figured out what type of source you've used? Have you followed the sample pattern for that type as closely as possible?

☐ Have you used quotation marks and italics correctly for titles?

☐ Have you used the conventional punctuation—periods, commas, colons, parentheses—in each entry?

☐ Have you accurately recorded the name of the author, title, publisher, and so on?

☐ Have you checked the accuracy of the numbers in your entry—pages, volume, and dates?

☐ Have you correctly identified the medium of publication or reception, using a label such as Print, Web, CD, DVD, Film, Lecture, Performance, Radio, Television, or E-mail?

☐ Have you checked any entry from a citation management system as carefully as your own entries?

☐ Have you arranged your entries in alphabetical order?

☐ Have you checked your final list against your text citations to be sure that every source appears in both places?

☐ Have you double-spaced your list, like the rest of your paper, and allowed a one-inch margin on all sides?

☐ Have you begun the first line of each entry at the left margin and indented each additional line one-half inch? (Check your software for a "hanging" indentation option, usually in the Format/Paragraph Indentation-Special menu.)

CITING AND LISTING SOURCES IN APA STYLE

In APA style (the format recommended by the American Psychological Association and often required in courses in the social sciences), your sources are identified twice: first, briefly noting the author and the date as you refer to the source and later identifying the source in full in an alphabetical list of references at the end of your paper. As you use this style, keep in mind the two key questions: Who wrote it? What type of source is it? For more detailed advice, turn to the *Publication Manual of the American Psychological Association* (6th ed.; Washington, DC: APA, 2010), usually available in your campus bookstore and library.

APA DIRECTORY

CITING SOURCES IN YOUR TEXT

LISTING SOURCES AT THE END

Citing Sources in Your Text

The core of an APA citation is the author of the source. That person's last name links your use of the source in your paper with its full description in your list of references. Next comes the date of the source, which often establishes its currency or its classic status for readers. A common addition is a specific location, such as a page number (using "p." for "page" or "pp." for "pages"), that locates the material in the original source. Unless the source lacks page numbers or other locators, this information is required for quotations and recommended for paraphrases and key concepts. When you supply these elements in parentheses, separate them with commas: (Westin, 2013, p. 48). This basic form applies whatever the source—article, book, or web page. (See also p. 247.)

Who Wrote It?

Naming the author of a source is part of your ethical obligation as a researcher. As a writer, however, you can decide whether to tuck that name away in parentheses or to emphasize it in your discussion.

INDIVIDUAL AUTHOR NOT NAMED IN SENTENCE

Finding lying without other pathologies is unlikely (Healy, 2008, p. 11).

INDIVIDUAL AUTHOR NAMED IN SENTENCE

As Healy (2008) notes, other pathologies typically accompany lying (p. 11).

TWO AUTHORS

List the last names of coauthors in the order in which they appear in the source. Join the names with "and" if you mention them in your text and with an ampersand (&) if the citation is in parentheses.

Legal professionals may fear that psychologists' testimony will unfairly influence juries (Fulero & Wrightsman, 2009, p. 18).

In *Forensic Psychology*, Fulero and Wrightsman (2009) note that attorneys remain wary of influential testimony by psychologists (p. 18).

THREE OR MORE AUTHORS

For three to five authors, include all the last names in your first reference. In any later references, identify only the first author and add *et al.*

(for "and others"), whether in the text or in parentheses. For six authors or more, simply use the name of the first author with *et al.* for all citations.

> Learning disabilities occur with each other, with emotional or attention disorders, or with social deficits (Fletcher, Lyon, Fuchs, & Barnes, 2006, p. 9). Fletcher et al. characterize this likelihood as "co-morbidity" (p. 9).

ORGANIZATION AUTHOR

> Important as nutrition is for healthy people, it is even more critical for cancer patients who may have specific dietary requirements such as the need for more protein (American Cancer Society, 2003, p. 7).

UNIDENTIFIED AUTHOR

When you don't know the author of a work, identify the source with a short title, beginning with the first few main words so it is easy to locate in your alphabetical list of references.

> Parents need to monitor their child's online activities ("Social Networking," 2012).

SAME AUTHOR WITH MULTIPLE WORKS

> Five significant trends in parent-school relations have evolved (Grimley, 2012) since the original multistate study (Grimley, 1987).

DIFFERENT AUTHORS WITH MULTIPLE WORKS

Within a single citation, list the authors of multiple works in alphabetical order (as in your reference list). Separate the works with semicolons.

> Several studies were designed to determine reasons for minority underperformance in educational attainment (Bowen & Bok, 1998; Charles, Dinwiddie, & Massey, 2004; Glazer, 1997).

What Type of Source Is It?

Naming the author and adding the date are the essentials of the APA citation, but a few types of sources may present complications.

INDIRECT SOURCE

If possible, locate and cite the original source. Otherwise, begin your citation with "as cited in," and then name your source.

> According to Claude Fischer, the belief in individualism favors "the individual over the group or institution" (as cited in Hansen, 2005, p. 5).

GOVERNMENT OR ORGANIZATION DOCUMENT

If no specific author is identified, treat the sponsoring agency as the author, and give its full name in the first citation in your text. If the name is complicated or commonly shortened, you may add an abbreviation in brackets. In later citations, use just the abbreviation and the date.

> The *2005 National Gang Threat Assessment* (National Alliance of Gang Investigators Associations [NAGIA], 2005, pp. vii–viii) identified regional trends that may help account for the city's recent gang violence.

Here is the next citation: (NAGIA, 2005)

PERSONAL COMMUNICATION

Personal communications—such as face-to-face interviews, letters, telephone conversations, memos, and e-mail—are not included in the reference list because your readers would not be able to find and use the originals. In the text of your paper, name your source, identify it as a personal communication, and supply the date of the communication.

> J. T. Moore (personal communication, November 10, 2013) has made specific suggestions for stimulating the local economy.

LONG QUOTATION

If you quote forty words or more, indent the quotation one-half inch and double-space it instead of using quotation marks. After it, add your citation with no additional period, including whatever information you have not already mentioned in your launch statement. The next example shows how Emily Lavery presented one of her sources in "A New Time: Female Education and Teachers in Western Territories" about education during the mid-1800s.

> Emma Willard and Catharine Beecher fought for female educational opportunities, such as a more inclusive curriculum and higher educational

opportunities. In 1848, Elizabeth Cady Stanton published the "Declaration of Sentiments" at the Seneca Falls Convention to address and rectify the wrongs done to women, including this resolution:

> That the speedy success of our cause depends upon the zealous and untiring efforts of both men and women, for the overthrow of the monopoly of the pulpit, and for securing to woman an equal participation with men in the various trades, professions, and commerce. (p. 73)

APA CITATION CHECKLIST

- ☐ Have you double-checked to be sure that you have acknowledged all material from a source?
- ☐ Have you placed your citation right after your quotation or reference to the source?
- ☐ Have you identified the author of each source in your text or in parentheses?
- ☐ Have you used the first few main words of the title to cite a work without an identified author?
- ☐ Have you noted the date (or added "n.d." for "no date") for each source?
- ☐ Have you added a page number or other location wherever needed?
- ☐ Have you checked your final draft to be sure that every source cited in your text also appears in your list of references?

Listing Sources at the End

In APA style, your list of sources appears at the end of your paper. Begin a new page with the title References centered. Double-space your list, and organize it alphabetically by authors' last names (or by titles for works without an identified author). If you need to list several works by the same author, arrange these by date, moving from earliest to most recent. (See the checklist on pp. 253–54.)

As you prepare your entries, begin with the last name and initials of the author. The various author formats apply whatever your source—

article, book, web page, or other material. Then find the type of source you have used in this section, and follow its pattern in your entry. Keep in mind these two key questions that are used to organize the sample entries that follow: Who wrote it? What type of source is it?

Who Wrote It?

INDIVIDUAL AUTHOR

O'Reilly, B. (2006). *Culture warrior.* New York, NY: Broadway Books.

TWO AUTHORS

Boggs, C., & Pollard, T. (2007). *The Hollywood war machine: U.S. militarism and popular culture.* Boulder, CO: Paradigm.

THREE OR MORE AUTHORS

Provide names for three to six authors; for seven or more, simply use *et al.* instead of adding more names.

Schiller, B., Hill, C., & Wall, S. (2012). *The economy today.* New York, NY: McGraw-Hill.

SAME AUTHOR WITH MULTIPLE WORKS

Arrange the titles by date, the earliest first. If some share the same date, arrange them alphabetically and letter them after the date.

Gould, S. J. (1996). *Full house: The spread of excellence from Plato to Darwin.* New York, NY: Harmony.

Gould, S. J. (2003a). *The hedgehog, the fox, and the magister's pox: Mending the gap between science and the humanities.* New York, NY: Harmony.

Gould, S. J. (2003b). *Triumph and tragedy in Mudville: A lifelong passion for baseball.* New York, NY: Norton.

ORGANIZATION AUTHOR

American Lung Association. (2012). *New standards bring cleaner air to you.* Washington, DC: Author.

UNIDENTIFIED AUTHOR

> Environment awareness: No child left inside. (2007, February 10). *The*
> *Economist, 382*, 32–33.

What Type of Source Is It?

Once you have found the appropriate author format, look for the type of source and the specific entry that best matches yours. Mix and match the patterns shown here as needed.

Article in a Printed or Electronic Periodical

ARTICLE FROM A JOURNAL PAGINATED BY VOLUME

If the pages in all the issues for the year's volume are numbered consecutively, no issue number is needed. Italicize the volume number as well as the title of the journal.

> Barker, T. (2009). Hong Kong film, Hollywood and the new global cinema:
> No film is an island. *Asian Journal of Social Science, 37*, 970–971.
> doi:10.1163/156848409X12526657425668

ARTICLE FROM A JOURNAL PAGINATED BY ISSUE

If each issue begins with page 1, add the issue number in parentheses with no space after the volume number. Use italics for the journal title and the volume number but not for the issue number.

> Kissam, E. (2005). The fulcrum for immigrant civic engagement. *Journal of*
> *Latino-Latin American Studies, 1*(4), 191–205.

ARTICLE FROM A JOURNAL WITH A DOI

Give volume, issue (if needed), and digital object identifier (DOI) numbers.

> Het, S., & Wolf, O. T. (2007). Mood changes in response to psychosocial
> stress in healthy young women: Effects of pretreatment with cortisol.
> *Behavioral Neuroscience, 121*(1), 11–20. doi:10.1037/0735-7044
> .121.1.11

ARTICLE FROM A JOURNAL WITHOUT A DOI

If an article you found online has no DOI, add the journal's home page URL.

> Doherty, S. D., & Rosen, T. (2006). Shark skin laceration. *Dermatology Online Journal, 12*(6), 6. Retrieved from http://dermatology.cdlib.org

**ARTICLE ACCESSED THROUGH A LIBRARY
OR SUBSCRIPTION DATABASE**

Supply any DOI, or search for and identify the home page of the journal. Name the database only for a source otherwise hard to find. If you access only the article's abstract, add "Abstract" in brackets after the title, or use it to begin the retrieval line.

> Nicol, S. (2012). Volunteering and young people. *Youth Studies Australia, 31*(3), 3–4. Retrieved from http://www.acys.info/ysa

ARTICLE FROM A PRINTED MAGAZINE

> Marsa, L. (2014, March). Infections infected. *Discover, 35,* 20–22.

ARTICLE FROM AN ONLINE MAGAZINE

> Levine, B. E. (2012, October 30). Does TV actually brainwash Americans? *Salon.com.* Retrieved from http://www.salon.com

ARTICLE FROM A PRINTED NEWSPAPER

> Stobbe, M. (2014, June 13). Teens drinking less, texting more. *The Denver Post,* p. 16A.

ARTICLE FROM AN ONLINE NEWSPAPER

> Davidson, A. (2012, November 20). Skills don't pay the bills. *The New York Times.* Retrieved from http://www.nytimes.com

Printed or Electronic Book

PRINTED BOOK

> Zelden, C. L. (2009). *The Supreme Court and elections.* Washington, DC: CQ Press.

ONLINE BOOK

> Oblinger, D. G., & Oblinger, J. L. (Eds.). (2005). *Educating the Net generation.* Retrieved from http://www.educause.edu/educatingthenetgen/

E-BOOK

> Goldemberg, J. (2012). *Energy: What everyone needs to know.* Retrieved from http://www.barnesandnoble.com/w/energy-jose-goldemberg /1110866917

MULTIVOLUME WORK

> Fink, G. (Ed.). (2007). *Encyclopedia of stress* (2nd ed., Vols. 1–4). San Diego, CA: Academic Press.

SELECTION FROM A PRINTED BOOK

> Martin, P. V., & Hummer, R. A. (2003). Fraternities and rape on campus. In M. Silberman (Ed.), *Violence and society: A reader* (pp. 215–222). Upper Saddle River, NJ: Prentice Hall.

SELECTION FROM AN ONLINE BOOK

> Brown, M. (2005). Learning spaces. In D. G. Oblinger & J. L. Oblinger (Eds.), *Educating the Net generation* (chap. 12). Retrieved from http://www .educause.edu/educatingthenetgen/

Printed or Electronic Report or Document

Many research reports and similar documents are collaborative products, prepared for government, academic, or other organizational sponsors. Start with the agency name if no specific author is identified. In parentheses, add any report number assigned by the agency right after the title. Add the publisher (unless also the author) before the URL.

PRINTED GOVERNMENT DOCUMENT

> U.S. Census Bureau. (2011). *Statistical abstract of the United States: 2012.* (131st ed.) (NTIS Order Number: PB2012965801). Washington, DC: Government Printing Office.

PRINTED RESEARCH REPORT

> Liu, J., Allspach, J. R., Feigenbaum, M., Oh, H.-J., & Burton, N. (2004).
> *A study of fatigue effects from the new SAT* (RR-04-46). Princeton, NJ:
> Educational Testing Service.

ONLINE RESEARCH REPORT

> National Institute on Drug Abuse. (2012). *Inhalant abuse* (NIH Publication
> No. 10-3818). Retrieved from http:// www.drugabuse.gov/sites
> /default/files/rrinhalants.pdf

ONLINE RESEARCH REPORT FROM A DATABASE

> Ross, D. B., & Driscoll, R. (2006). *Test anxiety: Age appropriate interventions.*
> Retrieved from ERIC database. (ED493897)

REPORT FROM AN ACADEMIC INSTITUTION

> Henderson, S., & Heinonen, O. (2012). *Nuclear Iran: A glossary of terms.*
> Cambridge, MA: Harvard Kennedy School, Belfer Center for Science and
> International Affairs.

Internet or Electronic Source

See the directory on page 243 for entries for other electronic sources,
including books and articles.

SECTION OR PAGE FROM A WEB DOCUMENT

Instead of referring to an entire website, whenever possible identify the
specific material that you have used by supplying its section number or
its own URL.

> Detweiler, L. (1993). What is the future of privacy on the Internet? In
> *Identity, privacy, and anonymity on the Internet* (sec. 2.12). Retrieved
> from http://cyber.eserver.org/identity.txt

DOCUMENT FROM A CAMPUS WEBSITE

Identify the university and sponsoring program or department (if applicable) before giving the URL for the specific page or document.

Allin, C. (2014). *Common sense for college students: How to do better than you thought possible.* Retrieved from Cornell College, Department of Politics website: http://www.cornellcollege.edu/politics/ resources -students/policies/common-sense-cwa.shtml

Visual or Audio Source

AUDIOTAPE OR RECORDING

Atandi Anyona, A., & Koons, R. (Writers). (2012). *Singing against apartheid: An audio essay* [Audio essay]. Retrieved from http://ethnomusicologyreview .ucla.edu/content/singing-against-apartheid-audio-essay

PROGRAM ON TELEVISION OR RADIO

McCabe, D., & Bower, D. (Director/Producer). (2014). Killer typhoon [Television series episode]. In C. Schmidt (Executive producer), *Nova.* Boston, MA: WGBH.

FILM

George, T., & Kitman Ho, A. (Producers). (2004). *Hotel Rwanda* [Motion picture]. United States: United Artists/Lions Gate.

APA REFERENCES CHECKLIST

☐ Have you started each entry with the correct pattern for the author's name? Have you left spaces between the initials for each author's name? Have you followed each initial with a period?

☐ Have you used "&," not "and," to add the last coauthor's name?

☐ Have you included the date in each entry?

☐ Have you followed the sample pattern for the type of source you have used?

☐ Have you used capitalization and italics correctly for the various titles in your entries?

☐ Have you included the conventional punctuation—periods, commas, colons, parentheses—in your entry?

☐ Have you accurately recorded the name of the author, title, publisher, and so on?

☐ Have you checked the accuracy of dates, pages, and other numbers?

☐ Have you correctly typed or pasted in the DOI or URL of each electronic source? Have you split a long URL only before a punctuation mark? Have you ended an entry with a URL or DOI without adding a final period?

☐ Have you arranged your entries in alphabetical order?

☐ Have you checked your final list of references against your text citations to be sure that every source appears in both places?

☐ Have you double-spaced your reference list, like the rest of your paper, and allowed an inch margin on all sides?

☐ Have you begun the first line of each entry at the left margin? Have you used your software to indent each additional line one-half inch (or five to seven spaces)?

☐ Have you checked any entry from a citation management system as carefully as your own entries?

Checklists, Tables, Figures, and Other Visuals

Revising

Editing and Proofreading

RESOURCES

Arguing

Integrating Sources

Crediting Sources

Acknowledgments (continued from page iv)

Benjamin S. Bloom, *Taxonomy of Educational Objectives, Handbook 1: Cognitive Domain.* Published by Allyn & Bacon, Boston, MA. Copyright © 1984 by Pearson Education. Reprinted by permission of the publisher.

Ann Carr, excerpt from "Deporting Resident Aliens: No Compassion, No Sense," from *America* 180.6 (February 27, 1999). Copyright © 1999 by America Press, Inc. Reprinted with permission.

Excerpt from "Disaster Planning for Libraries: Lessons from California State University, Northridge."

Tom Foster, "Can Artificial Meat Save the World?" *Popular Science*, Nov. 18, 2013. Reprinted by permission.

"How to Study Model," from Lucy Tribble MacDonald, Howtostudy.org, 2006. Copyright © 1998–2006 by Lucy Tribble MacDonald. Reprinted with permission.

Monica Luhar, "Being the Daughter of an Arranged Marriage," Alhambra Source: http://www.alhambrasource.org/stories/daughter-arranged-marriage April 25, 2013. Reprinted by permission.

John McCain. Adapted from "The Virtues of a Quiet Hero." From *This I Believe*. Copyright © 2005 by John McCain. Copyright © 2006 by This I Believe, Inc. Reprinted by permission of Henry Holt and Company, LLC.

Azadeh Moaveni, excerpt from *Lipstick Jihad: A Memoir of Growing Up Iranian in America and American in Iran.* Copyright © 2005 by Azadeh Moaveni. Reprinted with permission of Public Affairs Books, a member of Perseus Books Group, LLC.

Excerpt from "Preservation Basics: Why Preserve a Film?" Reprinted by permission of the National Film Preservation Foundation.

David Ropeik, "When Past Disasters Are Prologue," *Nautilus*, Issue 4, August 8, 2013. Reprinted by permission.

Robert Sapolsky, "On the Origin of Celebrity," *Nautilus*, Issue 5, Sept. 5, 2013. Reprinted by permission.

Audrey Schulman, "How to Be a Climate Hero," *Orion*, May/June 2008. Reprinted by permission.

From "Seeing Eye to Eye With Birds: Hand Feeding Wild Birds," http://www.birdwatching.com/stories/handfeeding.html. Copyright © 2014 Diane Porter. Reprinted by permission.

Clive Thompson, "Clive Thompson on 'The New Literacy,'" *WIRED*, August 24, 2009. Reprinted by permission of the author.

Index

Emphasis, revising for, 154
Endings. *See* Conclusions
"Epidemic of Childhood Obesity"
    (extract), 135
-es, adding to verbs, 176
Essay, MLA listing of, 238
et al., 231
Ethical appeals (ethos), 205
Ethos, 205
Evaluation
    claims of, 202–3
    in critical thinking, 32–33
    reading levels and, 21
    writing, 212–13
Evidence
    color, to enhance, 141
    selecting for persuasive support,
        41–42
    source selection and, 214–16
    statement-support pattern and, 44
    to support appeal, 204–6
    testing, 38–40
    types of, 39
    varied, examples of, 39
    visual, 138–42
Examples
    giving, 108, 110–12
    proof by, 208
Experience, drawing on, 115–17
Expert testimony, 37, 39
Explicit thesis, 68

F
Facts, 35–38
Fallacies
    logical, avoiding, 208
    recognizing, 208–9
Families and Faith (extract)
    (Bengtson), 114
Figures and graphs, 139–42
Film
    APA listing of, 253
    MLA listing of, 240
Film Preservation Guide, The (extract),
    106
Finley, Mary M., 124
Firsthand observation, 38, 39

Formal outline, 84–86
Formal sentence outline, 84–86
Format, editing, 194–96
Foster, Tom, 128–29
Fragments, sentence, 170–71
Freewriting, 52–54
Fused sentences, 171–72

G
Gender, pronoun-antecedent
    agreement and, 179–80
Generalization, 123
Generating ideas. *See also* Organizing
        ideas
    asking reporter's questions for,
        58–60
    from assignments, 48–50
    brainstorming for, 49–52
    doodling for, 54
    freewriting for, 52–54
    imagining for, 57–58
    keeping journal for, 61–62
    mapping for, 55–57
    preparing to write and, 63–65
    from reading, 22–23
    seeking motives for, 60–61
    sketching for, 54, 55
    writing process and, 23
Gerund, definition of, 178
Gladwell, Malcolm, 131–32
Goodman, Ellen, 107
Government document
    APA citation of, 246
    APA listing of, 251–52
    MLA listing of, 238–39
Grammar editing. *See also* Editing;
        Proofreading
    adjectives and adverbs, 181–82
    comma splices, 171–72
    common irregular verbs, 174–75
    fused sentences, 171–72
    past-tense verb forms, 172–73
    pronoun-antecedent agreement,
        179–81
    pronoun case, 177–79
    sentence fragments and, 170
    subject-verb agreement, 175–77

CORRECTION SYMBOLS

Many instructors use these abbreviations and symbols to mark errors in student papers. Refer to this chart to find out what they mean.

Boldface numbers refer to sections of the Quick Editing Guide (pp. 169–97)

abbr	faulty abbreviation		**,**	comma **C1**
ad	misuse of adverb or adjective **A7**		*no,*	no comma **C1**
agr	faulty agreement **A4, A6**		**;**	semicolon
appr	inappropriate language		**:**	colon
awk	awkward		**'**	apostrophe **C2**
cap	capital letter **D1**		**" "**	quotation marks **C3**
case	error in case **A5**		**. ? !**	period, question mark, exclamation point
coord	faulty coordination		**— () []**	dash, parentheses, brackets, ellipses
cs	comma splice **A2**		**...**	
dm	dangling modifier **B1**		*par,* ¶	new paragraph **D3**
exact	inexact language		*pass*	ineffective passive
frag	sentence fragment **A1**		*ref*	error in pronoun reference **A6**
fs	fused sentence **A2**		*rep*	careless repetition
gr	grammar **all of A**		*rev*	revise
hyph	error in use of hyphen		*run-on*	comma splice or fused sentence **A2**
inc	incomplete construction		*sp*	misspelled word **D2**
irreg	error in irregular verb **A3**		*sub*	faulty subordination
ital	italics (underlining)		*tense*	error in verb tense **A3**
lc	use lowercase letter **D1**		*v*	voice
mixed	mixed construction		*vb*	error in verb form **A3**
mm	misplaced modifier **B1**		*w*	wordy
mood	error in mood		*//*	faulty parallelism **B2**
ms	manuscript form **D3**		^	insert **D3**
nonst	nonstandard usage		*x*	obvious error
num	error in use of numbers		*#*	insert space
om	omitted word		⌒	close up space **D3**
p	error in punctuation **C**			